"By the pricking of my thumbs,
something wicked this way comes."
William Shakespeare, MacBeth

ONE NIGHT
in SALEM

The Hidden History of the American Witch

TROY TAYLOR

An American Hauntings Ink Book

ONE NIGHT IN SALEM
THE HIDDEN HISTORY OF THE
AMERICAN WITCH

ISBN: 978~1~958589~04~5

Published by American Hauntings Ink
PO BOX 249 ~ Jacksonville IL ~ 62651
www.americanhauntingsink.com

Cover Design by April Slaughter
Interior Design by Troy Taylor

Printed in the United States of America

TABLE OF CONTENTS

"All the wild witches, those most noble ladies,
For all their broom-sticks and their tears,
Their angry tears, are gone."
William Butler Yeats

"I am a witch. A real house-haunting, broom-
riding, cauldron-stirring witch."
Samantha Stephens

"The blackest chapter in the history of
Witchcraft lies not in the malevolence of
Witches but in the deliberate, gloating cruelty
of their prosecutors."
Theda Kenyon

INTRODUCTION

In January 1692, a handful of impressionable young girls who lived in the backwater village of Salem in the Massachusetts colony gathered to fight off the boredom of winter.

It was a hard life in that Puritan settlement. Hard work and prayer seemed to take up most of everyone's time. And during the long hours of every day, the villagers lived in fear. They feared hunger and disease and had a deep-seated terror of the unknown and of what lurked in the dark woods beyond the settlement.

It was in those forests and fields where the Devil lurked.

But perhaps more than anything, the Puritans feared their god - the god that punished them with bad weather and illness for their many sins.

They were always looking for sin. It had to be weeded out and expunged to keep the village safe. This uneasiness and anxiety caused the community to turn on some within their ranks - the eccentric, the elderly, the unusual, and the different among them. It was for their sins that their god might choose to punish them all. They had to purge the village of all who might incur their god's anger. It became convenient to accuse them of being witches and sorcerers who were in league with the Devil.

The fear felt by the adults in Salem was passed down to the children. The youngest in the community found no pleasure in growing up. They were meant to be seen, not heard, and expected to spend their days obeying their elders, doing their chores, and worshipping the god of their parents. They lived the same grim life they would live as adults. They learned to farm, hunt, cook, sew, and maintain the home. There was little that broke the monotony of their days and nights.

Not surprisingly, the tedious lives of Puritan children created boredom, especially during the long and dreary winter months. In turn, boredom led to mischief, and the innocent curiosity of that group of young girls about something outside their religious faith spun wildly out of control.

They had a notion to "try their fortunes," hoping to learn the identity of their future husbands by using an old divining trick of dropping an egg white into a glass to see what patterns it formed. It was only meant to be harmless fun, arranged by a woman who should have known better.

Rumors spread that instead of predictions about their marriage prospects, the girls saw a sure sign of death instead - leading to shock, terror, strange antics, and whispered accusations.

Horror came to Salem, and America would never be the same again.

1. THROUGH THE AGES

Witchcraft came to America with the first European settlers.

Those daring travelers came here on sailing ships, crammed with people, animals, and whatever belongings they could bring with them. Sickness - including colds, fevers, and near-constant nausea from being tossed by the waves - plagued them during their journey. Many died, never reaching the New World at all.

Those who survived brought a piece of home with them through their histories and traditions. They brought their hopes, dreams, fears, horrors, and faith in their god. Some escaped persecution for their religious belief - only to become the persecutors in their new home.

The first New England settlers left Europe at a time when thousands were being accused, tortured, hanged, and burned for being witches. They came to America for a fresh start - and brought that fear of witches with them.

They knew about witchcraft firsthand. They feared it and maybe experienced it or, in some cases, even practiced it. They brought their beliefs in the supernatural with them to their new home across the sea. Some came to escape the Devil, only to find him waiting in the woods, forests, and fields of America.

But to understand how witchcraft came to America, we must first explore its origins in Old World.

And believe me, most of that exploration is not for the faint of heart.

THE ORIGINS OF WITCHCRAFT

Witchcraft had its beginnings in ancient times as a form of nature worship and a means by which people sought to control the world around them and the elemental forces of both the visible and invisible worlds. In essence, the power of witchcraft had always been the effective exercise of mind over matter, although it was often carried out through potions, spells, rituals, and ceremonies, which were used to focus energy on achieving the wants and needs of the witch.

Stories of witches are as old as recorded time - and so are the stories of those who feared and hated them.

Hypatia of Alexandria wasn't your average woman of the fifth century. Her father taught her mathematics, philosophy, and astronomy - something reserved for only men at the time - and crowds gathered to hear her speak about Plato and Aristotle. These ideas didn't sit well with Christians in the region. It also didn't help that she was a pagan, though she believed in religious tolerance for all. Accused of being a witch, a mob of primarily Christians pulled her from her chariot one day in 415 C.E., stripped her, brutally beat her, and burned her to death. All of her academic work was destroyed.

Hypatia of Alexandria

It's one of the first documented accounts of a "witch" being murdered, but such an event was nothing new. People have been worrying about witches for more than 4,000 years now. More often than not, these witches were, like Hypatia, just people who lived outside the norms of society in one way or another. And though both men and women have practiced all sorts of magic - or have been accused of doing so - most of the fear and hatred toward witches have been directed at women. Anytime a powerful woman was outside the status quo, someone seemed to be around to frame that woman as evil, unruly, or potentially dangerous.

SAUL AND THE WITCH OF ENDOR

Saul perceived that it was Samuel, & he stooped with his face to the ground, & bowed himself.
1 Samuel.ch.28.v.14.

Pub. by Hogg & Co, Paternoster row

In the Old Testament, King Saul is said to have consulted the Witch of Endor so that she could ask the dead prophet, Samuel, how he might defeat his enemies. Samuel responds that it is the fate of all men to surrender power to another. The witch in the story is not evil - she is merely a medium who uses a talisman to summon a benign spirit on the king's orders. However, Saul had expressly forbidden his subjects to dabble in the occult. It is the king who attempts to deceive the witch by disguising himself and flaunting his own law when it suits him. Even so, the Old Testament writers took a dim view of anything connected to witchcraft.

In Exodus, it was written, "Thou shalt not suffer a witch to live." Or at least that's how it was translated in the 1500s when persecuting witches was one of the primary goals of the Church.

There's even the apocryphal bible story of Lilith, Adam's first wife, who was kicked out of the Garden of Eden for disobedience. In many versions of the story, she became a witch known to eat children.

Eating kids, or so the stories went, was apparently a favorite pastime of witches in ancient cultures. Often, the witches were childless hags in all the old stories. Roman lore offered tales of the Strix, a night owl who could assume the form of a woman and then fly around and eat children. She is thought to have influenced the Slavic tales of the Baba Yaga, also known for her diet of tiny humans.

The Roman scribes Horace, Ovid, Lucan, and Apuleius created the iconic image of the witch as a withered old hag who mixed up vile potions in a huge pot and skulked around graveyards with her familiars.

The Golden Ass, written in the second century, was the first full-length story of witchcraft. Although it was a satire that followed the author's misadventures after he smeared himself with a witch's ointment, there was a serious lesson to be learned from it - that meddling with things we don't understand can be dangerous.

The Greeks also told stories of witches, seers, and sorcerers. They consulted oracles and practiced forms of magic. Their spells were often for good, or at least morally ambivalent, reasons. In the *Odyssey*, Homer's hero summons the spirit of the seer Tiresias and encounters the witch Circe, neither of whom is evil.

Later, the poet Theocritus conjured up the image of a broken-hearted girl who prayed to Hecate, the goddess of night, magic, and necromancy, so that her faithless lover would return her arms.

Another legend involved a young man named Glaukias, and this ancient story is the oldest text to refer to a witches' love spell as "drawing down the moon." Glaukias was so in love with the beautiful Chrysis that he feared he would die of grief if he could never see her again. So, he consulted a magician who invoked Hecate. Glaukias was instructed to make a clay image of his beloved and stick bronze needles into it while speaking the words,

"I pierce thee that thou should think of me." The spell proved successful, for Chrysis ran to the lovesick young man and threw her arms around him, swearing undying devotion.

Every culture worldwide, even in the ancient Americas, recognized the power of magic - good and evil. Healers used their powers to assist their communities, while witches abused their powers to prey on the unlucky. In a few civilizations, sorcery served as a spiritual refuge for some and to explain the unexplainable. But, as is often the case, witches were used as scapegoats, too. They were blamed for illnesses, misfortune, disease, and even the fall of rulers and governments.

But witchcraft in the ancient world was never feared, as it would be after the rise of Christianity when the line between witchcraft and the works of the Devil would begin to blur. When the Christian Church held most of the religious world in the grip of both devotion and fear, nothing about witchcraft would ever be the same again.

THE WAR AGAINST THE PAGANS

Before Rome adopted the Christian faith as one of its religions, Christianity was simply another of the many cults competing for support among the people during the early centuries of the Common Era. It was persecuted by those in power and deeply split into different factions and beliefs. None of the cultists seemed to be able to agree on anything. They spent much of their time in hiding, and their belief systems - especially regarding the role of women in the cult - were wildly contradictory.

But all that changed with the emergence of Constantine as Rome's Emperor. Christianity achieved its first formal acceptance, leading to the exclusion of all other faiths. The pagan gods, followed by the common people and the practitioners of magic, were abruptly erased.

Before winning a battle against rival Maxentius in 312 CE, Constantine claimed to have had a vision of a cross appearing in the sky with the words *in hoc signo vinces* - in this sign, you will be victorious - and he soon adopted the cross as his emblem. The following year, he issued the famous Edict of Milan, which gave the Christian religion lawful status in the empire.

More than a half-century after Constantine's reign, Christianity became the empire's official faith. All statues, writings, and buildings dedicated to the pagan gods were destroyed, and all pagan faiths were outlawed. Under earlier Roman law, those who used magic to harm others - or were suspected of doing so - could be executed. Under the Christian emperors that followed Constantine, anyone who practiced magic or worshipped the pagan gods were immediately executed. For the pagans, the Roman Empire had become a difficult and dangerous place. They were jailed, murdered, and fed to the lions in the Coliseum - just as the Christians had been. It was the first case of the persecuted becoming the persecutors - but it would not be the last.

Christianity began to spread outward from Rome in the following centuries, marching along with the Roman legions as they conquered the far-flung lands of the empire.

It was in Europe -- in the lands occupied by the Celts, the Germanic tribes, and the Norsemen -- that the Romans met their greatest resistance. The people who lived in those lands had their own gods and goddesses, which they believed to be more powerful than the new religion of the invaders.

And they may have been right.

While the new religion of Christianity continues to dominate the world today, the old gods have never gone away. They inspired the Wicca, folk magic, and witchcraft movements that still exist today.

THE PAGANS OF THE NORTH

The history of the Celts is a bit of a mystery. It seems the more we try to learn about them, the less we actually know. Part of this is because they had little to no written traditions. This means that much of the information gleaned about their lives and deaths came from contemporary Roman writers, who were intent on portraying them as savages because of their non-Christian beliefs. So, we do our best, often focusing on how their traditions are reflected by the beliefs of those who came after them.

Celtic magic is closely connected to one of the most fascinating groups from European history - the Druids. The modern revival of Druidism conjures up images of people in long, flowing robes holding ceremonies at Stonehenge, but, in truth, little is known about their practices, their beliefs, or the gods they worshipped. This is partly because the Druids used oral tradition to pass their knowledge from one generation to another.

It has been said they relied heavily on the spoken word because it used the power of the mind in ways that written texts did not.

The Druids were said to be the intermediaries between the Celts and their gods.

This may or may not be true, but the bulk of their knowledge died with them, whatever the reason.

One thing we know is that the Druids were the intermediaries between the Celtic people and their gods and held immense power in their society.

The magic of the Druids was highly ritualistic and revolved around divination, shapeshifting, spellcasting, and control of the weather. Most of their magic and religious rituals were performed during the day, often in sacred oak forests, which is why the Druids have been linked so closely to the oak tree over the centuries, symbolizing nature and the wisdom of the earth.

One of the primary roles of a Druid was as a spiritual and magical advisor to the leader of the tribe. They also served as teachers, healers, and judges. It seems that Druids were almost exclusively male, though some writers did leave records of women performing similar roles.

The Druids offer merely a glimpse of sacred Celtic society. After their destruction by the Romans, then the Church, an entire magical tradition was almost completely lost.

There is little evidence that the pagans in different parts of Europe had many gods in common, although the Norse gods spread widely, thanks to the Viking raids on foreign lands, especially the British Isles.

However, one figure that did turn up among several cultures was the Horned God, whom the Celts worshiped. He has remained important in modern witchcraft and figured into most of early-century Europe's ceremonies, rituals, and gatherings.

The Horned God was born at the winter solstice when the days start to get longer. He marries the Goddess at Beltane and dies at the summer solstice when the days begin to get shorter. In some cultures, he was known as the Oak King for winter - and the Holly King at midsummer. He served as a representation of the endless pattern of life, death, and rebirth. He was also reputedly the leader of the Wild Hunt, the ghostly, nocturnal procession of the dead.

The Horned God of the Celts

Unfortunately, due to the stag horns of this old god, Christians stole his image to portray the Devil, using it as propaganda when it came time to try and suppress the older gods of the people.

Magic and witchcraft were also prevalent among the Germanic and Teutonic people who lived across much of Northern Europe during these early centuries. Many of their practices remain largely intact - namely, the making of wax figures and the use of needles, fire, or water to inflict harm upon the person the figure represented.

Meanwhile, the Visigoths found it necessary to pass laws in the sixth century that punished "storm makers" who threatened to ruin a farmer's crops unless he paid them with protection money.

The Norse Völvas that practiced Seithr in their histories.

Elsewhere, Anglo-Saxon magic ranged from simple charms to find love and remove warts to elaborate spells worked to destroy an enemy.

One of the best-preserved traditions of Northern Europe was the Norse form of magic known as *Seithr*. This kind of witchcraft was widespread and detailed in many Norse histories.

According to folklore, seithr was primarily practiced at night by women known as *Völvas*. They were supposed to have ridden out at night on animals such as bears and wolves to meet other witches - nightly meetings that the Church would later describe as being like the Sabbat festivals to honor the Devil.

Historically speaking, the actual practice of *Seithr* has been compared to shamanistic magic. It usually involved a woman sitting on a platform or high seat and then using chants or spells to achieve a trance-like state. She would then answer questions on subjects like the coming weather and seasons, where to find wild game, and predictions of love between young couples. While *Seithr* was occasionally associated with harmful magic, it was more often this kind of helpful divination.

That was the case with most stories of traveling seers and witches in this region. This may be explained by the fact that Christianity came much later to parts of Scandinavia than most of Europe. Thanks to this, there were fewer negative stories spread about *Seithr* by the Church to try and subdue the pagans of these lands.

The goddess most associated with *Seithr* is Freya, the most renowned goddess of the Norsemen and the most beautiful. She was associated with many things, including sex, magic, death, and fertility. When Freya mourns for her lost husband, the land goes cold and barren with the coming of winter. When she finds him again, and they return home, this marked the arrival of spring. The ebb and flow of the seasons and the mother goddess and her male consort, who dies and is reborn, were central to the mythology of the Norsemen and remain part of modern witchcraft.

Freya, the Norse goddess most closely associated with Seithr.

Freya has also been linked with another Norse goddess, Frigg, the wife of Odin. Frigg, like Freya, was also associated with childbirth, and the two of them are sometimes represented as two parts of the Triple Goddess - the young maid, the woman, and the crone - with the goddess Skadi, mistress of the hunt, making up the third aspect.

Odin was, of course, the highest god in the Norse pantheon and was closely identified with magic. After sacrificing one of his eyes for wisdom and knowledge, he became the great All Father and was, among other things, the god of magic.

REBELLION

As the Roman legions spread Christianity throughout the empire, in many places, like Britain, the new religion shared equal status with the gods of the Norse invaders who conquered the region and with the ancient pagan rites that had been passed down among the people for generations.

At first, anyway.

Even after the arrival of St. Augustine and the building of the Canterbury Cathedral a few hundred years later, the Britons were not convinced they needed to convert and worship the new god.

Kings, Queens, and the greater part of nobility were much quicker to accept it. Even though the Roman Empire only lasted into the fifth century, Christianity had become identified in the eyes of other societies with those civilized virtues that Rome still epitomized - virtues to which those societies also aspired. Thanks to this, the elites in most other European societies quickly adopted the faith. In time, many of those same rules, after being blackmailed by fanatical and militant priests with threats of hellfire and damnation, handed over much of their wealth for the building of churches, abbeys, and priories.

It is harder to know just how quickly and deeply Christianity spread among ordinary members of society. But it does seem clear that, for some, Christianity was appealing became many pagans couldn't see a huge difference between their old faith and the new one. Like the pagan religions, Christianity had minor deities - the saints - who could work miracles and heal the sick and whose very bones could provide healing and protection from evil spirits. They were, it seemed, good magicians whose magic was as strong as their pagan equivalents. And the fact that the faithful would visit the saints' shrines, wear amulets with their name or likeness, or carry relics with them for good luck, helped cement the new religion into the people's lives. In those early days, Christianity promised what the pagan faiths could offer and sometimes even more.

By the height of the Middle Ages, the Church had succeeded in imposing the Christian faith on much of the land.

While many of the major pagan sites remain today, far more were destroyed by the Church, replaced with churches, wiping out the traces of the old gods.

Many sites considered sacred to the pagans, often marked by monolithic stone circles and monuments, were built over by the Church, wiping out the physical traces of the old gods.

Pagan festivals were erased and turned into Christian celebrations of the seasons, like Christmas and Easter. At the Church's insistence, celebrations to mark the summer solstice and the winter equinox were condemned as witches' gatherings so that rural communities would be too frightened to revive them.

The Church tried eradicating the older religion while adopting some of its myths, including the virgin birth. It showed up in the Church's belief systems even though the pagans had used it as a traditional method of endorsing prophets for centuries. It hadn't been mentioned in the Bible before that - it was added in the 1500s.

Even the birth date of the Christian messiah, December 25, came from the cult of Mithra and the Roman feast of Saturnalia. The iconic image of the Madonna and Child? It was taken from the Egyptian story of Isis and Horus.

The message of all this was clear and easy to understand - the Christian god was right and powerful, and all others were false.

But not everyone listened. At first, the new rules established by the Christians had little effect on ordinary people. They continued their pagan beliefs, often baptized as Christians, but continued their worship of the old gods. They attended church because the lord of the manor ordered them to do so, but they relied on the old gods when they needed rain, good harvests, protection from misfortune, or other blessings.

As the Christian churches were built on the ancient sites, the people sought to appease the fertility gods by slipping the images of phalluses under the altars.

As more people began to put their faith in the Christian god, the Holy Virgin, and the saints, the Church was still not powerful enough to suppress the pagan feasts, so it simply replaced them. In many cases, though, the old traditions remained. On the eve of May Day, the day of Beltane, young men still jumped over bonfires and carried young women off into the darkness. On May Day, young people kept up the custom of dancing around a phallus - now disguised under the new name of the Maypole. The winter solstice turned into a celebration of the birth of the new god, and although attendance was required at church on Christmas day, the people had until Twelfth Night, on January 6, for merrymaking.

The ancient pagan festivals were slowly replaced by the Church, turning them into a religious feasts in honor of various saints.

And during these feasts, the Church usually overlooked at least two deadly sins - gluttony and lust. The Church was still allowing the people some leeway regarding the old religion because many of the rules created in the years to come had not yet come into being.

But that was soon going to change.

One of the most important new rules was when Rome decreed that all its priests should be celibate. The tens of thousands of young men who served as parish priests were now told they had to lead a life of chastity, which was asking the impossible. Before this decree, they had lived normal lives as married men and were now expected to leave their wives and suppress their urges through prayer. These were men who had not condemned their flocks for their pagan festivals and celebrations. Some of them even joined in. They knew about the old religions and, as they never menaced their own, they allowed the pagan rites to continue.

But all that began to change as the power of the Church grew, and its tolerance for the old gods started to disappear. It turned those gods into monsters and servants of the Devil. For instance, Pan, the playful woodland sprite and granter of sexual potency, began to be demonized as a purveyor of mortal sin. His followers were condemned as servants of an unholy master. The Church even borrowed his goat legs and hooves and attached them to the physical manifestation of the Devil himself.

It didn't take much for the Church to turn the woodland god Pan into their symbol of the Devil.

Had the Church possessed the strength of its own convictions, it would have waited patiently for the old ways to die out on their own, but it saw its authority

challenged by a pagan tradition that saw nothing sinful about sex. The pagans embraced it, and sex was part of many of its festivals, especially during planting season and when the gods were asked to grant fertility.

But to Church officials, sex became the greatest of all sins. It began to dominate the Church's thinking in a way that can only be seen as pathological.

First, the Church decreed that sex could only be sanctioned by marriage and then only to produce children. Sex was to take place as seldom as possible - if you're a priest, not at all - and kissing, fondling, attempting to have sex, and even thinking about sex was all sinful. To desire a member of the opposite sex, even without physical contact, was also a sin. Even desiring one's own wife was as sinful as desiring a buxom young woman spotted in the marketplace. If a man loved his wife too passionately, that was a sin equal to adultery.

Masturbation was another sin with which the Church was obsessed, and it held the most significant number of penalties. In five brief codes forbidding sex, 22 paragraphs dealt with various types of sodomy and bestiality, but 25 paragraphs dealt with masturbation alone. It was considered murder because a man's spilled see would never be used to create a child.

The sex act itself - when it was permitted to be performed - was strictly regulated and controlled. No position other than the "missionary position" -- the man on top of the woman -- was permitted. Women were not allowed to be on top, and a rear entry position was regarded with the greatest amount of horror because it was thought to offer the greatest amount of pleasure. Confessors were instructed to specifically ask married couples if they had dared indulge in this position, and if they admitted to it, they were made to do penance for seven years.

When the Church proclaimed that intercourse was illegal on Sundays, Wednesdays, and Fridays, it effectively removed the equivalent of five months of the year from possible corruption by sexual pleasure.

The Church then decided to enforce abstinence for 40 days before Easter and another 40 days before Christmas, removing the equivalent of eight months from everyone's sex calendar.

It also seemed sensible to the clergy to prohibit intercourse for three days before Holy Communion, which required regular attendance. From the remaining four months of possible sexual activity during the year, another month had been removed.

The frustrated populace was left with the equivalent of about two months during the year in which they might, for procreation alone, have sex without any sensations of pleasure. If a child had been born to them and were delivered at a particular time of the year that would fit into the wrong time of the Church calendar, their faith would prevent them from having sex for a year or more.

The Church maintained that it had created such stringent and ruthless rules to save the souls of its weakest members. However, such an extreme ban on sexual activity had never been enacted by Christ and was not supported by anything in the Bible.

So, you can likely guess what began to happen when people started to compare the old ways of life to the strict new rules of the Church - a quiet rebellion began.

The pagan traditions of the old gods had been lying dormant but had never gone away entirely. It's easy to understand how appealing the tales of the old ways, the old customs, and old religion - with its emphasis on fertility and sex rituals - seemed to the young. They listened to the older folks recall wild orgies in the woods and bodies of women past child-bearing age serving as "living altars" for young men with little experience.

The Church made it clear that women were the source of all fleshly evil - the exact opposite of what the old religions had taught.

In the Middle Ages, women were not only the property of their husbands but bore the burden of being held responsible for all sexual guilt. After all, it was a woman who had caused the fall from grace when she had tempted man in the Garden of Eden. Without Eve's deviousness, he would have otherwise indeed remained pure.

The Church believed that the mere presence of a woman could attract evil. Women were considered a necessary evil, a desirable calamity, a domestic peril, and a deadly fascination. In the infamous *Malleus Maleficarum*, an infamous witch-finders manual, the authors stated:

> *A woman is beautiful to look upon, contaminating to the touch, and deadly to keep. She is a foe to friendship, a necessary evil and a natural temptation. She is a domestic danger and an evil of nature, painted with fair colors. A liar by nature, she seethes with anger and impatience in her whole soul. Since women are feeble in both mind and body, it is not surprising that they should come under the spell of witchcraft more than men would succumb. A woman is more carnal than a man. All witchcraft comes from carnal lust, which in a woman is insatiable.*

This hatred of women did not date back to the early days of the Christian Church. At that time, women had equal roles to men. They were permitted to preach, heal, baptize, and perform exorcisms. Over the course of a few centuries, all that changed. By the Middle Ages, women had lost all their rights. The Church leaders hated women - perhaps because they lusted after them so much.

The Church's oppressive ways - and repression of women - eventually backfired, and the old religions began to return. But this was not accepted gracefully. In retaliation, the Church brings about the deaths of hundreds of thousands of innocent lives during the witch hunts and inquisitions of the Middle Ages.

To the Church, the old religions were inhabited by demons personified as the Devil, the enemy of the Church. The people had different ideas. To them, the old gods offered freedom from oppression and punishment. They had no satisfaction in a new religion that failed to provide an outlet for their carnal needs. They had more faith in the old gods as providers of good harvest and healthy babies than in a sad figure that hung pitifully from a cross. After all, no amount of fasting, prayer, and sexual abstinence stopped the Black Death until that terrible plague killed millions.

Sabbats became a regular part of pagan country life ~ acts of rebellion against the stringent rules of the Church and a return to the old ways that had been lost.

A painting by Francisco Goya

As the old ways returned, Sabbats became a regular feature of country life throughout Western Europe, and nothing was wicked about them. For the common people, who were poor and often worked from dawn to dusk, they offered joy and excitement - something that the Church certainly didn't provide.

A Sabbat was usually held during a full moon; about four times each year, a Grand Sabbat was held when several villages gathered to celebrate the feast days of the old gods. They included Candlemas on February 2, Beltane on May 1, Lammas Night on August 1, and Samhain at the end of October.

Those who attended these celebrations contributed poultry, game, fruit, cakes, honey, and home-brewed drinks to the gatherings held in open fields or forest clearings.

A local man represented the horned god of fertility. He dressed for the part as a goat or stag and was honored in his place. He and a village elder would offer advice and provide herbal remedies to those who sought healing. He also led the music, drinking, and games. After everyone had gotten plenty to eat and, likely, too much to drink, the ritual orgy would begin, aiding crops and cattle fertility.

And it was that aspect of the Sabbats that got the attention of the Church - the wrong kind of attention, of course.

A second Goya painting shows how the pagan Sabbats of the old gods began to be viewed by the Church as witchcraft and worshipping the Devil.

Unable to stop the common folk from celebrating the old ways, the Church doubled down, assisted by the Reformation. That movement began as an attempt to reform the Church. Many of its leaders were troubled by what they saw as false doctrines and malpractices within the Church, particularly involving the buying and selling of church positions and what was seen as considerable corruption within the Church's hierarchy, even reaching as high as the Pope.

The Reformation swept away the priests who had been tolerant of the pagans. A new kind of clergy came along who were earnest, outspoken, and puritanical men who took their religion very seriously and were determined to force their beliefs on everyone else. They declared that the old religions were now Satanic and that those who kept the old traditions were witches and committed heresy against God and the Church. The traditional festivals and feasts became gatherings of witches, and the broom, once a symbol of the sacred hearth, became an evil tool. The sex rituals - well, I don't have to tell you what they thought of that.

This was the first time witchcraft had been tied together with the Devil, but it would not be the last. In reality, though, witchcraft and Satanism were two very different things and vastly different philosophies, and the Church would always be around to thank for the mix-up.

They did all they could to stamp out the last remnants of the old gods, and soon, the bulk of the population had changed from nominal Christians who still followed some of the old ways to devout believers in the teachings of the Church. This change was not accomplished by prayer or the priests - it was caused by fear.

Branded as witches, those who continued to follow the old ways would not only be tormented in Hell for eternity but also have a terrible time on earth. The witch hunts had begun, and sheer terror was felt by those who might be accused of attending a Sabbat, taking part in a fertility ritual, or asking one of the old gods for a blessing for their crops. The threat of being tortured or burned alive at the stake managed to do what no amount of prayer and abstinence could accomplish - it caused most to abandon the old gods and become good Christians.

They simply had no other choice.

"THE BURNING TIMES"

The widespread execution of alleged witches - which lasted from the late Middle Ages to the early eighteenth century - is the most controversial period in the history of witchcraft. Even the name for this period - the "Burning Times" - is controversial because it implies that all accused witches were burned at the stake. They weren't. Most were hanged, but the name stands for a terror campaign that was waged over several centuries and ended with the deaths of perhaps as many as 100,000 people.

However, how many died is unimportant in the greater scheme of things. What's more important is asking why anyone had to die at all. The "Burning Times" has become known as one of the most shameful periods in history.

There is no one starting place for the witch craze in Europe. From as early as the twelfth century, there had been a slow increase in the arrest, trial, and execution of alleged heretics against the teachings of the Church. Witchcraft was said to involve the participant making a pact with the Devil to receive their supernatural powers, thus rejecting God, making it a serious form of heresy.

It became even more serious when Pope John XXII sanctioned a witch hunt in the belief that his enemies were plotting to murder him by magical means.

His suspicions turned out to be well-founded.

Three bishops - under torture, of course -- admitted to testing their powers by putting a curse on a wax image of the pope's nephew. The boy subsequently died. Encouraged by their success, they made images of the pope and his closest advisors and tried to smuggle them into the papal court in loaves of bread. But the plot was uncovered, and the sorcerers were allegedly found with poisons, herbs, toads, and the hair of a hanged man - all ingredients for their alleged spells. The plot's leader claimed to be innocent but was flayed alive, and his body burned.

More accusations of witchcraft and treachery followed.

In 1335, two women, Catherine Delort and Anne-Marie de Georgel, were tried in Toulouse, France, and confessed that over 20 years, they had attended witch gatherings and had given themselves to the Devil. They testified to drinking foul liquids, eating the flesh of infants, making poisons, and casting spells against people they disliked. There was no evidence that anything they claimed was true, but the court had their confessions, so both women were executed.

In 1441, astronomer Roger Bolingbroke, along with Thomas Southwell, a Canon of St. Peter's Westminster, and a woman named Margery Goodmayne, were all charged with having conspired against the life of England's King Henry VI by sorcery. The plot was masterminded by Dame Eleanor, daughter of Lord Cobham. Southwell died in the Tower of London, Margery Goodmayne was burned at the stake, and Bolingbroke was

Elizabeth Woodville ~ the so-called "White Queen" ~ whose mother allegedly used witchcraft to convince Edward IV to marry her.

dragged through the streets behind a horse before being hanged, drawn, and quartered. After publicly admitting her guilt in the affair, Dame Eleanor was pardoned.

During the reign of Edward IV, the Duchess of Bedford was accused of using witchcraft to entice the king into marrying Elizabeth Woodville. He later had two sons with her, both of whom vanished and were reportedly murdered in the Tower. The charges against the duchess were later dismissed - but that was not the end of the story.

After Edward's death, his one-time mistress, Jane Shore, was convicted of using witchcraft against Edward's successor, Richard III. However, the common people, who loved her, refused to believe the charges. She was forced to walk the streets with a sign around her neck declaring that she was a harlot, but the crowds met her with nothing but sympathy and affection.

In 1477, an accused witch named Antoine Rose was brought to trial. She testified that she had told a neighbor she needed money, so he took her to a Sabbat, where she was persuaded to enter a pact with the Devil. He appeared to her in the form of a large, black dog, and everyone present kissed his hindquarters. She added that the men who were present had sexual intercourse with the women in rear-entry style. They were told to take the communion host, hold it in their mouths, and then spit it out and trample it. They were given potions for making people and cattle ill and told to do as much harm to others as possible.

These accounts, and others, appeared over the course of almost a century. However, things took a darker turn on December 5, 1484, when Pope Innocent VIII declared open war on witchcraft by forming what became known as the Spanish Inquisition.

THE INQUISITION THAT NO ONE EXPECTED

The Pope empowered inquisitors appointed by the Church to participate in trials for heresy, to override the decisions of local courts, to proceed against persons of any rank, and to punish all those found guilty of practicing witchcraft.

It was believed that practitioners of witchcraft had become so numerous that, by casting spells, inciting rebellion, and endorsing other nefarious activities, they had become a menace to the Church and the Christian way of life.

The persecution of witches in Europe lasted for nearly 300 years.

In 1487, a Dominican friar named Tomas de Torquemada was appointed as the Grand Inquisitor of Spain. Under the patronage of the fanatical Queen Isabella, he began a reign of terror that is still remembered today as one of the darkest periods in the history of the world.

The fanatical Queen Isabella of Spain helped to start the reign of terror that was known as the Spanish Inquisition. It was led by the Grand Inquisitor, Tomas de Torquemada.

The tortures used to extract "confessions" from accused witches and heretics were brutal.

The Inquisition was given exceptional powers. It followed no rules of evidence. It rejected the basic principle of common law that a person is innocent until proven guilty and lacked legal representation for the accused.

Worst of all, even when it proved to its own satisfaction that a victim was guilty, they could not be executed until a full confession had been made. If a confession was not voluntarily offered, the Inquisition had the authority to extract one by torture, using the most heinous means imaginable.

A confession was followed by being burned alive at the stake. On the bright side - if there could really be any bright side to being burned alive - since they had confessed, the witch's soul now had the chance to enter heaven.

For nearly three centuries, thousands of men and mostly women met their deaths at the hands of executioners as victims of the witch hunters. Witchcraft persecution swept over the continent in waves. Many of those dragged before the Inquisition had been denounced by their neighbors out of spite or because they were old or mentally ill. Some might have been heard talking to themselves or to a cat or other animal. The Inquisition stated that such animals were a witch's "familiar." These supernatural entities took the physical form of living creatures and assisted witches with their magic. This was a sure sign, their accusers said, that they were in league with the Devil.

Others were accused because they were known to use herbs and roots to make natural remedies or because they told fortunes. Many went to their deaths for looking at their neighbors the wrong way, a look that might turn into an accusation of the "evil eye."

The tortures of the Inquisition were dark and brutal; believe it or not, the inquisitors had a sort of "instruction manual" to use. It was written by two German priests -- Jacobus Sprenger and Heinrich Kramer - and called *Malleus Maleficarum*, or the "Witches' Hammer," when translated into English.

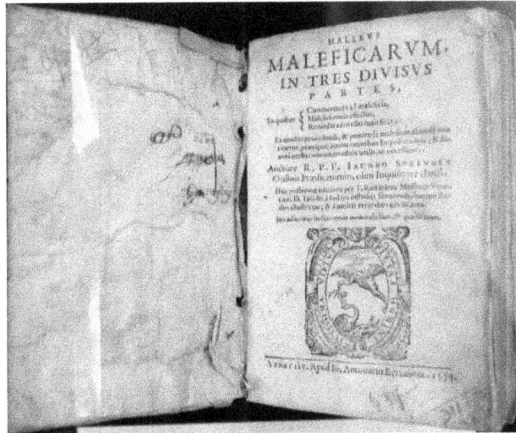

The infamous Malleus Maleficarum, or the "Witches' Hammer," a horrific volume of ways to torture witches ~ mostly women, of course.

And it was translated, thanks to its rabid popularity. It was first published in 1486, and many editions followed the first. The appalling book was written to be an examination of witchcraft, as well as a set of lengthy instructions about how to deal with its menace. It remains one of the most horrifying books ever written and caused the death of thousands during the Inquisition.

Like every other official in the Church, the authors of the book and the Inquisitors who followed its directions were obsessed with sex. Torturers were directed to obtain confessions from women by mutilating their breasts, driving nails into their rectums, and shoving red-hot pokers into their vaginas.

Once an accused woman was imprisoned because of those who claimed to see her use her "evil powers" - such witnesses could include jealous neighbors, rejected lovers, or relatives who wanted her money or property - she was as good as dead. The Inquisition charged that no witch could be condemned to death unless she confessed to every sinful act. This left judges with no choice but to torture the accused in ways that were so horrific that they would admit to anything to end the pain, even if it meant being put to death for the imaginary acts of witchcraft. The judges turned the accused over to black-hooded torturers who, to extract confessions, hacked, burned, branded, stretched, starved, and raped them.

To the Inquisition, an accusation was the same as guilt. No lawyer would dare come to the accused person's aid for fear he might also be accused of witchcraft if he pled her case too well.

Examinations began with a search of the accused witch's entire body. She would be stripped naked as inquisitors searched for a "Devil's Mark," a red blemish that appeared on all who swore allegiance to Satan. Sometimes, all their hair would be removed in search of the mark, which could be anything from a pimple to a scratch, a cut, or even a birthmark. If no mark was found, it was assumed it was invisible, so other methods were needed. Long sharp pins were inserted into her flesh, looking for unseen marks insensitive to pain. They had been left on her body by the Devil's touch. The pins were stabbed into her breasts, stomach, back, and groin, and if she did not cry out, she was obviously a witch.

The accused were often branded with hot irons, had their nipples torn away with iron pincers, were stretched and broken on the rack, had their feet crushed in iron "boots," had sulfur inserted into their anus and vagina, were scalded with boiling oil, and even worse - if that's possible. It's not surprising that many accused witches confessed to anything their accusers suggested to them, preferring death over the continued agony of the torture chamber.

Once a confession was made, the witch had to stand before the judges and provide a detail of their misdeeds. According to law, the judges could not hear confessions unless they were made freely, which is why the accused had to be tortured into admitting that they practiced witchcraft. Once they confessed, they were allowed back into the Church, forgiven of their sins, and burned at the stake.

If they didn't confess, they were burned anyway, so it was a losing proposition no matter how you looked at it - unless you were a Church official. As far as they were concerned, the difference was whether a person died as guilty but sorry for what they had done or died just plain guilty. The fire was just as hot either way.

I think it's safe to say that most who were found guilty before the judges of the Inquisition left the courtroom kicking, screaming, and begging for their lives. However, some proudly bragged about having sex with the Devil, how often they roasted children and ate them, how many of their neighbors

An accusation of witchcraft usually led to death, whether the accused confessed or not. The majority of executed "witches" in Europe were burned at the stake, although many were hanged or killed in other ways, too. There were no witches burned at the stake in America, despite folklore and legends.

they had cursed, and what mischief they had directed their familiars to cause. These wild - and always nonsensical - confessions were eagerly recorded by the court's secretaries and were readily accepted by the Inquisition as an admission of guilt. Such stories were used for centuries to add to the lore of the witch and create frightening tales about what kind of havoc witches would wreak if left to their own devices and not brought to justice.

Some of those who confessed hoped that the stories would frighten the judges into freeing them. They offered curses and warnings about what would occur if they were sent to their death, but this did little good. They were never allowed to escape the horrors of the torture chamber. Torture, in cases where the witch confessed readily, was considered good for their soul and the best path to salvation.

The testimonies and confessions that came from the Inquisition became an accepted part of witchcraft lore. They would go on to influence how people saw witches, conjurers, and the cunning men and women of folk magic for centuries to come.

PERSECUTION

The Inquisition slowly died, but there would be more persecution to come. During the sixteenth and seventeenth centuries, more religious figures took it upon themselves to try and uncover and destroy witches they claimed were menacing their countries.

The hunting of "witches" soon became a thriving industry. Successful witch hunting involved a lot of people - judges, jailers, torturers, exorcists, woodcutters, scribes, and experts on the forces of darkness - and all of them needed to get paid. The livelihoods of many depended on the continued rooting out of witches.

It wasn't long before witch hunters discovered a foolproof method of enriching their profession. Under torture, almost any witch could be forced to name others they knew who also practiced witchcraft. That turned one trial into many others.

And the money started rolling in.

Across England, witch hunters began springing up everywhere. They received a fee for every witch they detected, meaning witches began to multiply, and tales of witches gained legendary status in the country.

Famously, in 1591, a Grand Sabbat was allegedly held by three covens in England for the purpose of destroying King James IV of Scotland, who would later be James I of England. You know, the king one version of the Bible was named after. The king was about to travel to Denmark to bring home his new bride, Princess Anne, and this seemed the perfect time to plan his destruction.

King James of England ~ the one with the Bible named after him ~ was a pious religious fanatic who kicked off a brutal witch hunt across the country in the late 1500's.

The Grand Master of the covens, John Fane, assigned specific duties to the group of witches, including obtaining a piece of the king's clothing, making a wax image of him, wrapping it in the cloth, and then burning it. Others attempted to poison the king, while others tried to use witchcraft to cause storms that would

destroy his ship at sea. One witch named a cat after the king and then drowned it, believing his ship would sink.

It didn't. In fact, none of the magic spells - if there actually were any - managed to work. At the subsequent trial, it was said that King James was so pious and holy that witchcraft refused to work against him.

But he was very unhappy.

When he returned to Scotland, he initiated the first great witch hunt in that country, hoping to root out those who had magically conspired against him.

John Fane and many of the others involved were arrested, tortured, brought to trial, and burned at the stake. The confessions that were extracted significantly added to the Scottish witchcraft legends - no matter how fanciful some of them seemed. Fane confessed to attending witch gatherings, creating ointments that allowed his coven to fly, and breaking into a church with assistance from a "hand of glory." This was the hand of a murdered man, cut from his corpse, then dipped in wax and used as a candle. Locks were said to open at its touch, and a deep sleep could be caused among anyone in the building entered by a man carrying such a token.

Over the next decade, scores of witches were executed in Scotland and, later, in England, too. Soon after James became king of England, Parliament quickly passed new laws against witchcraft, providing an automatic death penalty for anyone causing harm to people or property by witchcraft.

The king's newly authorized version of the Bible also translated references to witchcraft that had never been mentioned in the past. A misleading translation about people who practiced bad magic or poisoned others was included as a deliberate act of propaganda. It has had an enormous impact over the centuries, noting, "Thou shalt not suffer a witch to live."

The new legislation in England saw a rise in witchcraft trials. It became widely known that rooting out witches required the employment of professional witch hunters, or "prickers," as some people called them.

They resurrected a version of detection used by the Inquisition. They stripped their prisoners, blindfolded them, and then, after feeling all over the bodies for a place where the skin was hard, they pushed a pin into their bodies at that point. If the prisoner did not cry out or bleed, they were told to find the pin and pull it out. If their hand went to some other part of the body, it was accepted as proof that the Devil had touched the place where the pin had been inserted.

The accused was most definitely a witch.

"WITCH-FINDER GENERAL"

The witch trials in England were still erratic until the start of the Civil War in the 1640s. The country was in widespread turmoil as Royalists found with Parliamentarians for control.

Into this chaos stepped the man who became known as the most infamous witch-finder of the period, Matthew Hopkins. He, and his assistant, John Stearne, began a reign of terror during this period. Hopkins held or claimed to hold the office of "Witch-Finder General," although this title was never bestowed upon him by Parliament. He conducted witch hunts in Suffolk, Essex, Norfolk, and other eastern counties of Britain.

Hopkins was a Puritan, a former shipping clerk, and a religious fanatic who felt that he had been called to hunt witches for God after he overheard some women talking about meeting the Devil in 1644 - or so he claimed. He reported what he heard to the authorities, resulting in the hanging of 19 alleged witches. Four more of the women that he accused died in prison.

Believing that he was now on a mission from God, he began traveling to various towns and villages in Eastern England, claiming that Parliament had officially commissioned him to hunt witches - he wasn't, but he never let that stop him. His witch-finding career only lasted two years - from 1645 to 1647 - but they were busy years. Hopkins was paid well for his work, making as much in a single village as most men made in an entire year.

While torture was technically illegal in England, Hopkins used various other methods to extract confessions from his victims. He often employed sleep deprivation, a tactic still used by interrogators today, and a "swimming test" to see if the accused would float or sink in the water. The theory behind this was that witches had renounced their Christian baptism, so water would supernaturally reject them. If a prisoner floated on the surface of a pond or river, then she was likely a witch. If she sank to the bottom and drowned, she would be innocent. Of course, a finding of innocence was little comfort to the dead.

The career of Matthew Hopkins was cut short by tuberculosis, and he died in April 1647, probably saving hundreds of innocent lives.

But this was not the end of the English witch hunts.

During much of the English Civil War, the Puritans controlled the country. These religious fanatics strongly believed in rooting out all evil in England, and over the next 16 years, hundreds of men and women were drowned, whipped, and hanged as witches.

It would not be until 1660 when the war ended, and Charles II became king, that this period in history ended. Charles, only 30 years old and loved by the people, was considered a kind and just man. Not only did the witch hunts end, but he even called a halt to the hangings of the men who had murdered his father after 10 of them had been executed. "I am weary of hanging, let it rest," he said and spared the lives of the rest of the conspirators.

That's not to say that no witches were hanged after Charles took the throne, but the indiscriminate witch hunts finally ended. There were still random trials, hangings, and burnings until the nineteenth century. There can be no doubt that many hundreds of innocent people were accused of witchcraft and sent to their deaths at the end of a rope or burned at the stake.

But there were also a great many people who were guilty - of something. While many were executed for nothing more than being different, angering a neighbor, or engaging in sexual practices not approved of by the Church, there were also many burned at the stake who were murderers of children, poisoners, blackmailers, and worse.

Were a few legitimate executions enough to justify all the innocent lives lost? No - because their crimes were nearly as bad as those committed by the Puritan leaders who had allowed the witch hunts to spin out of control. They were guilty of crimes, too. They claimed a devotion to God and inflicted unspeakable cruelties on the innocent and those who could not defend themselves.

No longer in power, the Puritans fled England because they claimed to be suffering "religious persecution" by those who had now turned against them. The Puritans fled to America to escape that persecution - where they became the persecutors.

And they brought the witch hunts with them.

2. THE AMERICAN WITCH

The Puritans, America's first -- but certainly not last - religious fanatics, settled in New England. They wanted a place where they could worship as they saw fit, keeping their religion pure, hence the name.

But New England was not the only place to find witchcraft in seventeenth-century America. The belief in witches was prevalent throughout the entirety of the colonies at that time.

But prevalence was one thing; lunacy was another.

For example, in some regions -- like the Mid-Atlantic colonies, worries about witchcraft rarely led to any official action. In others, especially Puritan New England, witchcraft was a deeply rooted, malevolent presence. There, formal accusations involving whole communities and generating full-blown legal proceedings were possible, even likely.

Few other regions were so fanatical and relentless, yet witchcraft was still reported elsewhere in the colonies. Virginia was the site of the first British settlement in America, and Virginia was also the source of the earliest surviving report of witchcraft.

In 1626, the colony's general court heard charges against a woman named Joan Wright. During several years at the Kickotan plantation, Wright had earned the reputation of a "very bad woman" by telling fortunes - usually about impending deaths - yelling at neighbors, and, most ominously, uttering mysterious threats of harm to any who crossed her. Her targets included two men who had subsequently failed in hunting despite "coming to good game and very fair to shoot at" and another whose "plants

The Puritans, while carving civilization out of the wilderness of New England, brought their fanatical religious beliefs with them from the Old World, wreaking havoc and beginning the American witch hunts.

were all drowned." She was also accused of making an entire family "dangerously sore" - whatever that means.

In 1641, another court settled a dispute between two women - - Jane Rookins and George Busher's wife, whose name was not recorded. They had quarreled for years, but things peaked when Rookins denounced Busher as a witch. Busher's husband then sued for defamation on her behalf. Rookins claimed not to recall the alleged accusation but apologized anyway. The court took this as a sufficient resolution of the matter, adding simply that the defendant had to pay all the costs of the prosecution.

Different versions of this story were repeated many times in other communities across the region. Indeed, most recorded references to witchcraft in early Virginia come from defamation cases. There were about 20 of these, with roughly even splits between acquittals and convictions. Punishments, when ordered, typically involved paying a fine. Often, as with the case previously mentioned, a public apology was ordered. In one case, a plaintiff stated that her neighbors refused to "keep company" with her after she was accused of being a witch. There is evidence, too, that some of the individuals defamed had been subject to physical assault and felt their lives to be in danger.

Surviving historical records offer a glimpse of the suspicions aroused during the colonial era, of curses, for example, and of "spells." One woman was said to have uttered "a kind of prayer" against her neighbor that "neither he nor any of his family might prosper." Shortly after, sickness overtook the neighbor's family. Another man claimed "bewitchment" of his cow; another injury to his horse; yet another, the sudden and mysterious death of some chickens. Several described experiences of being "ridden" like a beast of burden by supposed witches, over long distances, usually at night. One incident left the victim "wearied nearly to death." There were occasional references to the Devil's "imps" and to shape-shifting -- people changing into a black cat or some other animal.

Accusations of witchcraft against the "outsiders" in communities ~ the odd, eccentric, elderly, and feared ~ became all too common in the American colonies.

There were also elaborate stories of counter-magical activity. In one instance, a woman who "thought herself to be bewitched" ordered a servant to "take a horseshoe and fling it into the oven, and when it was red-hot, to fling it into her urine." According to the servant, the remarkable tactic produced immediate and telling results: "So long as the horseshoe was hot, the witch was sick at heart, and when the iron was cold, she was well again."

A smaller group of cases involved the prosecution of witchcraft itself, not simply its link to defamation. Juries were sworn in, witnesses called, and defendants interrogated, all along the lines of traditional English legal practice. By the same token, the suspect's body was carefully examined by "ancient and knowing women" who searched for "teats, spots, and marks not usual on others." If found, these dermatological imperfections were attributed to the Devil and understood to be flesh that was used to suckle his imps. And at least a few suspected witches were ordered to be "tried in the water by ducking." This time-tested method of discovery meant that the accused would be immersed in a pool or a stream. If she floated too easily, the Devil was presumed to be at work on her behalf. If she sank - or better yet, drowned - then she was obviously innocent of the charges brought against her.

Virginia was the first colonial site for court proceedings over witchcraft, and it also turned out to be among the last. Some trials occurred as late as 1706.

Meanwhile, there were similar cases in adjacent Maryland. Most of these, though, involved slander. A typical case involved a man named Peter Godson who was confronted by his neighbor, Richard Manship, who had heard Godson saying that Manship's wife was a witch. Godson said that he had gone to Manship's home, and his wife, in a jesting way, placed two straws on the floor and told Godson that if she were a witch, he would not be able to step over them. Godson did step over them but claimed he was struck lame the following day, which he claimed proved that Mrs. Manship was a witch. Manship sued him for libel. Godson later retracted his accusation, and the court case against him was dismissed, but his friendship with Manship likely ended.

New York witnessed occasional witchcraft trials, including a lengthy one in 1665 that charged a Long Island couple named Ralph and Mary Hall with using certain "detestable and wicked arts, commonly called witchcraft and sorcery," to cause the illness of a neighbor, George Wood, and his infant child. In the end, though, there were no convictions. A jury found "some suspicions of guilt" in the woman, but not enough "to take away her life." Her husband was acquitted outright.

Other, more casual implications of witchcraft were scattered through New York legal records until the late 1600s, with only a few rising to the level of legally actionable slander and one involving the banishment of a witch who had moved there from Connecticut.

Pennsylvania was founded in 1682, later than many of the other colonies, so it had a briefer involvement with the witchcraft of the era. The Quakers, who made up most of the population in those days, had little to do with such things, but a handful of cases did surface. In 1684, William Penn and his council conducted a full-blown prosecution of charges against members of the colony's Swedish minority. Two women, Margaret Mattson and Greta Hendrickson stood accused of bewitching cows and practicing other "sorceries" over a span of at least 20 years. The jury returned an unusual form of split verdict: "guilty on the common fame of a witch, but not guilty in manner and form as she stands indicted."

I'm not sure what that means either.

In 1701, a Philadelphia butcher and his wife were charged with slander for identifying a neighbor couple as the cause of a "very sudden illness in a certain strange woman lately arrived in town." The plaintiffs claimed as a result to be "suffering much in their reputation, and by that means in their trade." The strange woman, perhaps their lodger, had been found with "several pins in her breasts" and other seeming indicators of witchcraft. The case, however, "being inquired into, and found trifling, was dismissed."

The word "trifling" that appeared in the record was one not found in any other case of the preceding century. By this point, concern with witchcraft -- at least official concern with witchcraft -- was beginning to fade.

It becomes clear that it had never amounted to much outside New England. It was undoubtedly a part of local culture, and it certainly could attract a great deal of attention around particular persons for short periods. However, the sum of its effects was modest.

There were few executions, few clear-cut findings of guilt, and only occasional prosecutions -- and the majority of those for slander only, with the roles of the accused witch and accusing victim turned around. For the most part, America never came close to the kind of witchcraft frenzy seen in the Old World.

For the most part, anyway - because things turn pretty grim when we look at the history of witches in New England.

And we can thank our friends, the Puritans, for that.

The Puritans of New England hold a special place in American history - and it's not necessarily good. Two groups of Puritans settled in America - the Mayflower group, who arrived at Plymouth in 1620, and the much larger contingent, who arrived in Boston about a decade later.

The Puritans have been cast as ground-breaking social reformers of their time, but, in truth, their faith was fundamentally reactive and strict in a way that was only backward, not forward-thinking at all. It was founded because of their perception that the English

The Puritans felt the need to "cleanse" all religion to meet their standards, which was undesirable and impossible for most people in colonial America ~ which would lead to serious problems in the years to come.

Church was "corrupt" and needed to be "purified," returning it to the principles of the early Christians - or at least their version of the early Christians. They believed English society was also compromised and wanted to restore it by recapturing the "brotherly" spirit of a simpler age. The Puritans believed, not without reason, that they had been born at a time of unprecedented change and lived in terrible fear of disorder and chaos. Their faith was meant to be reassuring, offering strength, hope, and a promise of a simple life. It was founded on the principle of control -- both control of the individual person and outward control among the community of "saints." Intense and unrelenting discipline, they believed, was the appropriate answer to disorder.

After leaving England and establishing new homes in America, Puritan leaders seized on the opportunity to start fresh in a place where the law of their god and the law of man were the same. They would worship as they saw fit, keeping the religion "pure," and form communities where those who broke the law were flaunting evil in the face of their god. They never considered democracy as we know it. There was no separation between church and state. Religion influenced all community and political decisions.

Their Bible-based religious convictions caused them to see the Devil as an enemy whom they always needed to be vigilant against. He always lurked nearby, ready to claim the souls of anyone at any time. For the Puritans, fear and superstition were simply a part of their daily lives.

Religion dominated every aspect of a community's existence. Life was not easy. Hard work and prayer consumed most of a person's time. If the Puritans wanted to improve their fortunes, they believed they should spend more time in prayerful worship of their god. There was genuine dread of failed crops or an insufficient food supply, illness and epidemics like smallpox and infections, Native American attacks, and even disputes and disagreements between neighbors. The wrath of their god was deemed responsible for anything that went wrong, from bad weather to disease. They believed God would reward you if you prayed harder and avoided temptation. Anger him, and your life will be destroyed.

Failed crops? Food shortages? Bad weather? Native American attacks? All these things were believed to be punishments from the god of the Puritans. Only by removing the wicked from their communities could they feel truly safe.

The Puritans worked hard to fight against the influences of the Devil and other religious faiths. However, they believed their most sinister challenge came not from a competing sect but rather from the old traditions of folk magic.

THE CUNNING FOLK

Folk magic crossed the ocean with the first wave of colonists and took root in America's cultural soil. Puritan ministers frequently referred to it in letters, writings, and sermons and condemned it as the practice of curing sickness and bringing good luck through conjuring.

Needless to say, they did not approve.

But folk magic was a lot older than the Puritan faith. The practitioners of the craft were known as "cunning" men and women, and they assisted people who came to them in times of need. Most of the time, it was to cure an illness or for divining,

The cunning folk were feared by the Puritans who served an important role in communities throughout the American colonies.

which was the use of occult methods to foretell the future or to find lost objects.

Folk magic was truly a matter of ordinary folk who knew something of traditional lore and sought to apply it the best way they could. They healed the sick using medicines and plants, providing treatments and cures in ways that established medicine of the time could not.

But, of course, Puritans - who believed that healing should only come from their god - muddied the waters of early American folk magic, hoping to scare their followers away from it. There was a fine line between beneficial magic - like healing and divining - and diabolical witchcraft. The difference, it seemed, was in the eye of the beholder.

What seemed to be beneficial could also hurt people. Image magic was considered especially potent and dangerous -- for example, using " poppets " to represent a living person. A poppet might be made from materials like a carved root, corn stalks, a fruit, paper, wax, a potato, clay, branches, or cloth stuffed with herbs. Any actions performed on the effigy would be transferred to the subject through sympathetic magic.

Treat the doll with kindness, and the intended recipient of the magic thrives. But pinch, prick, or twist the poppet, and the intended victim might fall ill, break into fits, or perhaps even suffer a fatal injury.

During searches of the homes of suspected witches, the discovery of a poppet would be used to show the accused was in league with the Devil, regardless of how the doll had been used.

The cunning folk practiced palmistry, the study of the hand to show a person's future, and divined the future using eyes, crystal balls, the stars, keys, scissors, tea leaves, and more. Under the right conditions and circumstances, just about anything could be used to look

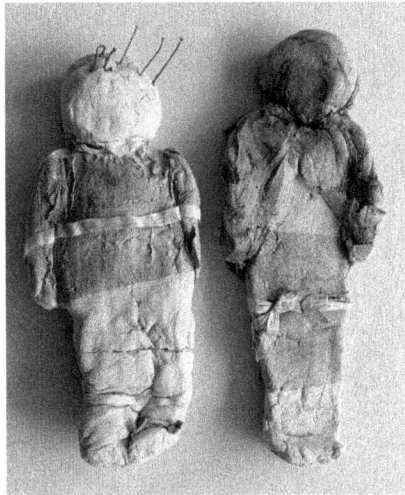

Folk magic poppets from my own collection, but similar in style to those used for centuries.

into the future, find lost objects, and return stolen goods, though the particulars of how many of them were used have been lost over the years.

Even though many folk magic practitioners would find themselves accused of witchcraft - in truth, a large part of what they did was to protect people from harmful magic.

They used charms, which involved the use of mysterious words and letter combinations and were sometimes written and sometimes spoken. There were secret healing phrases and charms of protection.

That protection extended into counter-magic that would be directed at a witch with nefarious intentions. For example, urine might be taken from a victim of harmful magic and poured into a witch's bottle - a glass vessel that could be used for good or evil. It would be infused with pins, nails, and various herbs and then heated over a fire. This was supposed to cause an immediate reaction -- scalding, burning, or some other painful sensation - in

Witch bottles were used as counter-magic against witches. They held pins, nails, herbs, and urine to break curses placed on people by a witch.

the perpetrator, whomever they might be. This way, identification, and retaliation were achieved in one stroke.

No matter how beneficial folk magic was, the clergy of New England kept up an intense and hate-filled opposition to it. To the Puritans, folk magic was a sacrilege, an affront to their own authority, and, most of all, to the power of their god. If the common people needed protection from the bad things in life, it must come from their god - and from nowhere else. Suffering should be relieved through "solemn prayer" and not by the workings of a conjurer. Their religion was divinely ordained, they stated. Conjuring and magic were not.

Puritan ministers knew that the best way to denigrate folk magic was to unfairly link it to witchcraft and the Devil. When asked about instances when folk magic worked, they replied that when it achieved its intended effect, then its source was surely the Devil himself.

Reverend Cotton Mather wrote, "Tis in the Devil's name that such things are done, and in God's name I do this day charge them as vile impieties." To ensure he got his point across, he added, "They are a sort of witches who thus employ themselves."

Reverend John Hale stated, "Magic serves the interest of those that have a vain curiosity to pry into things God has forbidden and concealed from discovery by lawful means."

Court records tell a story of how folk magic came under threat by the Puritans during this time. A case against a "doctor woman" named Ann Burt of Lynn, Massachusetts, was filed by several of her unhappy patients. According to one, Burt had prescribed potions from a certain "glass bottle," and after he drank it, he was even sicker. The same man claimed to have frightening encounters with "familiar" animals and then with Burt herself, seated "upon a gray horse." A second witness went to Burt to cure a sore throat and was told to smoke a pipe, after which she "fell into fits."

Another case against folk magic appeared in New Hampshire in 1680. A little boy fell ill, and a neighbor, thought to be adept at healing, offered to try a cure. Coming to the child's bedside wearing strange clothing and with her face "dabbed with molasses," she performed a ritual. The court record stated, "She smote the back of her hands together sundry times and spat in the fire. Then, having herbs on her hands, stood and rubbed them and strewn them about the hearth. Then she sat down and said, 'Woman, the child will be well,' and then she went out of the door."

Outside of the house, the ritual continued. According to the parents of the sick child, she turned back to face the house and stood "beating herself with her arms, as men do in the winter to heat their hands, and this she did three times while stooping down and gathering something off the ground in the interim." As it transpired, the child did not get well but died within a few days. The would-be healer was held responsible, and her supposed "remedy" was condemned as witchcraft.

As the controversy simmered, ordinary people were often caught in the middle. Resisting the clergy's pressure to choose between folk magic and the church, these people would remain Christians, remain churchgoers, remain adherents of the Puritan doctrine - yet would also avail themselves of magical "remedies" when need and opportunity presented themselves, risking the danger of being labeled as someone who used witchcraft, or even of being a witch themselves.

To the Puritans, a belief in witches - who carried out the evil deeds of the Devil - was as real as the constant threat of the Devil himself. Witchcraft was soon against the law in most New England colonies and was punishable by death.

The Puritans spent a lot of time convincing people that witches were everywhere in colonial New England, putting spells on livestock, cursing and killing babies, and more. This would set the stage for the trials that followed.

And for good reason, the Puritans believed.

Witches could put spells on livestock that made animals become ill or die. Witches even had the power to deform or even kill newborn babies. They believed it was the Devil at work, not the era's high infant mortality rates.

An inappropriate look, a pointed finger, or a harsh word might be construed as an evil curse. It was always worthwhile to keep an eye on anyone in the community who was more likely to be a witch. There were several tell-tale signs people were given from Puritan pulpits - a very old person, especially one with an odd appearance; someone who lived alone with a cat; someone difficult to get along with; a person known for immoral behavior; a woman who talked too much, or who was outspoken or strong-willed; a person who didn't attend church regularly; someone who had property disputes with others; a person who talked to themselves - who might be conversing with an invisible being; and many others.

Based on all that, witches were apparently quite plentiful in colonial America, but it will soon become clear that most accusations of witchcraft had little to do with actual magic.

AMERICAN WITCH HUNTS

Witches were everywhere in America.

Stories, rumors, legends, and gossip about witches spread from farm to farm and village to village throughout the colonies. Witches could be found among the settlers, but worse, there was also terror about diabolical magic being practiced by the Native Americans among them.

Such fears stretched back to the Old World. A large and constantly expanding amount of writing about American travel had cast the First Nations people as "servants of the Devil" - even though they had no idea who the Devil of the Christians was.

Puritan ministers and community leaders called them "consorters" and "minions of the Devil," and most of those accusations came about because of the Native American practices of traditional medicine, which the Puritans were suspicious about no matter who was using it.

The Africans that began arriving on American shores would have the same accusations made against them. Small groups had been arriving in the colonies as early as 1619. Of course, they were "immigrants" of a different sort since they had been kidnapped in

Africans brought to America in chains had their own beliefs in magic and witchcraft that was unacceptable to their white captors.

their homelands and transported to America against their will. Even though they were held in bondage as enslaved people, they would always fall under suspicion because of their persistence in practicing the traditions they brought from Africa and the Caribbean islands.

In their homelands, magical practice had been central to the supernatural belief systems of the people. To the colonists, such practices were to be feared. Many writings from this period refer to "conjurers" and "poison doctors" among the slave population. There were references to magic, charms, invocations, and substances such as "powders, roots, and herbs."

And while most of their magical practices were confined to the black population, white enslavers and townspeople feared harm from the sorcery practiced by their slaves - for very good reason. Too often, though, the enslaved people were punished for things that were not their fault.

If a white person died under mysterious circumstances, the slaves were usually blamed. Dozens, if not hundreds, of enslaved people, were suspected, accused, convicted, and put to death for acts of poisoning and murder by magic simply because the white authorities feared them so much.

But, as I've already mentioned, it wasn't the indigenous people or the enslaved people that the colonists truly feared. Diabolical danger, they knew, would come from their own kind - dark arts practiced by the settlers themselves.

The most dangerous witches, they knew, were within their own ranks. And they would do everything possible to weed them out - and destroy them.

"Thou shalt not suffer a witch to live," the Bible said, according to the fanatical King James, and the Puritans were determined to follow the scriptures to the letter.

There are records of witchcraft being practiced in Massachusetts as early as 1637. Although, honestly, this case seemed to have more to do with the fact that the accused was a woman rather than that she was a witch.

Anne Hutchinson, at the center of the controversy, seemed to challenge the very foundations of the Puritan establishment. The daughter of an Anglican minister, she was a unique presence for the time -- deeply thoughtful, eloquent, visionary, and charismatic. The mother of 15 children, she was an obviously energetic woman who worked as a midwife and

When Anne Hutchinson began drawing attention to herself with her biblical teachings, accusations of witchcraft soon followed.

held Bible study groups in addition to running a large household. Anne had a large following composed of Boston folk who attended her special worship meetings, and this served as another element about her that attracted attention.

A woman "attracting attention" always led to bad things with the Puritans in charge.

Governor John Winthrop, her chief antagonist, referred to her as a "prophetess," and the term does seem appropriate. Anne was greatly admired by many but drew suspicion from many others. Her prophecies were laced with such wit that no one knew whether or not to take them seriously. But to the Puritans, a woman with a sense of humor was almost as bad as being a witch.

Two years after she arrived in Massachusetts, Anne's gifts - said to be "beyond nature" - got her into trouble. As Governor Winthrop wrote, she was brought before the authorities because her doings "gave cause of suspicion of witchcraft."

As it turned out, she was never formally accused of being a witch. Her trial, conviction, and subsequent banishment focused instead on opinions that she had that went against the Puritan faith and for defying authority. She was also charged with being "deluded by the Devil" into believing a woman could have religious knowledge.

In addition, two of her friends, Jane Hawkins and Mary Dyer, were also accused. Jane, like Anne, was a midwife whose practice allegedly included the use of magical fertility potions. As a result, according to Winthrop, she became "notorious for familiarity with the Devil."

Mary and Anne had both experienced problematic childbirths. In Mary's case, the baby was stillborn and was badly deformed. Jane, too, gave birth to a severely deformed baby, who died within minutes. Such "monstrous" births - as they were regarded at the time - were a clear sign of some diabolical influence.

The only reason suspicions against the women did not immediately lead to witchcraft was the usual prelude to a witchcraft trial - which was the gradual, piece-by-piece build-up of suspicion and doubt over many years, accompanied by neighborhood gossip - was lacking in the case.

All three women were recent arrivals to Boston, and so were their adversaries. In a sense, neither side knew the other well enough to support a full measure of witchcraft allegations. In fact, there were no witchcraft trials at all during the quarter-century following the landing of the *Mayflower* in Plymouth Harbor in 1620.

People needed to get to know one another better before they could start accusing each other of frolicking with the Devil. Once they started, though, the trials went on until almost the end of the century.

The first real proceedings against a suspected witch occurred in Windsor, Connecticut, in 1647. On May 26 of that year, a woman named Alice Young had the unfortunate distinction of being New England's first legally certified witch - and the first to be punished by hanging.

Little is known about Alice other than that she was married to a carpenter named John Young and was the mother of at least one daughter. She and her husband had settled in the community in 1640. After his wife's hanging, John sold his land and moved away.

The witch trial of Alice Young in Connecticut ended with her hanging in 1647. It was one the first execution for witchcraft in America. It would not be the last.

Barely a year after Alice's execution, the nearby town of Wethersfield had its own witch trial. Little remains of the written record, and it states only: "The jury finds the bill of indictment against Mary Johnson, that by her own confession she is guilty of familiarity with the Devil."

Mary Johnson "confessed" to witchcraft in Connecticut barely a year after Alice Young was hanged. She claimed she'd had sex with the Devil. After her confession, she was also hanged.

Later writings by Cotton Mather offer a bit more information. Mary was evidently a domestic servant, and Mather noted that the Devil often played tricks on her master at Mary's request. He wrote, "She said that her first familiarity with the Devil came through discontent and wishing the Devil to do that and t'other thing, whereupon the Devil appeared unto her, tendering what services might best content her."

So, in other words, she was accused of having sex with the Devil, which progressed to her carrying on with young men in town before allegedly murdering a child.

I should add that Mary apparently "confessed" to all this and was summarily hanged. I think there is much more to this story - reading between the scant lines available - but we'll never likely know what was behind the accusations and confession.

After that, the communities surrounding Massachusetts Bay became infamous for the number of witch trials.

A little-known case in 1648 resulted in the execution of a woman referred to only as Goodwife Kendall.

Another trial that same year, against Margaret Jones of Charlestown, brought the same outcome. Margaret had been acting as a healer and fortune-teller, and stories that spread about her many successes raised suspicions about her. Her medicines healed the sick, yet she showed "such a malignant touch as many persons who she stroked or touched with any affection or displeasure were taken with deafness or vomiting or other pains or sickness."

When searched for the Devil's Mark, she was found to have "an apparent teat in her secret parts." A witness to her nights in prison as she awaited her trial testified about the comings and goings of a "familiar" spirit in the shape of a "little child."

Over the next few years, a different kind of legal case began appearing in the colony's records - suits for slander. Many were filed on behalf of women against the neighbors who had defamed them by suggesting - or openly accusing - that they were involved in witchcraft. Records show that some women were even accused of "conducting meetings" - a euphemism for having sex with - the Devil in their home.

A more serious and substantial case was filed in Springfield, Massachusetts, in 1652. At the center of the events was a married couple, Hugh and Mary Parsons. Mary was accused of murdering her infant son. Numerous accounts and depositions were filed against them both. The list of supernatural events of which they were accused included mysterious disappearances, strange illnesses, injuries, "threatening speeches" -- especially by Hugh Parsons - and, perhaps most important, causing "fits" in several innocent victims.

Mary Parsons, a mother grieving the recent death of her child, confessed to accusations of witchcraft in Massachusetts in 1652. She was hanged after her trial.

Mary, likely mad with grief over the loss of her child, admitted her guilt and confessed to "a night when I was with my husband and Goodwife Merrick and Bessie Sewell in Goodman Stebbins' lot... We were sometimes like cats and sometimes in our own shape, and we were a-plotting for some good cheer."

She was quickly convicted and executed.

Although Hugh denied participating in any of it, he was also convicted and condemned to death. However, the verdict was reversed, and he fled the colony for Rhode Island.

Whatever happened to the others named in Mary's "confession" is unknown, but what is clear is that Springfield was in a state of chaos during the many months of the unfolding events since participants in the trial had come from over half the families in town.

Another memorable case occurred in Boston in 1656, although the groundwork for it had been laid years before. The defendant, Ann Hibbens, came from a prominent household in Boston. Her husband, William, was a wealthy merchant and an admired civic leader, a magistrate, and a member of the Court of Assistants, the colony's highest governing body. There is no doubt that Ann shared in the prestige of her husband's position, and yet, her personality was so abrasive that it frequently caused problems for her - including being accused of witchcraft.

Problems started in 1640 when she became involved in a bitter dispute with a group of carpenters hired to refurbish her house. She accused them of cheating her, likely as a way of getting out of paying their entire bill. A resultant lawsuit in civil court was resolved in her favor, but the way she pursued the case was so aggressive that her church called on her to apologize for her "grievous manner." Ann refused, which led to her being admonished by Puritan authorities and then excommunicated. Her husband pleaded on her behalf, yet he admitted that she had been "uncharitable" and "un-Christian-like" on many occasions. The authorities also accused her of wronging her husband, but Ann simply ignored them.

As the years passed, Ann had other problems with the townspeople of Boston, but little could be done about her because of her husband's standing in the community. But when William died in 1654, Ann lost her protection. It was only a matter of months before she was accused and arraigned on charges of witchcraft. The details of her trial have been lost, but the outcome is known - she was convicted and hanged as a witch.

Around this same period, suspicion was aroused toward several people against whom rumors of witchcraft would circulate for decades. Eunice Cole of Hampton, New Hampshire, was one of them. There was also Elizabeth Godman of New Haven, Connecticut; Jane James of Marblehead, Massachusetts; and John Godfrey of Andover, Massachusetts. These individuals all fit a classic pattern - they were troublesome people accused of witchcraft; they could not shake the suspicions against them and were subjected to repeated prosecutions.

John Godfrey's story was particularly remarkable. In one respect, it was unusual because he was a man. Within the relatively small group of accused men, most were husbands of women suspected of being witches. Their guilt was always one of association.

But John Godfrey was different. So many people so hated him that he became an exception to the rule.

Unmarried and with no kin at all, he arrived in the Massachusetts colony around 1642. Almost immediately, he was mixed up in several lawsuits. And things would only get worse. Before he was through, he would set a record for lawsuits, even among people who loved to sue one another. Suits and countersuits piled up by the dozens - for debt, breach of promise, defamation, abuse, contempt for authority, and more. He sued most of his neighbors and won more times than he lost.

Rude, angry, mean, and downright unlikable, John Godfrey managed to survive several accusations of witchcraft by his neighbors. He was taken to court five different times but never charged.

He was also charged with all kinds of criminal conduct in his quest for "justice." He was accused of arson, theft, perjury, and physical assault.

And not surprisingly, since he was a thorn in the side of nearly everyone he knew. He was accused time and time again of practicing witchcraft.

He was an unlikeable man, continually at odds with his community over a score of personal and usually mundane affairs. He was angry, rough, and threatening. These were characteristics that New Englanders expected from their "witches," and the accusations against him followed a typical pattern.

In other words, if you made enough people angry at you in that time and place, you could expect to be accused of being a witch at some point - it was the perfect way to put people in their place.

However, it is notable that Godfrey remained at large to fight with his Essex County neighbors for more than three decades until he died in 1675. He was hauled into court five times under formal indictment for witchcraft - a capital crime -yet he narrowly escaped conviction all five times.

One jury did declare him "suspiciously guilty of witchcraft, but not legally guilty according to the law and evidence we have received," but that was as close as he came to the gallows.

Put on notice, again and again, and he just kept coming back for more. No one could ever really explain why Godfrey insisted on antagonizing people so much, but he simply refused to go away. Irritating or not, you have to sort of admire his nerve.

I guess you would say that Eunice Cole was the female version of John Godfrey. She was also repeatedly accused and even prosecuted for witchcraft, but she was somehow never convicted. She was described as uncommonly rough and abrasive and known for her "unseemly speech" and physical altercations. Her reputation was widely known and would long outlive her. Tales of her witchcraft became a part of local folklore, passed down from one generation to the next, and even today, people in Hampton know her name and tell stories of her alleged misdeeds.

The stories of Elizabeth Godman and Jane James were variations on the same theme. For both women, there were years of suspicion, occasional court trials, and acquittals each time, always accompanied by a stern warning to clean up their act. Both became part of local folklore, as familiar as Sabbath services, autumn harvests, and barn raisings.

In the 1660s, New England experienced its first "witchcraft panic" - and "panic" is the best way to describe it. Accusations again alleged witches spread and multiplied like a contagion, each new accusation being fed by the one before it.

It began in Hartford, Connecticut, and while its exact origin remains unknown, it seems to have started with the "very strange fits" of a young woman in town. As they developed, "her tongue was improved by a demon to express things which she herself knew nothing of." She apparently also began to speak in German - a language she allegedly didn't know -- and then revealed "mischievous designs by such and such persons" against several neighbors.

"Mischievous designs" being witchcraft, of course.

The Hartford "Witchcraft Panic" of 1662 began with strange first being suffered by a young woman in town and ended with several deaths.

One of the accused was a certain "lewd and ignorant woman" named Rebecca Greensmith, who was already in jail on charges of witchcraft. This just seemed like piling on. Regardless, she was examined by a group of ministers and magistrates who managed to get a pretty impressive confession out of her.

She said she was well-acquainted with the Devil, and he'd had "carnal knowledge of her body." She also described gatherings of witches that had been held near her home. Some of the witches arrived in different shapes, including one who "came flying amongst them in the shape of a crow."

No one knows why she confessed to the things she did, although one witness to her interrogation said that Rebecca felt "as if her flesh had been pulled from her bones, and so she could not deny her guilt any longer."

That sounds a lot like torture to me.

No matter how they managed to get those things out of her, they were damning statements and more than enough to get her convicted and sentenced to death. Her husband was also executed for good measure, even though he claimed to be innocent until the end.

Since those "very strange fits" experienced by the unnamed young woman managed to root out a self-confessed witch who had

A test for witchcraft at the time consisted of putting the accused under water to see if they'd float. If they did, they wee witches. If they drowned, they were innocent. It was a lose~lose situation no matter what happened.

sex with the Devil and met with other witches in town, the authorities figured they'd see who else she wanted to point a finger at.

It turned out there were many people in Hartford and the neighboring towns of Wethersfield and Farmington who were hanging out in the woods with the Devil and his minions.

Many of the details about the "panic" have been lost over the years, but some reports remain. Suspicion fell on a particular married couple, so a group of townspeople decided to subject them to the notorious "ducking" test. They were tied at their hands and feet and thrown into the water. When they seemed to float "after the manner of a buoy," bystanders concluded the Devil must be holding them up.

This had once been a time-tested method of discovery for witches, but several ministers who were on hand insisted it was an ignorant superstition and tried to intervene. In the confusion, the couple managed to escape.

Others who ended up in the water were not so lucky. Others were also submerged to see if the Devil saved them, but they managed to drown. They were, of course, acquitted - although it didn't do them much good. Six others were convicted, and two of them were hanged.

In the 1670s, there were further incidents in Massachusetts, Connecticut, and even in rarely affected Rhode Island, where people were free to pretty much worship in whatever way they wanted.

But the middle part of the decade brought new challenges for the American colonies that were dire enough to make everyone forget about witches for a while.

The greatest distraction was King Phillip's War, a horrific race war that pitted white colonists and their Mohegan and Pequot allies against Native Americans from five other nations. The death toll was like nothing seen before or since in American history, with a casualty rate approaching 10 percent of the total colonist population and even higher among the Native Americans.

As a result, in the four years between 1675 and 1679, there was only one indictment for witchcraft. But at the war's end, the pace increased again, with six witch trials over the next four years. However, there were additional indictments in the half-dozen years after that, none of which resulted in convictions. It is worth noting that no one was executed for witchcraft anywhere in New England between 1663 and 1688.

It began to seem as though the witchcraft craze had run its course, but in 1688, a woman named Glover was accused of witchcraft in Boston. Her first name was not recorded. She was Irish, Gaelic-speaking, and likely a Catholic, all of which would have made her seem suspicious to most New Englanders of the day. Her accusers - and supposed victims - lived on a neighboring farm and hired Mistress Glover to do their laundry.

A familiar series of events followed - a dispute, angry words, fear of retaliation, and then "fits" among the neighbor's children. The result was a trial ending with a conviction, confession, and execution.

During the proceedings, other suspects were named, and the people of Boston became alarmed by the possibility of more witches in their midst. The local clergy became involved, including the famed Puritan minister Cotton Mather, but eventually, the children's "fits" stopped, and a sense of normalcy returned to the community.

A Irish Catholic woman only called "Goodwife Glover" was accused of witchcraft in Boston in 1688. It was the first to end with a hanging in 25 years, but it would not be the last.

The Irish woman's case was the first witchcraft case in New England to end with hanging in 25 years - but it would not be the last.

As the final decade of the seventeenth century began, New Englanders were disturbed and frightened by the events at home and throughout the colonies. On the political and military front, the major European powers and their colonial possessions were at war. In America, this meant that New England was at war with New France (Canada), and there were sporadic incidents of violence taking place in the wilderness along the border. There had been attacks on villages in New Hampshire, New York, and Maine, which was then part of Massachusetts.

In the early 1690s, more than a dozen women were accused of being witches in New England. They were dragged into court and neighbors and former friends testified against them, telling stories of imaginary wrongs. Luckily, most were found to be innocent of the "crimes."

Perhaps even more frightening was the revival of the "witchcraft panic" that had seized the region a few years before.

Accusations surfaced in Boston, New Haven, and Northampton. In 1692, a significant outbreak gripped the coastal Connecticut towns of Stamford and Fairfield.

These events began in March in the home of a locally prominent family when a servant girl named Katherine Branch suddenly "fell into fits." The details followed a long-established precedent -- wild physical contortions, trances, fainting spells, cursing and blasphemies, suggestive sexual acts, spectral confrontations with the Devil, and finally, the naming of her supposed witch "tormentors."

Once again, it all happened in the presence of numerous enthralled onlookers, all of whom were willing to carry the tales to family and friends.

After the names of the witches were announced, no fewer than six women were brought under suspicion. A special court was convened, and dozens of witnesses testified about their dealings with the accused.

They all spoke of quarrels, threats made and received, cows that died mysteriously, and strange "injuries" of every sort. The proceedings continued throughout the summer, and the atmosphere surrounding the trials was both angry and circus-like.

The townspeople were divided into opposing factions, some supporting the trials and others doubting or dismissing the various charges outright. The doubters included several members of the court and a group of ministers, who called the whole thing a ridiculous charade. In the end, the cooler heads prevailed, and only two of the suspects were indicted. They were tried before a jury, and only one woman was pronounced guilty. A committee of magistrates eventually freed her.

But at almost the exact moment that Katherine Branch was first seized by the "fits" that led to her accusing six women in her community of witchcraft, something similar occurred about 100 miles to the north.

In a small village in Massachusetts, a group of impressionable young girls had a notion to "try their fortunes," hoping to learn the identity of their future husbands by using the old divining trick of dropping an egg white into a glass of water to see what patterns might form.

Instead of a glimpse into the future, the girls allegedly saw an omen of death, which would cause shock, terror, strange antics, and whispered accusations in their town.

The horror of the Salem Witch Trials was about to begin.

3. THE DEVIL CAME TO SALEM

Over the last few centuries, the backwater village of Salem has become infamous for the witch trials that occurred there in 1692. It should be equally as infamous for hosting the first real outbreak of religious mania.

Historians often say that America has been a nation of extremes throughout its relatively short history. It should be no surprise that its religious faiths can also be described the same way - extreme.

The witch trials could not have happened without the Puritans. They left England to escape persecution. They, in turn, came to America to persecute others. Anyone who disagreed with them was then purified, which is how they earned their self-righteous title.

The Puritans who settled in New England had no intention of letting go of their unyielding Bible-based convictions. The faith they had in their god influenced all community decisions. If their strict standards were relaxed, it left room for the Devil to slip inside. The Devil was, of course, the enemy and could claim the souls of anyone at any time.

The village of Salem was settled in 1626. Four years later, the Puritans dominated every aspect of its existence. Community leaders taught the people to live in fear of almost everything. A general feeling of helplessness and a terror of the unknown permeated the village. The uneasiness and anxiety of the village created the perfect climate for seeking scapegoats - any affliction could be attributed to the eccentric, the difficult, the elderly, or those not pious enough. It was convenient to accuse them of being witches or sorcerers, in league with the Devil and his demons, no matter how irrational it seems to us today.

The days and nights of the Puritans were hard, long and empty of joy. The adults lived a grim existence of work and prayer, and the children were never allowed to be children at all. They were taught the skills they would need as adults, worked all day on chores, attended church, and studied the Bible. Their days and nights were just as monotonous as those of their parents, perhaps even more so.

Salem Village was a small backwater town that likely would have faded into the historical record if not for the terrifying trials that took place there in 1692.

The boredom of this mundane existence would lead to the mischief that created the witchcraft hysteria of 1692.

There were no witches in Salem.

There was religious fanaticism that would alter the way that Americans would look at witchcraft for centuries to come.

And it all started because several young girls showed an innocent curiosity in something outside their religious faith and allowed what happened next to spin wildly out of control.

There had been plenty of other accusations of witchcraft in New England before the events in Salem, so what made these events so different? For one thing, unlike larger towns like Boston, Salem was not wealthy, and its residents were not well-

Reverend Samuel Parris

educated. It was a rural community with an adult population of only around 215 people at that time. But even among those small numbers, various factions quarreled with each other, causing jealousy and friction. Since outbreaks of "witchcraft" had less to do with the supernatural and more to do with hatred and fear, Salem was the perfect place for the events that followed to occur.

Ironically, the hysteria in the village began in the home of Reverend Samuel Parris, the relatively inexperienced pastor of the Salem Village Church. He'd been at the pulpit since only 1689 but was regarded as a pious and strict Puritan minister.

Within the Parris household lived the reverend, his wife, his nine-year-old daughter, Elizabeth, a quiet and nervous child, and his 11-year-old niece, Abigail Williams, a bold little girl who dominated her younger cousin. The two girls had been thoroughly indoctrinated into the Puritan faith, with its fear of the Devil, demons, and, of course, witchcraft. Little is known about the reverend's wife, except that she was a devout woman who spent most of her time doing charitable work in the village.

Parris had lived in Barbados for a time and brought two enslaved black people to Salem with him - John Indian, who did outside work, and his wife Tituba, who cooked and cleaned. The children were primarily cared for by Tituba, and with idle time on their hands, they were always eager to be entertained by her stories about her island home and a culture so different from their isolated Puritan world.

Tituba's traditions revolved around magic, ghosts, and necromancy - the opposite of Puritan beliefs. She told fortunes and read palms and told the girls about magic. In secret, Elizabeth

Tituba entertained Elizabeth, Abigail, and soon, some of their friends, with simple magic from her island home. This would soon have dire results for Tituba and many others in the community.

and Abigail huddled near the kitchen hearth, and Tituba enthralled them with stories of the occult, made even more exciting because they were so forbidden.

The girls became proud of their secret knowledge and boasted about it to some of the other girls in the village. These girls then quietly joined Elizabeth and Abigail to hear Tituba's stories and see fortune-telling and palm-reading demonstrations. The secret meetings broke up the monotony of cold January days in New England, although if their parents had discovered what the girls were hearing, they would have been mortified. And the girls knew it. The gatherings created excitement and uneasiness, tinged with fear and guilt. They knew they had gone well beyond the boundaries of accepted Puritan teachings.

It was inevitable that terrible things were going to happen.

The first sign of a serious problem occurred when Elizabeth and Abigail began displaying "peculiar" behavior. They gazed emptily at the ceiling above and seemed to be experiencing abnormal muscular contractions, twitches, and fits. Reverend Parris and his wife quickly summoned the village doctor, William Griggs, for advice. Unsurprisingly, he had no idea what was wrong with them since nothing like what we'd consider medicine was being practiced in those days. His conclusion? "An evil hand is on them," he announced and solemnly issued a disturbing medical opinion that the girls had been afflicted by witchcraft.

This was hardly a surprising diagnosis for the time. Most physicians accepted witchcraft as a valid explanation for certain maladies -- like the "fits" and other inexplicable symptoms being suffered by the girls. No doctor in the seventeenth century was familiar with a psychological disorder like "hysteria." What was wrong with the girls could only be interpreted within the bounds of Puritan thought and belief.

Some would claim that the girls were acting - faking the whole thing - but it's more likely that Elizabeth and Abigail were highly impressionable and believed strongly in what the Devil, magic, and witchcraft could do to hurt them. They had frightened their way into a genuine state of hysteria. In addition, as news of the girls' mysterious condition spread throughout the community, the affliction also spread, and there were soon complaints of similar symptoms reported by other girls.

Dr. Griggs had inadvertently started the hysteria by failing to provide a better medical diagnosis for the two girls. To everyone in the village, his conclusion that "an evil hand is on them" was clear - the girls were victims of witchcraft.

No one knew what to do for the girls except to pray for them. Reverend Parris summoned several other ministers, and they offered sincere and fervent entreaties to their god on behalf of the afflicted girls. But Elizabeth and Abigail seemed to worsen.

Their bodies became oddly contorted, then stiffened. Their breathing was labored, and they cried loudly, complaining of horrible pains. They suffered fits of dizziness and spells during which they crawled about on all fours and made horrible animal noises. Prayer proved to be of no avail. Accounts stated that the girls screamed as though touched with burning coals whenever sacred words were said over their bodies.

It was clear that they were being attacked by witchcraft, but who was working with the Devil in Salem Village? Who had bewitched the two girls? Whoever it was, that person had to be found and stopped.

The girls were asked who their tormentors were, but no one could not get a straight answer from either of them. They were honestly unable to identify anyone. Unfortunately, village leaders and the clergy could not allow the situation to continue without finding someone to blame.

But one village resident, Mrs. Mary Sibley - described by one historian as a "true Puritan busybody" - decided she would get to the bottom of the problem. She had located an old recipe that forced someone afflicted by magic to identify the witch who was responsible. Mary Sibley gave the recipe to Tituba and persuaded the enslaved person to make the "witch cake," which consisted of rye meal and the urine of Elizabeth and Abigail. If the family dog ate the cake - and the two girls were truly bewitched - the dog would also begin to act as though bewitched.

But the cake was never made. When Reverend Parris learned of Mrs. Sibley's plan, he furiously condemned it as folk magic, declaring that it was the same as "going to the Devil for help against the Devil." He said the Devil was already among them, and unless the village witch could be identified, he would consume them all.

The girls became increasingly frightened and agitated. They knew they were now in a position where they had to identify

Left ~ Illustration of Sarah Good

Above ~ Sarah Osborne during her trial in an illustration.

someone as a witch. They had no choice - their elders, who could be both intimidating and punishing, insisted on it. So, they accused not one but three local women as those responsible for their suffering. They named Tituba, Sarah Good, and Sarah Osborne.

Why those three? Anyone who lived in Salem at the time could understand. Tituba's stories of the occult and magic had started it all. She was also a woman of color, which made her suspicious in the white Puritan backwoods New England community. Sarah Good was a poor, disheveled, homeless woman who roamed the streets begging for shelter for herself and her children. Sarah Osborne's reputation was questioned simply because she had stopped attending church.

Warrants were issued for the arrest of the three unfortunate women on February 29, 1692, and they were ordered to present themselves before local magistrates. Allegations were being made by Elizabeth and Abigail, as well as eight other girls who were now "afflicted" by witchcraft.

Reverend and Mrs. Parris, frantic at the turn of events, moved Elizabeth away from Salem to live with family friends. But Abigail and the other girls stayed in the village. One of the girls was 12-year-old Ann Putnam, the malicious daughter of a neurotic, gossipy mother who would be responsible for scores of rumors spread about town. Another of the afflicted girls was Mercy Lewis, a high-strung servant who worked for the Putnam family. Mary Warren was 20 and a servant for the John Proctor family. Elizabeth Booth, 18, lived near the Proctors. Another of the afflicted was Sarah Churchill, a servant for the George Jacobs family. There was also Elizabeth Hubbard, 17, the niece of Dr. Griggs' wife. Susannah Sheldon was 18, and 17-year-old Mary Walcott's father was the parish deacon.

Salem did not have an official courthouse when the legal proceedings against the accused began, so the prisoners were brought to Ingersoll's Tavern to be questioned by the magistrates. There was such excitement in the village over what was happening that even the

Ingersoll's Tavern

strict Puritans put aside their work to gather and watch. So many men, women, and children jammed into the tavern that the inquiry had to be moved to the village meetinghouse to question the women before two judges, John Hathorne, and Jonathan Corwin.

Hathorne began his questions with Sarah Good, but it quickly became apparent that he was not impartial. He had no doubts about the dangers of witchcraft, and his tone suggested that he already believed Sarah to be guilty - he just needed her to confess.

"Sarah Good, what evil spirit have you familiarity with?" he asked her.

"None," she replied.

"Have you no contract with the Devil?"

Sarah shook her head. "No!"

"Why do you hurt these children?"

"I do not hurt them. I scorn it," she told him.

"Who do you employ then to do it?"

"I employ nobody!"

"What creature do you employ then?" he persisted.

"No creature! I am falsely accused!"

The afflicted girls, who were all present, were then questioned, and Judge Hathorne asked if Sarah Good was causing their suffering.

Judge John Hathorne

Yes, they told him, it was she. They suddenly fell to the floor and began to convulse and scream as if they were in terrible pain.

Judge Hathorne, who watched the outburst, turned his attention back to Sarah. "Sarah Good," he asked intently, "do you not see now what you have done? Why do you torment these poor children?"

But Sarah didn't waver. Ignoring the judge's accusatory tone and the theatrics of the afflicted girls, she repeated that she'd had nothing to do with what was happening to the girls - but then she blamed it all on Sarah Osborne. Any sympathy we might have for Sarah Good, with her hungry children and homelessness, was lost at that moment.

Sarah Osborne was brought before the judges, and she also proclaimed her innocence. But in the middle of insisting that she was not guilty, she allowed that it might have been her "specter" that was responsible for the bewitching, or perhaps the Devil had disguised himself to look like her. However, she maintained she'd had no contact whatsoever with him.

When Tituba was questioned, she maintained her innocence at first, then changed her testimony and told the judges that she'd had interactions with the Devil. Some believe that she was beaten into a confession by Reverend Parris, but it's more likely that she was just telling the Puritan judges what they wanted to hear - perhaps fearing worse punishments if she didn't.

Tituba confessed to anything she could think of, and it was nearly impossible to stop once she started. She claimed that the Devil had come to her and asked her to serve him. In exchange for her loyalty, he'd promised her splendid possessions. She acknowledged that she had signed the "Devil's Book" and added that Sarah Good and Sarah Osborne had also made their marks within the pages, using ink that was "red like blood."

She said there were four women - the two Sarahs and two women she did not know - who had hurt the afflicted girls. She said the "specter of a tall man dressed in black" had threatened her with injury if she did not hurt the girls, but she would not. The specter was adept at shapeshifting, changing from a man to a dog or even to a pig.

She had flown to Sabbaths with the Devil - sailing through the air on wooden poles -- accompanied by a hog, two red cats, and the winged head of a cat that belonged to Sarah Osborne. She also had a familiar that was a "yellow dog" and "a thing with a head like a woman, with two legs and wings." Sarah Good had a "yellow bird" that served her as her familiar.

Tituba - who knew how to spin a good story and likely even hysterically believed some of what she was saying - confessed that an evil specter had attacked the girls. She quickly added, though, that she'd not acted of her own free will. She had been coerced into witchery by evil magic.

The court readily accepted her testimony. It was evident to them that the uneducated enslaved person had been deceived by the Devil and was an innocent victim of the witches. Evidence of this was given as Tituba also became "possessed," rolling her eyes, frothing at the mouth, and screaming that a demon was attacking her for having spoken out against the forces of darkness. Her husband also got involved in the ruse and roared, blasphemed, and threw himself onto the courtroom floor, also apparently in agony. The court believed he was also another victim of the horror that had come to Salem.

The afflicted girls were present when Tituba testified, and at first, they reacted with an outbreak of violent contortions but then calmed down as she spoke.

Meanwhile, those gathered in the meetinghouse watched with both fascination and horror. They were shocked to learn that the Devil was at work in their little village. The judges had noted that Tituba said nine marks had been made in the Devil's Book. That meant there were still six other witches in the village - who were they?

Hysteria quickly gripped the community.

In early March 1692, the three accused women were sent to jail in Boston while their fates were being decided. The jail's horrible conditions took their toll on Sarah Good. She died behind bars in May. Tituba and Sarah Osborne remained locked away.

During this time, Salem was a hornet's nest of fear and worry about those among them who were witches and had not yet been identified. The community was on the verge of losing its collective mind. At least a dozen people came forward - including some who may have honestly believed what they were saying - claiming to have seen the "shapes" of others sticking pins into dolls and casting spells on livestock.

The closeness of living in a small town cut two ways. Beneath the surface of polite and neighborly behavior, there were often resentments and jealousies. Using witchcraft as an excuse, neighbors could get back at neighbors for all kinds of slights and wrongs, both real and imagined. A man who might have used foul language against a neighbor might now be accused of "cursing" that neighbor. When an illness occurred among the neighbor's sheep, hogs, or cattle, the first man might be blamed. When such incidents were offered in court, they were introduced as incontrovertible evidence of witchcraft.

Community leaders ordered March 11, 1692, to be a day of prayer and fasting to combat the wickedness that seemed to envelop the village. It also turned out to be the day young Ann Putnam began screaming in pain, alleging that she was a victim of another witchcraft attack. Who could be responsible for the newest evil doings?

Ann accused a woman named Martha Corey.

Villagers were shocked. Unlike the dubious reputations of Sarah Good, Sarah Osborne, and Tituba, she was an upstanding member of the community and church.

But Martha had made an error in judgment when the witch hysteria first gripped Salem -- skeptical of the claims of the afflicted girls,

Artist's depiction of Martha Corey and her persecutors

she neither attended the court appearances of the accused nor did she want her husband, Giles, to attend them. Rumors claimed that she was inclined not to believe the accusations, and those rumors spread through the village. This started further gossip that perhaps Martha Corey herself was a witch, but for most, this seemed too hard to believe. Before church leaders could even consider such an allegation, they thought it best to speak with her privately.

The "afflicted girls" reacted violently whenever any of the accused women were brought before them during the hearings. If the girls acted possessed in the presence of the accused, it was assumed they were guilty.

However, before confronting Martha Corey, clergymen questioned Ann Putnam for further details about the specter that afflicted her. However, she said she had none - she couldn't see the apparition because Mrs. Corey had momentarily blinded her.

The visit by two church officials - Ezekiel Cheever and Edward Putnam - to the Corey home went badly. Martha acted as though she had been expecting them. She told them, "I know what you come for. You are come to talk with me about being a witch, but I am none. I cannot help people's talking of me."

Martha remained skeptical about the goings-on in town and, again, badly misjudged the people of Salem. She overlooked the fact that those who believed in witchcraft could easily rationalize the idea that even a woman who appeared to be pious could still do the work of the Devil.

Martha was arrested on Monday, March 21. She had been in church the previous day, disregarding the rumors about her because she was certain of her innocence.

She denied that she had tormented the girls with witchcraft when taken before the magistrates. If she was not responsible, she was asked, who was? She replied, "I do not know. How should I know? I am a gospel woman."

The afflicted girls who were present immediately screamed, "Gospel witch! Gospel witch!" Ann Putnam added that she saw Martha Corey's specter and another woman invoke the Devil.

Martha quickly replied, "We must not believe these distracted children!" But the girls showed no signs of calming down. At one point, court records state that Martha bit her lip, likely from nervousness, and at the same time, the girls screamed that they were being bitten. Then one of them yelled that she saw a "black man" - an apparition that, like all the others, wasn't visible to anyone else -- whisper something to Martha. This sent the crowd gathered in the meetinghouse into hysterics. The girls continued to scream and cry and were sufficiently convincing enough that Martha Corey joined the other accused in jail.

The hysteria in the village was gaining strength, and the news that Abigail Williams had seen the specter of a woman named Rebecca Nurse quickly spread. Once again, many were baffled by the accusations against Rebecca. She was admired and respected, a kind woman with a large and loving family. Her husband owned considerable land, and they lived on a comfortable farm.

Everyone seemed to like them - or did they? Some in Salem resented the position and affluence of the Nurse family. They were also private people, not given to excessive socializing. Worst of all, the Nurses were also skeptical of the claims of the afflicted girls. To many in Salem, this suggested they were unsympathetic to those bedeviled by witchcraft.

The accusation that Rebecca's malevolent specter had been seen was sufficient grounds to bring the elderly woman from her sickbed to stand before the magistrates for questioning. She faced her accusers in late March with the afflicted girls performing

Rebecca Nurse in chains.

their usual fits, contortions, and shrieks. They, of course, blamed Rebecca for the torture they were enduring.

And if the girls' accusations were not enough, Rebecca now faced a new allegation from Ann Putnam's mother, also named Ann. She and her husband swore that Rebecca had "enticed them to wickedness" and had injured Ann with her magic.

Rebecca Nurse, who suffered from hearing loss, must have been bewildered by the charges against her. She protested, insisting that she was not guilty.

But that only spurred on the elder Ann Putnam, who was emotionally unstable at best. She began to hurl more accusations at Rebecca angrily. "Did you not bring the black man with you? Did you not bid me to tempt God and die?" she screamed, spit flying from her lips.

"Oh Lord, help me!" Rebecca begged.

But apparently, her god didn't hear her pleas.

The new accusations sent the afflicted girls into another frenzy. Whether truly hysterical or acting for attention, the commotion inside the meetinghouse was approaching bedlam. The girls uttered more frightening cries, contorted, and convulsed on the floor.

Judge John Hathorne chose to accept the girls' performance as evidence of Rebecca's guilt. He demanded of her, "Do you not see what a solemn condition they are in? When your hands are loose, the persons are afflicted."

Hathorne also noted that Rebecca did not cry. It was a belief at the time that witches could not shed tears. Rebecca replied to his insinuations that she was just as deeply moved as anyone would be but preferred not to display her feelings. The judge waved this away and said that he believed Rebecca was guilty unless she claimed that the girls and Mrs. Putnam were lying.

"I cannot tell what to think of it," Rebecca replied.

The judges continued to hammer away at the allegation that Rebecca's specter had harmed her accusers. She told them that she could not stop that - she had no control over the shape the Devil might take.

Meanwhile, the afflicted girls stepped up their antics. They cried out that the black man had returned and was now whispering to Rebecca and claimed they saw birds encircling her. Whichever way she turned; the girls imitated her. One of the afflicted, Mary Walcott, spoke up and said she'd seen Rebecca's apparition and that she had contributed to the death of several Salem residents. The crowd in the meetinghouse became so loudly agitated at this that it became difficult to hear the proceedings. When the judges finally restored order, they sent Rebecca Nurse to the Boston jail.

The village was soon being whipped into a frenzy. The wild rumors, the fear of lurking devils, and the fire and brimstone sermons at the church created a disturbing atmosphere. It was obvious to all that worse things were on the way.

Perhaps the most bizarre - and certainly most unjust - arrest for practicing witchcraft was that of Dorcas Good, the five-year-old daughter of Sarah Good. In my opinion, this marks the peak of the collective insanity in Salem. Before the judges, little Dorcas "confessed" that she, like her mother, was a witch. She told the court that her familiar was a snake that sucked out her blood. As "proof," she showed the magistrates a small blister on her hand. That was enough for them to send her to jail.

Fear and suspicion spread through the village like a plague, although some tried to resist it. Visiting minister Reverend Deodat Lawson had warned villagers from the pulpit that they should be careful of false accusations. However, few of the parishioners apparently bothered to listen at the time.

And then there were those who remained stubbornly skeptical about the whole business. One of them was a hardworking farmer named John Proctor, who had become angry after the public displays put on by the afflicted girls. He was especially irritated that one of them was Mary Warren, whom he's employed in his home. He sarcastically noted that if the girls were given a chance, they'd accuse everyone in the village of being a witch. His solution to the whole mess was for the girls to be whipped.

It should be no surprise that John Proctor and his wife, Elizabeth, were soon behind bars. They had been accused of witchcraft.

Rebecca Nurse's sister, Sarah Cloyse, had been understandably distressed by the accusations made against her sister, knowing they were outrageous and untrue. During a church service in early April, she heard Reverend Parris make a biblical reference that implied Rebecca was in league with the Devil. In a fit of anger, Sarah left the meetinghouse, banging the door when she exited so that everyone present could hear the noise.

Any guesses as to the next person accused of witchcraft?

It didn't take long for the afflicted girls to claim they had witnessed the specter of none other than Sarah Cloyse. Before the magistrates, John Indian, the husband of Tituba, claimed that Sarah had used sorcery to harm him.

But she stood her ground. "When did I hurt thee?" she demanded.

"A great many times," he replied.

One victim after another was jailed and forced to wait for a formal trial about being accused of witchcraft by one of the "afflicted girls."

"Oh, you are a grievous liar," Sarah snapped.

Asked by Reverend Parris, the afflicted girls predictably answered that they had witnessed ceremonies in which the Devil gave communion to several witches, including Sarah, her sister, Rebecca, and Sarah Good. Hearing these accusations against her, Sarah collapsed. The afflicted girls reacted by mocking her. The meetinghouse burst into a commotion while the girls convulsed into fits and spasms.

The judges used the girls' behavior as evidence against the accused - even though the behavior existed almost entirely to make the prisoner feel as unsettled as possible. If the accused lifted her eyes, the girls all lifted theirs; if she rubbed her face, the girls did the same; if she coughed, the girls all coughed, and so on. If the prisoner denied the charges brought against her, the girls went into a frenzy, howling and throwing themselves on the floor.

Still worse, they were sometimes to make the sole decision of innocence or guilt. One by one, the girls stood before the prisoner, and she was forced to take each of their hands. If an afflicted girl continued to rave and thrash about the accused was innocent, but if she became quiet, it was assumed that the accused had halted their magic, and so was obviously guilty.

The girls had a terrifying effect on the hearings and the rest of the village. They were constantly seeing "specters" all over the place. So unshakable had the belief in them become that at the girl's direction, the villagers stabbed with swords and pitchforks at the empty air where the apparitions were supposed to be.

People in Salem who feared being accused or "cried out," as it was called, began to leave the village. Among them was John Willard, the deputy constable, who had arrested several of the accused witches. In a sudden fit of disgust, he turned on the afflicted girls, accused them of being frauds, and said that they should be hanged for what they had done. The girls retaliated against him by claiming they had seen his "specter" strangling his nephew, a young man who had recently died. Willard tried to flee but was captured and chained up in prison, accused of having witched to death several other people.

By now, a panel of five more judges from Boston had joined those in Salem. Whether intentional or not, the fact that judges from a higher court had taken an interest in what was happening in the village elevated the controversy to a new level. It was no longer a matter of just local business. The mania in the small community became news that gripped the entire Massachusetts colony.

Later in April, there were four more arrests on charges of witchcraft -- Bridget Bishop, Abigail Hobbs, Martha Corey's 80-year-old husband Giles, and John Proctor's servant Mary Warren - who was herself one of the afflicted girls. There were questions about Mary's arrest - she had been an accuser, why was she now being charged? Likely she was badly shaken by the arrest of the Proctors for whom she'd worked. Her behavior became erratic, and she was now confused about her time as a victim. When the other tormented girls got wind of Mary's doubts, they quickly tried to quiet her loose talk by claiming that she had bewitched them and had signed the Devil's Book.

When she was brought before the judges, it only took a glance from her to cause the other girls to begin to scream and convulse.

Mary became emotionally overwhelmed - and it wasn't an act. She was genuinely terrified and became so hysterical that she was removed from court and taken to jail. Several weeks later, she admitted to being a witch but blamed John and Elizabeth Proctor and others for her misfortunes. By confessing, Mary probably saved her own

Mary Warren, who had been one of the "afflicted girls," was badly shaken by the arrests of her employers and was soon accused of witchcraft herself.

life. She was freed and again considered one of the afflicted girls. Typically, those who confessed to being witches were spared the gallows. Those who maintained their innocence were invariably convicted and condemned to hang.

When Bridget Bishop, Abigail Hobbs, and Giles Corey were questioned, both Bishop and Corey insisted they were not guilty of witchcraft. But their pleas were in vain - as soon as the afflicted girls looked at them, they fell into outbursts of fits and contortions.

Abigail Hobbs, however, confessed to everything, telling the magistrates that she had "sold herself body and soul to the old boy" - meaning the Devil, of course. She told the judges that she practiced witchcraft, attended meetings of sorcerers, and drank "red wine with red bread." She was jailed along with the others, but she implicated nine more people during her confession. Before April was over, warrants were issued for Abigail's parents - William and Deliverance Hobbs - Susanna Martin and Mary Easty, the sister of Rebecca Nurse and Sarah Cloyse.

Shaken by her arrest and the questioning that followed, Deliverance Hobbs began to question her own sanity - could she be a witch and not know it? Rattled and overwhelmed, she confessed to practicing witchcraft and offered the names of other witches in the village. Her husband, William, outraged by the treatment of his wife, insisted that they were both innocent of all charges, which landed him in jail.

Mary Easty, when questioned, kept control of her emotions but was also jailed. On the other hand, Susanna Martin didn't take the courtroom proceedings seriously and even laughed at one point. She was skeptical of the afflicted girls and called them liars. As she was being taken to jail, she remarked, "A false tongue will never make a guilty person."

A short time later, Mary Easty was freed from jail. Her manner impressed officials so much that they started to believe she was not guilty. But her freedom didn't last long. Whether genuinely fearful or just malicious, the afflicted girls grew hysterical, especially Mercy Lewis, whose fits frightened everyone who witnessed them. When she cried out Mary's name, the poor woman was placed back behind bars.

Around this time, the afflicted girls decided to announce the identity of another prominent witch - Reverend George Burroughs, who had been a minister in Salem several years before.

His time in the village had been unpleasant. Many Salem residents hadn't warmed to him, and his wife died while he lived in town. He'd also had difficulty getting the salary owed to him, primarily because of a disagreement between himself and the Putnam family.

I'm sure it was just a coincidence that Ann Putnam had been the afflicted girl who accused him of witchcraft.

When Burroughs left Salem, he moved to Maine and remarried, but even so, Ann claimed she had been visited by two ghosts, who told her Reverend Burroughs had murdered them. The apparitions were those of the minister's dead wives, long since passed on.

Even though they were shocked at the idea that a minister would be involved in witchcraft and murder, the magistrates quickly dispatched officers to the parish where Burroughs now lived. They stormed

Reverend George Burroughs was a former Salem minister who'd had disagreements with several prominent local families. He was hauled back to Salem, also accused of witchcraft.

into his home in the middle of a meal and dragged him unwillingly back to Salem. Despite being a minister, he received no special treatment, perhaps because he didn't show proper Puritan piety. Ann Putnam testified against him, as did Mercy Lewis, claiming Burroughs had conducted witches' gatherings. Deliverance Hobbs confirmed their stories, and others agreed.

When asked how he could have done this while hundreds of miles away from Salem, Burroughs was amazed to hear that he had bedeviled the innocent in Salem as a sinister "specter," just like the other alleged witnesses. His history of disagreements with the Putnams and other people in town wasn't in his best interests. He quickly found himself in jail.

While these events were happening in Salem, a new royal governor from England arrived in the colony. After learning of the widespread hysteria around witchcraft accusations, Sir William Phips decided he needed to deal with something that could become a calamity. It was no longer confined to one village - it was affecting the entire colony.

Phips arrived in the village with Increase Mather, the father of famed Puritan minister Cotton Mather and later, president of Harvard University. Mather had been prominent in earlier witch trials in Boston and wanted to see what all the fuss in Salem was about. Sir William was counting on his advice to get the situation under control.

After decreeing that all those accused of witchcraft be left chained in their cells, he turned the business of trying them over to the courts. A special court was formed with Deputy Governor William Stoughton as president. The court would bring the accused witches to trial and render a verdict in each case with no appeals permitted. Six other judges were also named for the special court - four from Boston, one from Salem, and one from Haverhill.

The accused were no longer being questioned - they were now going on trial for their lives.

As for Sir William, he was only interested in getting together a military expedition against the French in Canada. He personally wanted nothing to do with what was going on in Salem.

Bridget Bishop was the first to stand trial. Her position in the community undoubtedly contributed to her dilemma. Bridget, in her 50s, was twice widowed and was the successful proprietor of a local inn. She also stood out in the community for her wearing of "brightly colored" clothes, which was abhorred by the Puritans who traditionally wore dark, modest clothing. She didn't help her case by appearing in court wearing a "lace-trimmed scarlet bodice."

There had been accusations of witchcraft against her for years, even by her late husband. There were suspicions that she practiced folk magic, offering healing cures to ailing people. Combining the suspicions with how she lived, dressed, and prospered, she became an easy target.

When women assigned by the court examined Bridget's body, they found an "excrescence of flesh," believed to be a teat or a nipple used by the witch's familiar to feed from her breast. She also didn't help herself by stating that she was not guilty. "I am innocent to a witch," she said. "I know not what a witch is."

Judge Hathorne attacked this statement by asking how she could be sure she was not one if she didn't know what a witch was. Bridget was unable to find an answer that would suit the court. She was pronounced guilty and was hanged on June 10, 1692.

Bridget Bishop was obviously a victim of the hysteria, but she might have also been one of the only actual practitioners of magic in Salem at the time. We would consider her part of the "cunning folk." She and several others had delved into spells for healing, divination, and fortune-telling, and later, when work was being done in the house where she had once lived, poppets - "small images with stuck with pins" - were found carefully hidden away. She had dabbled in folk magic, which was not the work of the Devil, but in Salem in those days, it was all that was needed to send her to the gallows.

Bridget Bishop became the first of the accused to be hanged at Salem, but she would not be the last.

During the Salem trials, religious hysteria peaked when the judges allowed "spectral evidence" to be admitted in court. This evidence claimed that specters or apparitions of witches tormented and inflicted pain on the innocent. But the specters could only be seen by those who were bewitched. The Salem judges allowed these claims - along with unsupported allegations and hearsay. This seems mind-boggling to us today, but in the religious climate of New England in the seventeenth century, it seemed perfectly reasonable.

But not everyone was convinced that "spectral evidence" was enough to warrant an execution. Cotton Mather, who was consulted for advice during the trials, gave the issue a great deal of thought. Although he was undoubtedly a fervent believer that witches were the handmaidens of the Devil, he advised against putting too much emphasis on "spectral evidence" in determining the guilt of the accused.

Other respected ministers throughout Massachusetts also weighed in. Every reply stated wholeheartedly that witches were a genuine danger and threat to God-fearing Christians. However, most wanted more than merely spectral or unseen evidence as absolute proof of a crime. But once the accused were determined to be witches, they wanted them hanged.

So, if ministers throughout the colony questioned the reliability of "spectral evidence," why was it so universally allowed during the Salem trials?

Chief Judge and Deputy Governor William Stoughton.

Stoughton strongly believed that such evidence should be permitted. He had no doubt, he said, that the Devil could take the shape of those who were guilty. Some of the consulting ministers may have disagreed with his beliefs, but his position was so important that he prevailed. "Spectral evidence" would be allowed when the witch trials continued that summer.

In late June 1692, the fates of Sarah Good, Elizabeth Howe, Susanna Martin, Sarah Wilds, and Rebecca Nurse were also sealed. Four of them were found guilty and sentenced to hang. Only Rebecca Nurse had been found not guilty. Her good reputation served her well - at first.

Rebecca's many friends and family members were brave enough to testify on her behalf, and she was found innocent of the crimes for which she was accused. Instantly, though, the courtroom was plunged into chaos. The afflicted girls howled, pulled their hair, and rolled around on the floor, screaming that the woman was guilty.

Unbelievably, Judge Stoughton ordered Rebecca to be returned to the courtroom and ordered the verdict to be reconsidered. This time, she was - no surprise - found to be guilty.

Stunned and angry, her family appealed to Governor Phips, who granted a stay of execution. But the afflicted girls began claiming they were being tortured by Rebecca's specter, begging

the judges to hang her. Judge Stoughton ended the delay, and on Tuesday, July 19, she and the other four women were hanged as witches in Salem.

As Sarah Good waited for the rope to end her life, she again proclaimed her innocence and then rebuked the Reverend Nicholas Noyes, who stood nearby and accused her of being a witch.

"You are a liar," she sneered at him. "I am no more a witch than you are a wizard, and if you take away my life, God will give you blood to drink."

Eerily, Sarah's prediction came true. Years later, Noyes choked to death on his own blood following a throat hemorrhage.

The terror continued to spread. Scores of people continued to be accused, and the court continued its travesty of justice. The fear of being charged as a witch became so pervasive that many turned on the neighbors who'd always lived peacefully next to them. It was better to be an accuser than one of the accused, seemed to be the common way of thinking.

Many of those charged had learned that the way to avoid the gallows was to admit to practicing witchcraft, even though they never had. They fabricated stories about their involvement with magic and sorcery; while untrue, it saved their lives. Those who insisted they were innocent and refused to confess to things they hadn't done faced relentless questioning and even torture - only to confess to things they hadn't done anyway. They did whatever they could to get the harassment and pain to stop. Then, under intense pressure from officials, they'd accuse others of witchcraft, and the panic went on and on.

Again, there was no doubt that some individuals secretly practiced magic in Puritan communities, but none of it was the kind of magic that officials were charging. Fantasy had overtaken reality, and the combination of fear, superstition, and coercion fed the flames of hysteria so intensely that some of the cunning folk - primarily women - became convinced they were in league with the Devil after all.

In July, John Proctor, still in the dismal confines of the jail, wrote to local ministers to plead that the witch trials be moved to Boston with new judges on the bench. He was confident that the "witch hunts" were based mainly on lies and intimidation. But his letters had little effect.

In early August, John and his wife, Elizabeth, stood trial, as did Reverend George Burroughs and three others. More than 30 people from Ipswich, Massachusetts, where John Proctor had once lived, appealed to the judges on his behalf, hoping to save his life. Nearly two dozen neighbors from Salem also offered support. But their efforts were in vain - John and Elizabeth were declared guilty, along with the others. Only Elizabeth was spared from being hanged. She was pregnant at the time, and under Puritan law, the killing of her innocent unborn child was forbidden.

Reverend Burroughs, who had always claimed that witches and devils were genuine, now protested against using "spectral evidence," insisting that witches could not harm the innocent using apparitions. But the word of the afflicted girls against him was simply too powerful. He was also condemned to die on the gallows.

George Jacobs was convicted on the word of his granddaughter, Margaret. When she had been arrested on witchcraft charges, she had offered his name because she feared being tortured and hanged. Although she later stated in court that her confession had been coerced and that her testimony had been "false and untrue," it had no effect on the fate of her grandfather, who was sentenced to be hanged.

When August 19 - the day of execution - arrived, Reverend Burroughs again proclaimed his innocence and followed this with a perfect recitation of the Lord's Prayer. Many of those gathered knew that a witch was supposed to be unable to recite that prayer and pointed out the contradiction. But Reverend Cotton Mather stepped in and assured the crowd that Burroughs was guilty. He urged those assembled not to be swayed otherwise - Burroughs was an ordained minister, so he could perfectly recite the Lord's Prayer and still be a sorcerer. "The Devil is never more the Devil than when he most appears like an angel of light," Mather told them.

Burroughs and the others were hanged.

The trials and executions continued. In September, 15 more people were sentenced to death. On just one day, September 22, eight were hanged, including Martha Corey. Several of the convicted pleaded to the governor, judges, and clergy for clemency, but their appeals fell on deaf ears.

Giles Corey, Martha's husband, had also been accused of practicing witchcraft. Although the older man knew he was not guilty, he also understood that if he claimed to be innocent, he'd be convicted anyway. A proud man, he refused to falsely plead guilty to save his life and satisfy his accusers. So, Corey refused to enter a plea at all. In fact, he did not utter a single word in court. When questioned by the judges, he said nothing. Therefore, under Puritan law, he could not be brought to trial.

But he paid the price for his bold silence.

The court made no allowance for Giles' advanced

In court, Giles Corey refused to utter a word and his silence would not allow him to be tried under Puritan law. Regardless, he paid a terrible price when he was crushed to death by stones.

age when they decided on his brutal punishment. He was laid on the ground while heavy stones were placed on him until he was crushed to death under their weight. He suffered intensely for two days before he finally died.

His courage, composure, and resolve deeply affected the residents of Salem - and the first seeds of doubt about the reality of the witch trials had been sown at last.

Following the executions that took place in September, the court recessed with plans to reconvene later in the fall - it never happened.

By October, more than the seasons had changed in Salem. There had been a marked shift in the villagers' attitude about the trials. People were beginning to speak out and question their fairness.

Increase Mather delivered an address to his fellow clergy speaking out against "spectral evidence" and reprimanded those who accepted the unreliable accusations of "confessed witches." He added, "We ought not to practice witchcraft to discover witches. I would rather see ten suspected witches go free than execute even one innocent."

Unfortunately, it was too late for that.

But others spoke out, too. An influential Boston merchant named Thomas Brattle published a letter in which he objected to how the Salem trials had been conducted. He noted how easily the magistrates had accepted the words of the afflicted girls and others who'd made accusations without deeply questioning their motivations. Like most people of the time, Brattle believed the Devil was at work but thought many of the girls' claims were the result of their imaginations. He concluded that some of the confessions seemed obviously coerced, while others were made by the demented and the deluded.

A magistrate from Salisbury, Robert Pike, wrote that he was skeptical of both what the afflicted girls claimed and the types of highly questionable evidence that were permitted to convict someone of witchcraft. He stated that he did not doubt the reality of witches but suggested the Devil was doing his nefarious work through the afflicted, not the witches. Because of this, innocent people were sometimes accused because the Devil commanded the afflicted to falsely blame the righteous.

But it was Governor Phips who finally ended the whole thing. He returned from the Canadian border and was dismayed that his special court had not found a solution to the problem. In fact, it seemed to have made things worse. The jails in Salem and Boston

A widely distributed image that illustrated the "Last Hanging" in Salem. By the spring of 1693, the hysteria had finally come to an end.

were still packed with people who had not yet been tried. Still, more people - mainly women - were accused daily of being witches. And the afflicted girls showed no signs of being released from the Devil's grasp - or their own hysteria or maliciousness, depending on whom you asked.

In addition to the personal misery suffered by the accused locked up in the dirty, overcrowded dungeons, the witch madness created problems for the entire colony. The commotion of the past several months had led many to disregard their farms, shops, and trades.

In other words, the witch craze was costing the government money, and that couldn't be allowed to continue.

Not only that, but many of the colony's residents had fled, worried they might be accused of witchcraft, too. It was not an unwarranted fear. Allegations had been made about people from all walks of life - how soon before they started to be made against even important individuals whose reputations should be beyond reproach, like the governor's own wife?

This had to be stopped. In October, Sir William ordered that no one else would be jailed except in extreme cases. He also decreed that, in the future, "spectral evidence" would be inadmissible in his courts. This made trying the other defendants nearly impossible, but laws had to be followed. Those that remained in jail finally had their day in court in January 1693, when 52 people were brought to trial. All were found to be not guilty, except for three who confessed. Those three were sentenced to hang, but the royal attorney general stepped in and ruled that the evidence against those to be hanged was insufficient. Governor Phips commuted their sentences.

He then ordered the jails to be emptied of suspected witches, but bizarrely, before they could be released, they were required to pay for the food and expenses incurred while they were in jail. Most didn't have the money. It was an added insult to the innocent who had already suffered, and some never overcame the hardships and costs - physically, financially, and emotionally. Under the law at the time, those who couldn't pay had their property confiscated and spent the rest of their lives with nothing.

But at least the Salem witch hysteria had come to an end.

By the spring of 1693, the witch hunts were over, but the hard feelings they created between villagers would linger for years. The accusations, harsh words, and bitter memories created permanent rifts between former friends and neighbors. Many of those who fled Salem during the hysteria chose never to return.

Once public sentiment shifted away from the "afflicted girls," they withdrew from sight. Only Ann Putnam publicly admitted the wrong that she'd taken part in. In 1706, she requested to be allowed back as a member of the church in Salem Village, and Reverend Joseph Green read her apology from the pulpit. In the spirit of healing, she was forgiven and allowed to return to the church.

But not all were forgiven.

Many were angered at Reverend Parris for his rush when he demanded the children accuse others of supposedly bewitching them. The most furious were, of course, the relatives of those jailed, tortured, and executed. They refused to forgive what he'd done. Some even chastised him for his treatment of his former slave, Tituba, when she was released from jail. She could not legally own property and was without resources when it came time to pay for her expenses behind bars. Reverend Parris refused to help her. It wasn't until a kind man came forward and paid her jail costs that Tituba was freed. Parris was forced to leave Salem in 1697, and he never returned.

The minister who followed, Reverend Green, devoted considerable time and effort to easing the tension and hostilities in the community. No one was blameless, he said, but no compensation was possible for those who lost their lives.

Eventually, most people realized that the insanity in Salem was a deception created by fear and religious extremism. Throughout the Massachusetts colony, January 4, 1697, was set aside as a day of fasting and prayer to ask "God's forgiveness" for the tragedy of the witch trials.

One of the judges, Samuel Sewall, wrote a letter that his minister read to the congregation. Sewall acknowledged his terrible mistake when he condemned innocent people to death. He wrote that all he could do now was plead for absolution from God and his fellow men and women.

Most of the other trial judges also admitted their mistakes, especially in believing that "spectral evidence" was sufficient to send someone to the gallows. They begged for forgiveness and deeply apologized, saying they'd fall under the power of a strong "delusion."

Of course, one judge never apologized at all, believing that he'd done nothing wrong - the chief judge, William Stoughton.

But no matter how many apologies were made, mere words couldn't erase the damage that had been done.

Twenty innocents died in Salem - 19 hanged and one crushed to death - and more than 150 had been jailed, and of those accused, 50 confessed to being witches, likely under the threat of torture. Several died in jail, undoubtedly because of the deplorable conditions.

And then there was little Dorcas Good, the five-year-old sent to jail as a witch. She nearly went insane from her experiences and the subsequent trauma. She remained mentally ill for the rest of her life.

An apology was an inadequate gesture in response to the horror that had occurred.

So, what happened in Salem?

Experts have blamed fraud, class conflict, sexual repression, accidental poisoning, hysteria, actual witchcraft, and, of course, religious extremism. Likely no one explanation will suffice. It was probably a combination of these things, but there is no doubt that the religious extremism of the Puritans was the leading cause.

If not for their willingness to blame the Devil and witchcraft for every illness, crop failure, and bit of bad luck in and around the village, the madness in Salem would have never occurred.

Salem - and much of New England - had teetered on the edge of madness and permanently changed the way that Americans would think about witchcraft and folk magic. The events of 1692 cast a shadow over the country's history and influenced the opinions and fears about witches for centuries to come.

Because even after Salem, the very idea of witchcraft would continue to lead to murder, mayhem, lynch mobs, and more.

4. AMERICAN FOLK MAGIC

For the most part, they just sort of stopped.

The witch hunts, I mean. Salem may have been the peak of the madness when it came to hunting American witches, but it was not the end. More trouble followed. More elderly, eccentric, or just plain mean people in small communities throughout the colonies were accused of witchcraft. Some were placed on trial, a few were convicted, a few were hanged, and then it all seemed to fade away, and the seventeenth century became the eighteenth in the American colonies.

Matters more pressing took everyone's attention - war, droughts, religious conflicts, and problems with Native Americans among them. There had also been seeds of doubt planted about the fairness of the witch trials. Many questioned the extraordinary ways they had been conducted, the evidence that had been allowed, and the painful methods used to extract confessions. Most admitted that they themselves would confess to just about anything if someone were dumping them in a lake to see if they'd float.

But just because the witch trials ended, it didn't mean that suspicion about some members of communities came to a halt.

And it also didn't mean that witchcraft wasn't practiced anymore - because folk magic and conjuring had never gone away.

No matter what may have been happening with the religious and civil authorities of the time, for the everyday folk, belief in witchcraft and its powers persisted. Such a belief rarely linked magic with the Devil, though. Instead, people accepted that certain men and women had powers and secret knowledge and were expected to be respected or feared - or, more accurately, a little of both.

These people are the cunning men and wise women mentioned earlier. They had existed before the times of the witch trials and had somehow survived those persecutions. They were the practitioners of folk magic and healing that the Puritans had both hated and feared, and they continued to practice their craft in small towns and on farms throughout America.

But don't misunderstand - some of the cunning folk had been tried and executed as witches. However, they were, more often than not, able to avoid persecution thanks to the respect they held in communities where they provided valuable services. It is their survival that manages to provide the continuity between the modern day and the ancient practices of witchcraft tradition.

But for many people, those who practiced folk magic were not necessarily considered witches. Even though they were believed to have the same or similar occult powers as witches, it was thought by most ordinary people that a witch used their powers for evil purposes, in league with the Devil. In fact, one of the primary roles of those who engaged in folk magic was to help people whom witches had cursed - their opposite numbers, so to speak.

That's how most people felt anyway. There would always be religious extremists and those who imposed their morality on others who would consider the cunning folk witches and evil - no matter how helpful they might be. When it comes to witchcraft, perception is everything.

The interesting thing about folk magic is that there was a correct way to do it. Depending on what part of the country, hillside, or holler a family was from, it might practice it differently. The differences mostly came from where the families came from - predominantly Scottish and Irish - and what they'd brought with them from home. Some families used candles for rituals, and others used oil lamps. Some hung corn cobs over doorways for good luck, while others used horseshoes.

Immigrants brought folk magic to America, but when it arrived and set down its roots, it became a uniquely American form of witchcraft. The methods used to practice it became little fragments of family histories like an heirloom passed down by oral tradition.

While folk magic was practiced throughout the country, including in Puritan New England, most history focuses on practitioners in the mountain regions, specifically Appalachia and the Ozarks. Since most Ozark folk magic seems to be an offshoot of that practiced in Appalachian - and brought west by settlers to that area - I think the best way to introduce it historically to readers is to focus on the way it became such an integral part of Appalachian life.

Explaining the history of the Appalachian region would take more pages than this book will allow, so I want to focus on the area of East Tennessee and the surrounding areas of Virginia, West Virginia, and North Carolina - in other words, the *heart* of Appalachia.

By the late seventeenth century, when immigrants first began arriving, the Cherokee had become the region's dominant tribe and had established communities scattered around the mountains and valleys. A Cherokee legend recorded in the eighteenth century says that when the Cherokee first arrived in the region, they found "moon-eyed" people living in the mountains. They were called "moon-eyed" because they couldn't see well during the day. They had white skin, light hair, and gray eyes. There were said to have been in the buildings of ancient ruins found scattered in the hills. The Cherokee drove off the "moon-eyed" people, sending them west.

Cherokee society is matriarchal - a person's lineage is traced through their mother - and women were held in high regard. This

The folk magic traditions of Appalachia were combined from the beliefs of European settlers and the Native Americans who first inhabited the region.

respect for elderly women also became a part of the white culture, and "grannies" are given great respect to this day. Each Cherokee woman belonged to a family clan, and no one could marry within their own clan. When a man wanted marriage, he had to build the woman a house. If she wanted a divorce, she would gather his things while he was away and set them on the porch. She got to keep everything else, including the house and children. Her uncles and brothers would take over teaching her sons to hunt, pray, and fight. This kind of structure became common among most settling white families, too.

When those first settlers arrived in the late seventeenth century, there was hostility with the native people. The Cherokee freely gave land to the new arrivals, but the white men wanted more. And they took it and spilled blood for it. Agreements were broken, and the natives were often mistreated.

But not by everyone. Many of the new settlers treated the First Nations people with respect and lived among them peacefully, which is how many of the Cherokee's myths, stories, crafts, and medicinal knowledge found their way into American folk magic.

In 1830, the Indian Removal Act was passed, and in less than a decade, the Cherokee had been moved west along the Trail of Tears. Of the 17,000 who were driven out of the mountains, between 2,000 and 6,000 died on the way to land west of the

Mississippi River. Those who stayed behind were forced into a secret existence in the hills and hollows of the mountains.

The remaining Cherokee were one secret of the Appalachians - folk magic practitioners were another. After

A long tradition of folk magic and healing began in the earliest days of Appalachian settlement.

the witch trials that bedeviled the early colonies conjure work was carefully hidden. According to the well-off church folk who sat in stiff pews every Sunday morning, anything magic was of the Devil himself. They didn't understand - like the Puritans - that sometimes people needed a little "special" help.

Folk magic gave ordinary folks a little hope. It was a way to have a little control over their circumstances and a sense that things would be all right, even in the poor circumstances they found themselves in. And it worked. It didn't make them rich, but it gave people a chance to maybe change things in their favor.

American folk magic is a melting pot of practices from the Irish, Scottish, German, and other European traditions and influences from African and Native American sources. For example, the use of rainwater in magic primarily originates from the British Isles. The use of graveyard dirt and dust comes from the Native Americans and the enslaved Africans brought to this land. The art of placing bowls and pans under the bed for workings and spells comes from Jewish folklore. The practice of throwing spells and remnants behind oneself into a stream comes from European traditions. And so on.

In almost every case, some things were added, or taken away, based on location, timing, and need. Generations changed and adapted them. Many spell recipes for the same purpose may include different ingredients or tools. For example, hotfoot powder - which makes people leave you alone or leave town - is usually made from hot peppers, spices, and sulfur. But those things weren't often found in the mountains, so most conjurers used black pepper and salt instead. Some used spiders, bugs, and other things that might scare people away.

When it comes to this kind of sympathetic magic, it's not always the ingredients - it's believing that it works. Superstition is the fuel that makes folk magic work. This doesn't make it primitive or backward. Superstition is one of the basic needs of humanity, like food, weather, hunting, childbearing, and labor. It guides us from accidentally causing harm to ourselves and offers protection from the same to others.

CHARMS AND PROTECTIONS

There were both men and women among the conjure folk. The men generally practiced the craft as a second job in addition to their primary employment, while for women, it was their only source of income. The men were often called "wizards" or "conjurers." Some took the title "doctor" to make themselves more respectable. Some called them "conjure folk," and most of the women were known as "granny" once they reached a certain age.

One thing that those who respected and paid for their services *never* called them, however, was "witch."

In folk magic, there is a difference between a witch and a doctor, healer, or conjurer. Witches were thought to have made pacts with the Devil, read the Bible backward, and consulted with demons to obtain their conjure knowledge. These beliefs date back to the era when the Puritans and others persecuted witches.

Among the mountain people, witches were thought to have been initiated into black magic - by shooting a silver bullet into the Bible, cursing God, or waiting for the Devil to arrive in the family cemetery and having sex with him. While most accounts of true witchcraft follow no such beliefs, the reputation of a conjure person was based on the community's attitude. As stated before, witchcraft is all about perception. One doctor might have been a born healer, and even though he might have mixed up some sort of revenge for a client's enemy, he was still regarded as "good" since the community believed he'd gotten his powers from their god.

On the other hand, the witch was susceptible to a much harder judgment. It was believed that the outcast older woman up in the hollow was mixing up poisons, dancing with the Devil, and cursing people all over town. There were stories of witches cursing cattle, harming crops, making people sick, causing birth defects, and worse.

In addition to their advice which was sought on matters of love, crops, health, and finding lost objects, one of the main functions of the conjure folk was protection and lifting curses. Spells for protection used everything from rainwater to moonshine, tobacco juice, graveyard dirt, red clay, silver, roots, herbs, bones, candles, bottles, knots, poppet dolls, and all manner of written charms and spells.

The people of the era had always been superstitious about everything from ghosts to lightning, death, and curses - basically anything that threatened their lives or fortunes.

The most important people in the household - and most needed protection from haunts, bogeymen, and the evil eye - were children. They were most susceptible to such threats in their early months, so it was customary to baptize and christen them as soon as possible. A flowering plant called yarrow was traditionally hung at the head of a baby's crib, and an iron nail could be driven into the crib post to protect the child from being taken by a witch. If a child got sick, folks would take her to a healer for medicine or prayer.

Chamomile-infused milk was also fed to an infant nightly for the first six months of its life to protect them from evil and keep them alive until dawn. When a child died from what was then known as "crib death," it was believed to be the work of a witch, so people did all they could to track down the offender and make sure it never happened again. Usually, this meant obtaining a "witch bottle" or spell from a conjurer, which would hopefully lead them to the devious witch.

In addition to children, people had to protect themselves. There were many things suggested by conjurers that could be done for a person's own protection - like carrying an iron nail in your left front pocket and hanging a horseshoe over your door. Turning it upside-down on Wednesday, Thursday, and Friday would eliminate any lingering ghosts in your house.

When storms and lightning were particularly threatening in the spring, folks were told to walk around and tap two stones together to make a barrier that lightning strikes couldn't penetrate. Wood from a lightning-struck tree could be turned into a charm offering protection.

When restless ghosts inhabited a house, residents were told to find a whole, unwashed potato and a small object that belonged to the deceased. The potato was cut in half, and each side was hollowed out so that the object would fit inside. The halves were then put back together, bound with red yarn, and pinned together with nails. It was then taken to the graveyard and left on the resting spot of the dead person. The spirit would then stay bound to the cemetery until they fully crossed over.

Other practices included hanging bunches of basil over windows to keep unwanted spirits out, hanging lavender to

protect from misfortune, and placing a dried corncob beneath a doorway to attract good fortune and keep illness away. For it to work, though, the corncob had to stay dry. If it molded, it took away the good luck.

To keep from being cursed, a person was told to tie up a lock of hair, a toenail clipping, and a stick from the eastern side of an oak tree with red string while invoking the name of the Father, Son, and Holy Ghost. It was said that you could not be cursed as long as that charm was around your neck. If you ever lost it, the person that found it could curse you.

To remove a curse, a conjure doctor would usually instruct a person to keep a piece of coal in a right pocket or shoe. Once the coal crumbled to dust, it had to be disposed of at a crossroads or under a willow tree near a stream. Once that was finished, the person had to return home a different way. If completed in the proper order, the curse would be put to rest.

In addition to getting rid of curses, most people also wanted to attract good luck. Horseshoes were a popular method, and so was keeping a jar of money by the front door to encourage money to keep coming in. Cornmeal was always sprinkled on the bottom of the empty jar before it was placed there to make a soft "dirt" on which the money would land. Most of the money in the jar would be collected by finding it outside or along the street. If a person found a coin, he was supposed to keep it in his left pocket until he could add it to the jar. Money from the jar could be spent, but it was never supposed to be totally empty and should always hold seven or more of one type of currency - like seven pennies, seven dimes, etc.

Four-leaf clovers were always lucky, and when found without looking for them, they were usually pressed into a Bible or placed into the inner lining of a shoe. Good luck also came from finding a heads-up penny which was then placed in the right shoe, or from a spider found nesting in a kitchen. It was a sign that the family would never go hungry as long as it was there. Seeing a new moon for the first time each month over your left shoulder was considered good luck, but not if you saw it through the trees.

A black cat's bones were considered lucky for gambling - even though they were considered notoriously bad luck under other circumstances. Conjurers would take the cat's skeleton to a creek where the water flowed toward the south and dropped in the bones. If one bone floated and went upstream, that was the lucky bone. Other variations call for the bones to be boiled in a pot of milk, and the first one that came to the surface was considered the lucky one.

Other items for luck were bones from the right paw of an opossum, deer horn points worn around the neck, and, of course, a rabbit's foot.

Conjurers also had a long list of things to avoid so you wouldn't end up with bad luck. It was bad luck to open an umbrella inside the house, to come in a door you didn't go out from, spill salt, burn sassafras or cedar in your home, or point at a graveyard with a new grave in it. You should never bring blooming dogwood into your house because it was believed to be the kind of wood Christ was nailed onto in the Bible. When a fish was caught, it had to be thanked, or bad luck would befall the home, and the cupboards would become bare. Also, women should never be allowed into a coal mine.

Many of these superstitions were taken to extremes, but such fears were understandable, especially among Appalachia's poor and often poverty-stricken inhabitants. Bad luck was terrifying and could literally end their lives as they knew it. Is it any wonder they turned to the conjure folk for help?

THE WAYS OF THE CONJURE FOLK

The tools of a cunning man or woman were more common than most realize. If for some reason, they didn't have - or couldn't afford - a tool they needed, they'd make do with what they had. Folk magic was, and is, the magic of common people, and if a scrap of newspaper, some yarn, and a candle were all they had, they made it work.

In almost every conjurer's kitchen, you'd find a mortar and pestle for grinding herbs. If they didn't have one, a large flat stone with a bit of a groove and a palm-sized river rock would do. Shovels were needed for digging up herbs, unearthing roots, burying works, or getting dirt - and gloves made that easier on the hands.

In folk magic, a broom is surrounded by lore. If a free-standing broom fell with no one around, unexpected company was on the way. If one swept over someone's feet, they'd go to jail. Sweep under their feet, and they'd never get married. There was also the tradition of jumping the broom at weddings for luck and fertility.

Brooms, of course, had a long tradition in witchcraft. The broom was used to sweep the porch - and the lawn - to eliminate any tricks that may have been placed on the property, especially at the edges.

When a house needed to be cleansed of evil or sickness, the broom's bristles were anointed with holy water. Salt was cast down on the floors, and then the house was swept from back to front, sweeping the salt out the door. When a troublesome person entered a house, salt and pepper was thrown in the tracks, then swept away so they'd never return. The used broom could then be placed upside down, bristles up, to keep them away for good.

Knives were also a staple in folk magic - anything from a kitchen knife to a pocketknife. Like the broom, they were objects of many traditions. When a bad storm was approaching, a person could go to the house's south side and drive the knife's hilt into the ground with the blade pointing up. This was to cut the storm or tornado in two, sending it around the home.

A person was never supposed to close a pocketknife that had been opened by someone else - it was bad luck. And if someone was given a knife as a gift, the receiver should always "buy it" from the giver for a penny. Otherwise, the blade could sever their relationship. Knives were used for protection, cutting away pain or fear, and as a remedy to wounds they might cause.

Yarn or string was always kept on hand - usually red - so that it could be used to tie up sachets, bind packets, hang charms, and even act as a charm itself.

Rags and handkerchiefs of various fabrics and colors were often used to make charm bags and poppet dolls. Rags could also be used to curse one's enemies, provide healing from sickness, and catch the morning dew to be used in works for love and healing. Washcloths and kitchen towels used repeatedly for stopping blood or as a compress were thought to become stronger with every use. Flannel was always a popular kind of cloth to be used because it was believed to bring good luck of its own. Most charm bags were made with flannel from old shirts.

Candles and oil lamps provided the only light back in the day, so they also became guides for spiritual work. Candles were rubbed with lard, butter, or oil, rolled in sifted herbs, or filled with herbs using a hole cut into the bottom. Herbs were also added to the oil in lamps. The color of the candles didn't matter as long as it got the job done.

A conjurer's kitchen would be filled with jars, canisters, and bags of every kind. Since many families canned their fruit and vegetables at the end of the growing season, it was just as easy to use the mason jars to store herbs, spices, roots, salts, flowers, and everything else they needed for spells and workings.

The workings required other ingredients, too. Nature's creeks, rivers, and lakes held magical qualities that were ascribed to them by the settlers, the enslaved Black people, and the Native Americans. They were turned into an array of different waters - mixed with herbs, moonshine, and whiskey - that were used in remedies and charms.

One crucial component of folk magic was rainwater. It was used for healing skin afflictions and in teas for spiritual and physical ailments. Its power stayed intact as long as it did not touch the ground. Rainwater was used to cure toothaches, remove witching from cattle, and many other things.

Creek water was often used as a base for teas and washes. It was also used for cleansing or removing curses from a person, but to work, it had to be free-flowing and "alive," so it could not be stored for that purpose.

As the most famous ingredient in folk magic, dew had powerful properties because it was considered the earth's "sweat."

If a person washed their face with morning dew before sunrise, they could clear up skin rashes. If they washed their chest with it, it was considered a cure for depression. A woman who wanted to gain a lover's affection washed their face, breasts, and private parts with dew while saying that person's name aloud. Women who wanted to get pregnant were told to roll around naked in dew under the full moon's light.

Certain kinds of stump water - found pooling in the rotting stump of a tree - were also considered beneficial. Since it had never touched the ground, its magic was intact - but only if it was collected on a full moon while the moon reflected in the water. To gather it required a silver ladle, walking backward to the stump, and remaining utterly silent while taking the water home. The Cherokee believed that stump water was a primary tool in healing, a tradition they passed on to the conjure folk.

Water mixed with tobacco juice was considered good

medicine for bug bites, rashes, wounds, and infections. The Cherokee taught the healers to chew tobacco and spit the liquid on snakebites, dog bites, bee stings, and cuts. Most healers kept it in their kitchens in a jar mixed with water.

Moonshine and whiskey were also used in healing for their antiseptic qualities - long before anyone understood what germs were. Both were good for colds and congestion and were good hand washes for cleansing, luck, and love. Sprinkling moonshine on the top of the head and wiping it on the neck was used as protection from haunts when visiting a graveyard. Three daily doses of "burnt whiskey" - setting a tablespoon on fire until the flame went out - was a cure for diarrhea. It was also a good offering to be left for the spirits, human or otherwise.

The use of dirt and dust was also important in folk magic. Dirt was believed to contain the spiritual essence of a place and, like water, could be used for many purposes. Charms using dirt - like bottles of spiritually charged water - were often buried in certain areas to absorb the spot's energy.

Mud was often applied to wounds, bug bites, and snakebites. Dirt from a church or a courthouse was often carried by people who wanted to avoid the law. Dust was often mixed with other ingredients and sprinkled into the shoes or on the clothing of the people it was intended for, sprinkled where they would walk over it, scattered around the home to act as protection, or added to teas by placing it in a bag and boiling it with the leaves.

Graveyard dirt - taken from the grave of a certain person or the cemetery itself - was used in healing remedies or in charms for love, gambling, protection, and cursing. When taken from a particular grave, it employed the spirit of that grave for the work at hand.

And that work was rarely good.

Dirt from a churchyard was used to remedy toothaches, wounds, and general sickness. It also provided protection from witchcraft, from a person's enemies, from the law, and to attract love. Dust from a church building could also be gathered and baked into bread or mixed with milk to treat illness. Church dirt was best collected on a Sunday, and its power was often increased by collecting and combining dirt from several churches.

Dirt from the railroad tracks was used to make charms for safe travel. This worked in the same way that dirt collected from coal mines and banks attracted wealth and money. Dirt from a police station helped a person avoid the law, or courthouse dirt helped achieve a positive outcome in court - all were very simple in their symbolism.

Dirt collected from a crossroads was thought to be some of the most powerful, but it had to be "paid for" by leaving three shiny dimes in the place where it was removed. This dirt could be used to remove obstacles from a person's path, call a lover home, encourage good luck, or just about anything connected to acquiring or removing something spiritual or material from a person's life.

Among the other jars in a conjurer's kitchen were jars filled with red clay, which was used with salt and pepper to protect from witchcraft. Animal excrement was used for cures and to protect livestock from being bewitched. Sulfur could be used for healing remedies and curses when mixed with dirt and black pepper. Water steeped with copper pennies was used to ease the pain of arthritis. If anyone could afford to have it around, silver and gold provided protection from the evil eye and misfortune. Gunpowder was used in works of good luck, cursing, and protection.

There were scores of herbs, too. Their uses were legion, from curses to protection, healing the sick, having children, and almost everything imaginable. Long before small towns and isolated communities had doctors, the conjure folk provided all the medicine they needed. Herbs and roots could be found in the forests and fields, including bloodroot, corn silk, dandelion, ginseng, goldenrod, potatoes, walnuts, and pawpaw, which protected from ghosts, laid curses, and healed the sick.

Workings were also cooked up using silver coins, feathers to ward off nightmares, various bones to conjure up lust and romance, and stones from graveyards and crossroads.

Among the conjure folk's tools were also books - many books at a time when books were not exactly common. They had books of spells, rituals, tarot cards, astrology, and fortune-telling. The written word was thought to contain power, and magical books sometimes took on their own supernatural power.

As well as owning books, the cunning folk created their own books on various subjects, including astrology, herbal medicine, and magic spells. Many also used books to record their practice, their ideas, and any helpful information they gleaned out in the wild.

But the most powerful book to most folk magic practitioners - - especially those in Appalachia - was the Bible. It was often used as a spell book of sorts. In Appalachia, the family Bible was used

to record births, deaths, marriages, and other events. Important dates filled the blank pages inside, as would makeshift family trees, pictures, certificates, newspaper clippings, and locks of baby hair. This gave the family Bible a connection to the past, where much of the power of folk magic came from.

But the Bible was also used to provide power when its words were spoken or written - like the "Blood Verse," which is Ezekiel, Chapter 16, verse 6. It was used to stop bleeding in both man and beast.

And when I passed by thee, and saw thee polluted in thine own blood, I said unto thee when thou was in thy blood, Live, yea, I said unto thee when thou was in thy blood, Live.

A verse from John was often recited when baking bread:

This is the bread that comes down from heaven, so that one may eat of it and not die.

Or a verse from Joel, recited while cooking:

Yea, the Lord will answer and say unto his people, Behold I send you corn, wine, and oil, and ye shall be satisfied therewith.

Practitioners of folk magic might also rub oil on stiff joints while reciting Proverbs, Chapter 16, verse 24:

Pleasant words are like a honeycomb, sweet to the soul and health to the bones.

Many of the conjurers believed that their gifts came directly from God. But being influenced by the Bible may lead some to presume that harm was never done using folk magic, but this wasn't the case. It could be used to stop pain and cause it, too. It didn't always go by the biblical idea of being kind to your neighbor.

It aligned more with the concept of "an eye for an eye, and a tooth for a tooth."

However, any curse or retaliation had to be justified, and the punishment had to fit the crime. If not, the scales would tip back on the conjurer since they created an imbalance.

DEATH AND DYING

In the same way that a family Bible puts the conjurer in touch with their ancestors, even the simplest things could sometimes do the same. And they were necessary. Ancestors and family heritage were of the utmost importance to workers of folk magic.

When those ancestors arrived in America, many had nothing but the wisdom and practices they brought with them. The same could be said for the white settlers and the enslaved people who arrived in chains. With folk magic, conjurers asked their ancestors to come to their aid, and in return, they were given offerings and honor.

Often those offerings involved food, which was a heavy part of Appalachian culture. The food came from what was readily available to the ordinary folk - ham, bacon, cord, cornbread, green beans, potatoes, venison, and more. Whether it was a family gathering, a funeral, a marriage, or a burial, when neighbors got together, food was at the center of it. It embodied the struggle and poverty of the people, as well as the love and pride they took in themselves and their community.

The memory of the dead was often based around the food and drinks they loved during their lifetime. On birthdays and anniversaries of the dead, favorite dishes were usually prepared with a prayer. Many families followed the tradition of leaving a space at the table for those who'd passed on.

As we'll soon see, food also had a place in some traditions regarding death and dying.

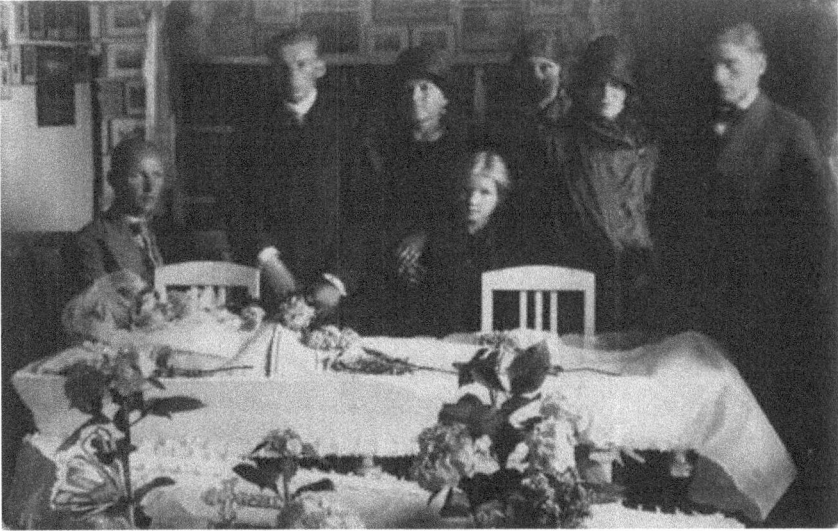

When a person died, it was generally believed that a local church bell should be rung for each year they lived, announcing their passing to the community. The body would then be washed and dressed and placed on a "cooling board," - which might be an old ironing board of a slab of wood passed down through a family. The chest and feet were tied to the board to prevent the body from rising, and a bowl of unmixed salt and earth was placed on the chest to prevent swelling and to keep the Devil away. Some tied a bag of salt around the neck of the corpse for the same reason.

Next, two pieces of silver money were placed on the eyes to prevent them from opening. The coins were also part of a very old tradition that the dead needed to pay the ferryman to cross the river to the other side.

On some occasions, what was called the "Sin Eater" would visit the deceased's home. The Sin Eater was an outcast from society, summoned upon the death of a loved one to eat a meal that had been placed on the corpse. When the plate was finished, the Sin Eater recited a few lines and absolved the deceased of their worldly sins, which afforded them passage into heaven and kept them from both the Devil and from wandering the earth. He then left without saying another word, only to appear again when he was needed.

The tradition of sin-eating became common in Ireland and Wales in the eighteenth and nineteenth centuries and was brought to America by immigrants.

Sin Eaters were paid for their service, though it was a small amount of money. There was a stigma attached to them, and they were considered a necessary evil. They were thought to be carrying the sins they ate along with them, which made them unclean, and they were shunned by neighbors and communities - if their identities were known. By taking on the sins of others, they were dooming themselves to isolation and, some believed, to damnation.

But most people had no idea who the Sin Eater in the community was since he always arrived in a black cloak and hood at the deceased's home. He did his business and went on his way. He remained anonymous and lived an ordinary life in the town or region.

Tales of sin-eating continued in isolated communities in North Carolina, West Virginia, Kentucky, and Virginia into the 1950s, and some say it still takes place today.

After a death, all the windows and doors of the house were left open to let the spirit out. If a family wanted to ensure they didn't return, they could also change the doorknob, lock, and rearrange the furniture.

The burial had to take place within three days, although never on a Sunday. If that rule was broken, another death might occur in the house that same year. Corpses were never taken out of a house head-first - always feet-first. If that was done, the dead might stay and haunt the house or beckon another family member to the grave.

The body was then carried to the cemetery by mule and wagon - but never across running water - and the wagon was required to stop at every crossroad so

Taking the dead to the graveyard in Appalachia

that the dead could catch up. If one could be afforded, a burial would take place in a plain pine box lined with cloth or quilts, or the corpse might be carefully wrapped in linen instead.

The digging of the grave had its own rules to follow. The weather was an essential part of it. When it rained, the dead were happy and would help the family through their grief. However, it was considered bad luck to rain into an empty grave.

The treatment of the grave before it was occupied could foretell deaths to come or at least misfortune. It was bad luck if the grave was left open overnight or over a Sunday, and the digging never started before sunrise of the day the body was buried. Many burials were held in the evening when the sun was setting.

If the diggers' shovels hit each other while digging, another death would soon follow. If a grave sank after a period of days, it was making room for another family member. If there is a bad storm soon after the burial, the deceased isn't at peace. The first person to leave the cemetery after the burying predicts the next death - if a man left first, the next death would be a man, and vice versa if it was a woman.

After the body was buried, the grave was covered with flowers from home. The tools used to dig it were left behind for three days in the shape of a cross to help the deceased's spirit and sanctify the grave. Along with the tools, a lighted lantern or candle was often left behind to lead the dead to the afterlife. Some even took home a handful of dirt from the grave to let the dead know they wouldn't be forgotten.

Because of the importance of ancestors in folk magic, the dead were honored daily. People were taught to never speak ill of the dead, walk over a grave, or dismiss their continued presence among the living. Shrines were kept for the dead -- especially those who were also conjurers -- filled with photographs, relics, locks of hair, and other belongings.

The veneration of ancestors also led to traditions concerning their graves. Often, families gathered to eat and then went to the cemetery to clean, dress, and decorate the graves of their dead. The graves of children were tended to first, then the older folks. Flowers, plates of food, toys for the children, liquor, and cigarettes were left on the graves.

After the graves of the family were honored, they moved on to the worn graves with illegible inscriptions. They washed them, picked them up, and placed flowers for their unknown occupants.

For those who practiced folk magic, the dead were never forgotten.

HEALING

In the days before modern medicine came to the rural regions of America, most folks relied on charms and remedies for their ailments, just as the people had been doing for hundreds of years.

Due to the poor hygiene of the time, warts were a common problem for most people. There were said to be some healers who could remove them with nothing more than a cloth and a spoken prayer, but most used slightly more complicated methods. One charm required a person to pick up the same number of stones as the number of warts he had from a creek that slowed south of west. Using one hand, he lowered it into the water by following the creek's current and picking up the stones one at a time. Each stone was touched to a wart three times, placed in a small pouch, and hung from a cow's horns or a fence post in a field. One variation had them left at a crossroads. Whoever opened the bag next would get warts.

Some healers had the gift of stopping blood. One method used a verse from the Bible but others used a damp rag that was left out overnight on Christmas Eve. The rag was then used throughout the years to stop wounds from bleeding. Sometimes a person would be given a red string to tie around their neck or left wrist to stop the blood. As long as it was knotted, the wound wouldn't bleed.

Water was another powerful medicine. Water collected at daybreak on Easter morning, Good Friday, or Ash Wednesday was said to be a cure for multiple illnesses. Rainwater from gutters applied to rashes would make them disappear, and water collected from stumps or grooves in boulders could be used in various medicines. Ocean water was said to heal anything from deep wounds to rheumatoid arthritis.

In addition to charms and healing waters, conjure folk also relied on home remedies and herbal medicines. For croup, they

An average Appalachian family had a lot of children, so folk magic about babies, children, and childbirth was practiced frequently.

prescribed the juices of a baked onion. Turpentine, cod liver oil, and lard were often mixed with herbs to prevent coughs. For common colds, two cloves of garlic were cut in half, and the two parts were tied to the bottom of the sick person's feet. Within an hour, their breath would smell like garlic, at which point the two half-cloves were thrown out the door. The other two halves took their place, and the process was repeated. After the second round, the sick person's feet were soaked in warm salt water, and the cold was "pulled out."

There were also many methods to assist in birth and with babies. Even before a child was born, conjurers stated that the mother's behavior would mark the baby. If she were whiny while pregnant, she would have a whiny child. If she made fun of a disabled person, her child would be born with that disability.

The first cup of water a mother carried after birth should be only a thimble full of water. She was to carry it from the front yard to the child without spilling a drop. This keeps the child from drooling too much when they're an infant. She also shouldn't cross running water until the child is one month old. Otherwise, it can bring illness to both mother and baby.

Conjurers had other wisdom about babies, too. These were mostly about divining if a woman was pregnant and about the birthing process. A popular method of determining if a woman was pregnant used an egg and a glass. First, the egg was rubbed over her belly in the sign of a cross. She then blew on the egg, and the healer dropped it into a glass of water. If the egg sank, the woman was with child. If it floated, she was not.

This practice was often paired with a way to divine the sex of the child. A gold wedding ring was suspended using three hairs from the expectant mother's head. She then lay on the floor with her head to the west, and the ring was dangled over her stomach while 23 Psalm from the Bible was recited. If the ring rotated in circles, it was a girl. If it swung back and forth, it was a boy.

If a woman wanted to be free from morning sickness, she was supposed to crawl over her lover to get out of bed when she awoke. This passed the symptoms on to him.

To ease birthing pains, a Bible was opened to the book of Matthew and placed on the women's chest or stomach. The location depended on the necessity. If the child was in danger, the stomach. If the mother was, the chest. A knife, arrowhead, or ax was also placed beneath a birthing bed to "cut the pain into pieces" and render it harmless.

In the case of possible hemorrhage during labor, chicken feathers were burned under the bed. The father gathered a bundle of six feathers plucked straight from the chicken.

If a child was stillborn, the mother needed a way to dry her milk without physical pain to add to her grief. A charm was devised for that - camphor on a cotton rag was placed on the child's grave to dry up the milk.

There are many charms devised to aid the health of a child and some to ease the parents' work. A stuttering child was believed to be cured by drinking water from a church bell or a baptismal pool.

To get a child - and mother - through the teething phase, the baby was given a dime with a hole put through it by a nail to wear around their neck. For a boy, the dime had to come from an aunt, and for a girl, it had to come from an uncle to be charmed. A child's gums could be rubbed with a silver thimble to ease discomfort. A deer-tooth necklace was also a powerful charm against teething pain, as was a necklace of strung elderberries that were dried and dipped in a creek on Easter morning.

CASTING FORTUNES

The early settlers were filled with a fear of the unknown. For the same reason that some colonists developed a fear of Native Americans, spirits, and witches, others put their faith in the workings of the grannies and the power doctors. They had their traditions of discerning the will of their god by following signs and listening to the wind, but sometimes divination by spells and charms was needed to ease the terrors of those they were trying to help.

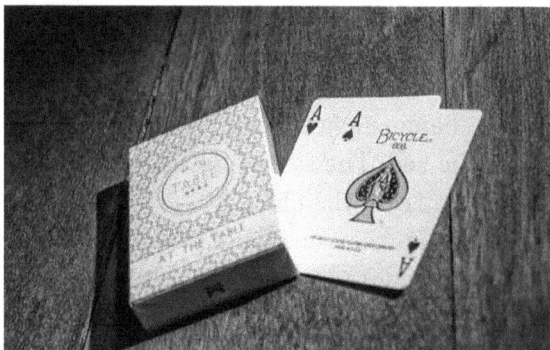

Aside from using a crystal for gazing and long layouts of cards, most divination methods were fairly simple - using "yes" or "no."

Playing cards could be used in this

way. A deck was shuffled three times, and three cards were drawn. The black suits meant no, and the red suits meant yes, so the probability was determined by two out of three cards.

Cards could also be used to determine a general overview of a person's life. The deck would be shuffled three times, and then the person looking for guidance would knock on the top three times. The stack was cut into two piles and then breathed on. Then, they were shuffled again. Starting from the top of the deck, every card would be turned over. When two of the same kinds of cards were found in a row, those cards were to be set aside in the order they came up. After the last card, the doubles were then interpreted.

Each set of cards had its own meanings, which sometimes varied depending on the conjurer. Kings usually meant money and business. Queens represented lovers. Jacks meant jealousy, while tens stood for dreams either fulfilled or thwarted, based on other cards. And so on. There were good cards and bad cards, depending on the cards that connected them.

There was also the "scattering" form of divination, which meant tossing sunflower or apple seeds on a handkerchief after whispering a question to them. If the seeds were spaced out after they landed, it meant yes. If they fell in groups, it meant no.

Another method called for placing something in a particular place and interpreting the letters and signs that formed. This was usually done with corn kernels thrown into a circle drawn in the dirt. The conjurer then found letters, shapes, and patterns from how they landed.

Reading tea leaves or coffee grounds was also a way to interpret

Water witches used dowsing to find water, treasure, and lost things. This was usually done using a forked stick.

signs and messages. The drink would be consumed to the last sip, leaving grounds or leaves behind. The granny would then breathe three times into the cup and cover it with a saucer. Then, the cup and saucer were passed over the person's head in a circle three times and then quickly turned upside down, so the mouth of the cup rested on the plate. Once any remaining liquid was drained, the remains could be interpreted.

Pendulums were also used for divination and when searching for buried treasure. The most common use was the wedding ring and pregnancy trick mentioned earlier. Some cunning folk could also hold a pendulum above a map and find lost things, missing people, buried money, and water.

Most of those who specialized in searching for the best place to dig a well - usually called "dowsers" or "water witches" - used a forked stick cut from a willow, cherry, pear, hazel, or hickory tree. Held by the two prongs, fists down, and the single branch pointing outward, it was kept at just the right tension before snapping. While holding the stick, they began to walk in various directions. As they approached the water underground, the stick would start to bob and wiggle, and as soon as they reached the source of it, it would point straight down.

Gazing, also known as scrying, could be done in several ways - looking into a well or bowl of water, gazing into a mirror with a cancel, or watching the smoke and how things burned.

An Irish form of scrying was brought to America with the use of hazelnuts, which were believed to be a symbol of knowledge and wisdom. They were often burned to answer specific questions, and answers came from whether they burned to ash or popped, broke, or jumped out of the fire.

The same kind of method was used with sheaves of wheat, barley, or corn stalks. Bundles were laid on hot coals one at a time. Depending on how they burned or the smoke they produced allowed conjurers to predict the outcome of events. The longer the items burned, the greater the influence. If the smoke drifted to the east or south, it was good. If it went north or west, it was bad. If the smoke stayed on the ground, the situation was hopeless.

To gaze with water, practitioners used water from a well placed in a white porcelain bowl. The smoke from burning chicken feathers was used to smudge the conjurer and the surface of the water, and then they would sit and gaze into the water while reciting these lines three times: "In the name of the Father, the Son, and the Holy Spirit, as far as the east is from the west, let me see..." The final word would be the person or place they were looking for.

By gazing into the water, images or words would form to provide the answers they sought.

Some also believed that by speaking those words and rubbing the water from the bowl on their eyes, they would dream of the things they wanted and needed to see.

Folk magic may have been carried to America by immigrants, but when it arrived here, it became a purely American type of witchcraft. And that's likely why it has stuck around for as long as it has and has become such an important part of the history of witchcraft in America.

5. AMERICAN WITCHCRAFT
AFTER SALEM

The madness of what happened at Salem had drained America of some of its fervor for the supernatural - for a time. As decades passed and the furor over witchcraft died down, the severe Puritan approach to life changed, too, largely a victim of its own excesses. American thinking and culture changed, but many of the old prejudices remained. In one incident, before the American Revolution, an anonymous Philadelphian, angered at the British-imposed Stamp Act, wrote a critical broadside that included a curse on the commissioner who administered the hated law. In 1787, in another incident also in Philadelphia, a crowd stoned to death a woman who was believed to be a witch.

But what followed the war was a time of tremendous cultural change in America. Never in the history of humanity had so many different people, their languages, cultures, customs, and beliefs been thrown together so quickly and chaotically in a new land.

Those who came to America faced a new environment that was almost a blank slate, waiting to be written on by new people and new traditions. The eastern seaboard of America had been virgin country when the first settlers arrived. Immigrant families' blood, sweat, and tears turned thousands of acres of forest into farmland in the early 1800s. Poverty, starvation, and disease were faced by most, yet within a generation, towns were started, industries created, roads built, and churches and schools constructed.

It is no surprise, then, that the magical beliefs that both concerned and comforted the early settlers were just as relevant to the lives of Americans long after those first settlers arrived on the country's shores.

The landscape of the country had changed around them. Forests became farms, villages became towns, and the rapidly expanding cities of the nineteenth century became the destination for millions of new arrivals, who brought more new customs and traditions to the land.

These new influences would bring their own ideas of magic and witchcraft into the melting pot of American culture, mixing with the conjure folk, the witches, and the magic practitioners that were already here.

Surprisingly, slavery, one of the nation's most hideous institutions, was one of the greatest influences on magic because of the African traditions it brought to the country. The first enslaved people arrived in America in 1619 and numbered into the hundreds of thousands by the nineteenth century.

Conditions for slave transport to America were horrendous. Most enslaved people had been bought or kidnapped from Africa's west coast. Chained, branded, and packed into ships for the journey, many did not survive. To add to their misery, they were often forced to exercise by dancing on the ships, a sacrilege of ancient traditions meant to honor spirits. If they refused, they were beaten. The cruel voyage across the ocean hastened the destruction of their belief systems and heritage.

The black men and women who endured this pain and humiliation found themselves in a strange land, torn from their families, communities, and culture. They held on to what they could, even as their faith was watered down by Christianity forced on them by their masters.

Africans were brought to America in chains and were bought and sold like cattle in public auctions. Their lives were spent in captivity, worked to the bone by their masters. Is it any wonder they turned to magic to ease the pain of their everyday lives?

But there were things they clung to on those southern plantations, like their healers and "witch doctors." The healer was a powerful figure who practiced sorcery and used magic spells, potions, powders, and herbal remedies. So-called traditional medicines and treatments that whites received at the time were usually much more dangerous.

The conjurers were also adept at calling on the spirits. The noted African American scholar W.E.B. DuBois wrote that conjurers were at the heart of black culture because they were critical to preserving the physical health of the enslaved people. He wrote that the conjurer "found his function as a healer of the sick, the interpreter of the unknown, the comforter of the sorrowing, the supernatural avenger of the wrong, and the one who expressed the longing, and disappointment of a stolen and oppressed people."

Black healers often treated blacks and whites - a seeming contradiction in a time of terrible inequality and brutality against enslaved people. But foremost, the conjurers helped people bear the burden of their captivity with all its abuses. They provided survival skills, a sense of community, and the promise of a better life in the next world.

Two centuries later, in the 1920s, Gilbert Osofsky wrote that Harlem in New York was home to many "spiritualists, herb doctors, medicine men, faith healers, palmists, and phrenologists" who were all practicing skills that could be traced back to the slave cultures of America's past.

Just as the Irish and Scottish immigrants who settled in Appalachia influenced the magical culture of the region, immigrants from a myriad of European countries brought their magic and witchcraft traditions to farms, towns, and cities across the land.

As strangers in a strange land, it's no surprise that many immigrants settled in the country. They often formed isolated communities among their own kind. They knew the language and the customs, but it wasn't home. Unsure of how to deal with illness and misfortune, many of them initially wrote home for help.

In 1885, Mrs. John Solomon, who lived in the Swedish community of Belgrade, Minnesota, became sick with an illness that refused to go away. Fearing that witchcraft caused it, she wrote to friends in Sweden for advice. At their suggestion, she mailed a conjurer a lock of her hair and a piece of clothing. The conjurer wrote back that she had been bewitched by an older woman who frequently came to the Solomons' home. She became convinced the witch was her husband's aunt and publicly accused her of witchcraft.

In 1901, the sister of a man named Peter Calabrese of Chicago also fell ill due to witchcraft. She didn't seek help locally either. Instead, she wrote home to Italy to see if the spell could be reversed.

Packed into crowded tenement neighborhoods in America's largest cities, immigrants found themselves as strangers in a strange land. Many turned to old customs and healing traditions that would often seem them accused of witchcraft.

There could also be misunderstandings with locals regarding folk magic practiced by immigrants. In 1871, a Dutch family named Stupemeyer settled in the Watson Street neighborhood of Detroit. It was not an area with a large Dutch population, and the family spoke no English. When Mr. Stupemeyer came down with a terrible fever, his wife tried several magical cures that baffled the neighbors. One saw the man with a bag of ash in one hand and a cup of cold water in the other - the idea being that the ash would absorb his fever and then be quenched by the water. The worried neighbors called a doctor, but his help was refused. After several days, a man who could speak Dutch was brought in and threatened Mrs. Stupemeyer with arrest if she didn't let a doctor tend to her husband.

Margaret Carr of Pittsburgh found herself in a tricky situation with locals in the fall of 1867. Her grandchild was sick with croup, and to cure it, she purchased a black cat from which she took three drops of blood to rub onto the child's swollen throat. Although a well-known treatment in Margaret's native Ireland, it wasn't so popular in her new neighborhood. They saw her need for blood from a black cat as proof that she was a witch. Fearful

The Five Points neighborhood of New York was regarded as the most dangerous in the city, filled with criminal gangs, political factions, prostitutes, and thieves. But even these hardened folks maintained a fear of witches and witchcraft.

of retribution, she hired a lawyer to plead her case in court and dispel the fear that she was a witch.

In January 1829, New York residents were spellbound over the stories of the "Five Points Witch." The neighborhood bore the nickname thanks to the five-pointed junction of roads, and starting in the 1820s, it became one of the most notorious places in the city. Mainly populated by African Americans and the Irish, it was the poorest, most violent, and vice-ridden place in New York, filled with crime, brothels, and barrooms. It was also home to several gangs, like the Dead Rabbits and the Forty Thieves, regarded as American history's first organized criminal gang.

Martha Ann Sloan and Catharine Lane were two of the residents of Five Points, and on January 20, 1829, they were arrested for the beating of a third woman, Mary Boman. The reason? Mary was a witch.

When brought before a magistrate, the two women pleaded self-defense because they were terrified of Mary's alleged powers. According to Catharine, Mary had bragged that a Mrs. Dexter would never get off her bed again - and now she was bedridden. Catharine had been asked to come and see her, but she was too scared, fearing that Mary's black magic would rub off on her.

Martha Sloan added that Mary had boasted of giving another girl a disease that could not be cured. That girl's face had become twisted and deformed by convulsions, so she was "terrible to look upon." Doctors had pronounced the affliction incurable.

Catharine also told the magistrate that she had seen Mary making human figures from rags and placing salt and pepper inside. She stuck pins and needles into them, muttering spells as they burned.

A sailor named Williams spoke up and confirmed Mary's reputation for witchcraft. He offered that her landlady believed she had injured several other tenants of the boarding house where she lived. Williams, however, made it clear that he did not believe in witches.

After hearing all the testimony, the magistrate went on record: "The charge of witchcraft is a somewhat curious one. It is not so serious now, as it would have been some centuries back, although it may have considerable effect upon the minds of the ignorant part of the community."

The women were bound over for trial on charges of assault and battery, and when they were asked to sign their names for bail, each made an X because both were illiterate.

Assuming that education was an antidote to such beliefs, the magistrate commented that it was no wonder they believed in witchcraft.

But the magistrate was wrong. There were still a great many people who believed in witchcraft in the nineteenth and twentieth centuries - and, of course, just as many who do so today.

Witchcraft after Salem was clearly not just a collection of legends, lore, and superstitions. It continued to be a matter of life and death, both souring and inspiring the American dream for many immigrants and enhancing and spoiling the lives of those who had been here for generations.

Witchcraft was an essential part of the cultural fabric of America. It was part of the story of the destruction of Native American life and the experience of slavery and emancipation. It was embedded in the lives of the immigrants and became a major part of the religious and social history of the nation.

WITCHES EVERYWHERE

As American religion and belief systems moved away from the strict Puritan and Calvinist faiths of the colonial era, the lore of witchcraft began to change. Witches were no longer being hanged in the public square, but the stigma of who might - or might not - be a witch was still strong in towns, villages, and cities all over the country.

Looking at the many accusations, assaults, and outright murders that occurred in the centuries after Salem, three types of accused witches seem to have been prominent.

There were those accused of being witches because they were *outsiders*, primarily women who gained a reputation because of where they lived, how they lived, what they looked like, and their social standing. Just like during the years of the witch trials, they were usually older women who called upon the charity of their

Vincennes, Indiana around 1906 when Margaret Gilmore was accused of being a witch.

neighbors to survive. The lore of the old woman who asks for help is denied and then accused of causing the misfortunes of those who denied her was one that dated back centuries - and it continued long after the colonial witch craze ended.

The turning of Margaret Gilmore of Vincennes, Indiana, into a witch was a similar story. Married three times, Margaret came to Vincennes in 1906 as a single, independent, middle-aged woman. She lived in a small shack and made her living selling eggs from her chickens and home-grown vegetables. At some point, she adopted a little girl named Bertha Anderson.

Margaret was apparently better educated, made more money than her neighbors, and didn't fit in well in the poor community where she lived. Rumors about her began to spread. Some claimed that she had not slept in 14 years and spent every night hammering mysterious on the floor of her home. She stood at her front door and called to the spirits, other stories claimed.

Soon, the local children began to regard her with fear. They fled in terror when she stepped out to sweep her porch with a broom.

And then a coincidence turned into an outright accusation.

In 1907, a neighbor's son, John Paris, accidentally injured one of Margaret's chickens. Soon, neighbors whispered to Paris that Margaret had been heard saying, "If that chicken dies, one of his children dies, too." The chicken died, and not long after, so did John Paris' two-year-old son. The cause of death was whooping cough - not witchcraft - but the neighborhood didn't care. John was urged to do something, and he went to the local justice of the peace and had a warrant sworn out against Margaret for "disturbing the peace." She was arrested and locked up in the Knox County Jail

Of course, the case went no further, and she was soon released, but the damage was done. She was innocent of any crime and had spent time in jail, and the newspapers had widely reported her status as a witch.

Margaret Gilmore quickly moved away from Vincennes.

As that case suggests, children often played a significant role in creating the outsider witch. I remember growing up in a small town with older women - and in one case, an unusual young girl - who was considered odd and witch-like. Most readers can say the same. Many were pestered by neighborhood kids and, in some cases, subjected to more serious harassment.

An elderly German woman in Cincinnati named Christina Meyer became the victim of children's persecution in 1878. The city was filled with German immigrants, so she didn't stand out because of her background. Instead, she got people curious about her because of her habit of sitting on the floor of her room in the boarding house where she lived with a candle between her feet, reading from an old book. She could be seen from the street, which got people's attention.

Some children in the neighborhood started a story that Christina was a witch and was reading a book of charms and spells

- not the Bible, which was more likely. They peered in her windows and drew protective crosses on her door and threshold.

Two teenage girls, Clara and Lena Roher, were especially troublesome. They, along with their parents, were also German immigrants and lived in the same boarding house. Their harassment of the older woman was incessant, and eventually, Christina grew so bothered by it that she prosecuted the two girls. Brought before the local court, the girls were lectured, and their father was forced to pay a $100 bond for each of them for their release.

Once again, the damage had been done, and Christina Meyer moved out of the boarding house and to another part of the city.

One of the most common afflictions suffered by those who crossed an outsider witch was the so-called "evil eye," which often appeared in sensational newspaper reports in the nineteenth and twentieth centuries. The idea that witches could cast spells by sight was widespread in many cultures, but, of course, most stories involved immigrant women, largely from Slavic and Mediterranean regions. Both young and old were believed to be vulnerable to its power, but most accusations involved illnesses in infants. It was much easier to blame a witch for a sick baby than accept it was bad hygiene and infant death tolls of the era.

For some, having the "evil eye" could be recognized in a woman with a heavy "unibrow" - these were mostly Italians, sorry. Unusually colored or particularly piercing eyes were also a sign. Having an "electric gaze" was a common description in many cases. Most apparent was a woman with a squint.

That trait appeared in a 1929 divorce case. Giuseppina Porcello, a Sicilian woman who had emigrated to the United States in 1920, had one eye that closed further than the other, making a squint. In 1928, she married her husband, Giuseppe. But the wedding wasn't followed by conjugal bliss. Just four days after the ceremony, Giuseppe accused her of casting an evil eye over him, which was the only reason he'd married her. He said he would die unless freed from her evil influence. He had visited several cunning women in Brooklyn to try and free himself from her curse but to no avail. It was best for all concerned when Giuseppina was granted her divorce.

In 1901, a German woman named Carrie Merckle lodged a complaint about her Greek neighbors at the police station near her home in Baltimore. Carrie was a laundress in the apartment building, and one day, she picked up the four-month-old child of the Greek family. Several hours later, the child became ill, and the family accused Carrie of casting an evil eye on it. They demanded that she spit in the baby's face - a common bit of counter magic in evil eye cases - and Carrie did so to avoid further confrontation.

But that wasn't the end of it. Carrie ended up having to leave her job because the Greeks had convinced all the neighbors that she had the evil eye. Unfortunately for Carrie, there wasn't much the police could do.

Another type of witch that commonly appeared in reports was the *conflict witch*, a figure that resulted from long-term feuds and unresolved tensions within families or between neighbors. Going against type, more men were regarded as conflict witches than women, although the *outsider* female still appeared frequently in stories and accounts. In almost every case, disputes emerged because of envy, jealousy, conflicting personalities, sexual passions, and financial frustrations. Accusations of witchcraft became like opening up a pressure valve, which could be devastating for individuals, families, and communities.

In 1796, accusations and suspicions within three related families led to terrible violence in Arundel, Maine - then part of Massachusetts. In the 1730s and 1740s, the three families - the Smiths, Cleaves, and Hiltons - had established themselves in the prosperous fishing town and became prominent in the community.

The events of 1796 centered around Elizabeth Hilton, daughter of Abraham Hilton, and his wife, Dorothy. Elizabeth had married Daniel Smith, son of Captain Daniel Smith and his wife, Hannah, but when he died, she became a widow. However, she could not count on her relatives in her sorrow because she had been accused of bewitching a neighbor and relative named John Hilton.

One night that October, John was walking home, just before dark, when Elizabeth appeared before him, walking about six yards away. He claimed he had a tool in his hand, and it began moving by itself as if it was trying to get away from him. Quickly putting two-and-two together, he assumed that Elizabeth's witchcraft caused this. He then decided to beat her with the tool to make the magic stop, but then, guided by some supernatural force, the tool turned and began beating John instead. He was now convinced and began publicly accusing Elizabeth of being a witch.

He needed to find a cure for the spell she'd cast on him and was aided in this by two of his nieces, Sarah and Molly Hilton, and by Dolly and Elizabeth Smith - the latter of whom was the sister-in-law of the accused. They boiled some of John's urine, a widely used method of dealing with witches, hoping it could break the spell. But nothing seemed to end John's mental torment.

The Smith and Hilton women began making death threats against the widow and then urged John to take matters into his own hands. On the night of October 15, he broke into Elizabeth's house, beat her, dragged her outside, and tried to strangle her. The other women were present, urging him to finish her off. Fortunately for all involved, Elizabeth didn't die.

The following month, all four women were tried for assault and battery. It isn't clear why John was not arrested and tried, though it could have been because of presumed insanity.

A man named Eaton Cleaves was a key witness for the defense. He was married to Miriam Smith, the sister of Daniel

Smith, another of Elizabeth's sisters-in-law. He testified in court that John Hilton had been of sound mind until the day he encountered Elizabeth on the road, and she had bewitched him.

But no matter how convincing Cleaves may have been, the four defendants were fined $100 each and kept in jail until the next court session decided their date of freedom.

One thing that court records failed to reveal was what had caused the family to turn on Elizabeth in the first place. That remains a mystery.

What isn't a mystery is what caused the accusations against Rose Downey in July 1898. One afternoon, the Irish immigrant showed up at the St. Louis coroner's office to report to the deputy coroner that her daughter-in-law had accused her of bewitching her three-month-old grandson to death.

Her daughter-in-law, Mary Downey, had arrived from Ireland three years earlier to visit relatives. While in St. Louis, she met and married Rose's son, Bernard, a foundry worker, in 1897. Their first child was born the following year. The infant that Rose allegedly killed was their second child. Mary would go on to lose

St. Louis in the early 1900s seems an odd time and place for accusations of witchcraft, but two cases emerged at this time.

nine other children over the years, but her first loss hurt terribly - and she went looking for a reason.

She chose her mother-in-law.

Another St. Louis case occurred in 1899. Hugh Lambey, a printer and son of Prussian immigrants, filed a divorce petition against his wife, Anna. He stated that Anna's belief in witchcraft and her preoccupation with charms and magical rituals had turned Hugh into the subject of ridicule and contempt among his neighbors and friends. He accused her of putting a love potion in his coffee, and it caused him "gastric upset" instead of feelings of passion. His divorce was granted. He remarried the following year.

A few years later, Eliza Norris of Worthington, Ohio, had the opposite problem. She brought a divorce suit against her husband, Amos, after 35 years of marriage. She testified for two hours about how her farmer husband practiced experimental witchery on her, aided by a book of spells he owned. He would seek out and swallow four-leaf clovers to enhance his powers and to make her fall sick. He would put seven $1 bills in his shirt pocket, place his right hand over it, and then touch her left elbow. Eliza got her divorce, too.

And then there was the *accidental witch*. Many accusations of witchcraft emerged not because people fit stereotypes or were in dispute with their alleged victims but because unlucky people sometimes showed up in the wrong place at the wrong time - including in dreams and nightmares - or did or said something entirely innocently but when a bad thing happened, their comments were seen as suspicious.

For instance, admiring glances and words at the sight of a beautiful baby got many people in trouble. In 1903, a legal case was filed in Chicago by Frank Galenski and his wife, owners of a grocery store, because they became convinced that an elderly customer, Francesca Krejewski, was a witch. One of their children fell ill after Francesca kissed them one day in the store. A doctor later diagnosed the child with blood poisoning.

Other acts of kindness by strangers ended up in similar ways. In 1883, a butcher's wife in Reading, Pennsylvania, named Malinda Balthazar, told a journalist: "None of the family are allowed to accept any gifts, and everything that comes into the family must be paid for." She told the reporter about a woman she knew well who offered her some very nice-looking pears. "I told her that we could not accept them as a gift," Mrs. Balthazar added. "Before she left, I bought the pears by paying her a cent."

Being a close friend didn't help either. In 1903, the police in Newark, New Jersey, listened to Mary Guth as she accused her best friend, Anna Lesnik, of having "witched" her with a cup of tea. "Ever since I drank that tea, I have felt queer," Mary said. "When I got out in the street, everything seemed turned wrong."

But Anna only rolled her eyes. "Mary talks nonsense," she told officers. "I gave her a cup of plain, ordinary tea, such as people drink every day."

DEALING WITH WITCHES

Thanks to the many cultures that made up America's population, there were numerous methods and rituals for identifying and dealing with witches.

We have talked about many of them already, including the notorious method of "ducking," which meant testing witches in water to see if they floated or drowned. The Puritans may have made that one popular, but believe it or not, people continued to use it as recently as 1730, even though it had long been condemned by the religious extremists who made it fashionable in the first place.

So~called "witch finders" searched a woman's body for any sign of a "witch's mark." If found, they were often pricked with a sharp object to see if the accused witch felt pain.

There was also "pricking," which meant sticking pins into areas on a woman's body thought to be made insensitive by the Devil's touch. I suspect this was more of a method of seeing a woman naked during a significantly suppressed time in history than it was about finding witches, but who am I to say? This was once an official method of identifying witches, used under the guise of the law, and even though it disappeared over time, traces of it remained for years.

In the Ozarks, it was thought that a sharp tool could be hidden in the seat of a chair so that just a small point of it came though. If a person sat on it without feeling it, they were a witch.

Of course, it was also believed in the Ozarks that a freshly cut onion would immediately turn sour and become poisonous in the presence of a witch. It was also said that a witch would become sick if they inadvertently smoked tobacco into which a little pawpaw bark had been inserted.

Another common method of detecting witchcraft at work used an egg. A raw egg was cracked and poured onto a plate or into a cup. It was then placed under the head or pillow of a child or adult believed to have been hexed. If an eye appeared in the egg, it was confirmation of witchcraft. If the egg white appeared cooked, it was a sign that the spell had been broken.

And then there are the pillows.

In 1883, it was reported that a woman in Pittsburgh had discovered a bundle of tightly woven feathers in the shape of a 15-inch alligator in her husband's pillow. The husband, an employee of the Oliver Wire Company named John Smith, had been sick with a lingering illness. His

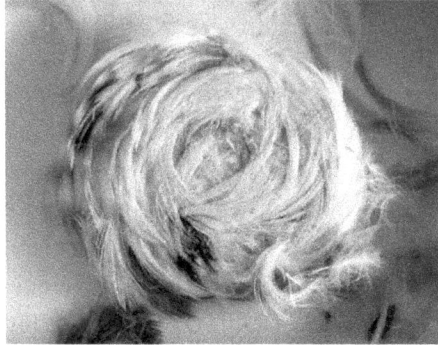

A "feather crown" found inside of a pillow. Many believed they were the work of a witch.

wife had cut open his pillow after an ill neighbor found a strange formation in the shape of flowers and crosses in his pillow.

Mrs. Smith didn't know what to make of the bizarre discovery, but neighbors assured her it was "the work of a witch." She kept the feathers for a few days but tired of people coming to the house and asking to see them, so she burned the feathers and her husband's bedding.

According to reports, his health was restored a few days later.

Stories of feather bundles in the shape of crowns and coffins go back centuries and seem to have originated with the Germans. The general interpretation was that the formations were created over time by a witch, and when the figure was complete, the sick person who used the pillow would die.

In 1896, Germans in Carondelet, Missouri, experienced an outbreak of pillow wreaths. A young woman named Neubauer fell ill while visiting her sister in town, and several women gathered to discuss the girl's strange sickness. The girl's sister was told to open the bedding to see if she found anything suspicious and was horrified to find several feather wreathes in pillows throughout the house. A woman named Spinning, who "knew a thing or two about witchcraft," was called in and ordered that the pillows all be burned.

In 1889, communal pillow-burning events occurred in Graafschap, Michigan, when the German immigrants cut open their pillows following several cases of supposed witchcraft. More than a dozen figures that looked like "crowns and chickens" were found when the pillows were cut open. A bonfire occurred the following day, even after a local minister delivered a sermon to try and "extinguish the excitement."

Once a suspected witch's identity was confirmed, carrying out rituals to counter their spells became necessary. Regrettably, most seemed to require some kind of bodily fluid. Urine was a popular one, as we have already discussed. If a bewitched person put a bottle of their own urine into a fire, the witch would be forced to reveal herself.

In another incident - in Goodhue County, Minnesota, in 1872 - a farmer's wife and young child became ill, and the family believed that a servant girl had cast a spell on them. Some of the wife's urine was boiled in a pot, and the servant girl was forced to inhale the fumes, thereby taking the spell back on herself. Her head was forced so low over the boiling liquid that her lips were scalded. Ugh - she understandably lodged a complaint with the county attorney.

Others required physical confrontation, like "scratching," - which meant getting the blood of the alleged witch to negate whatever spells and curses she'd cast. That was not, as you might imagine, easily accomplished.

Spit was also thought to have strong anti-witch properties in American. One tradition required coercing a witch into spitting on her victim. In 1876, Julia Welch, who had emigrated to New Jersey from Ireland 10 years earlier, was told that her bewitched child could only be saved by getting the suspected witch - another Irish woman named Mary Meehan - to "come and bless the child three times and cast three spits upon her." Meehan reluctantly agreed to this but changed her mind at the last minute.

Julia was then advised that the only alternative was to take a piece of Mary's clothing and burn it. Julia acted on this advice --- leading to her prosecution for assault.

She wasn't the first to run into legal trouble over this method. In Portland, Maine, in September 30, an Irishman was charged with assault after attacking a female neighbor with a razor, crying, "You old witch, I will be the death of you!" He then started slashing her clothing until neighbors came to her aid. In court, he claimed that the woman had bewitched his goats. He asked her to remove the spell, but she denied having anything to do with it. So, he decided to cut off part of her dress, burn it in his goats' presence, and break the witchery. The judge wasn't sympathetic and sent him to jail.

Some assaults had no ritual function at all - they were merely brutal attempts to force the alleged witches into retracting their spells. In 1860, Marias Ramirez, a wealthy American rancher in Texas, kidnapped a woman named Antonia Alanis in the belief that she had bewitched his son. A conjurer told him the witch had shot pigeon bones into the boy's head. Alanis was severely beaten for two weeks, but the son did not recover. She was tied up, and a fire was set under his feet - a torture that would force her to pull the pigeon bones from the sick boy's skull. Needless to say, it didn't work.

In June 1901, Frank Olding of Jasper, Indiana, came to believe that his neighbor, Catherine Ferry, a German woman in her sixties, was responsible for bewitching his horse. He was arrested for whipping, kicking, and punching her.

And it sometimes went further than that. In May 1822, a laborer named Joseph Lewis, who lived near Deep Creek in

Norfolk County, Virginia, was arrested for the murder of a free African American man named Jack Bass.

"I would like to do it again," he told the authorities.

He had killed Bass after a fortuneteller told him that Bass was responsible for bewitching Lewis and his wife. He was sentenced to 18 years in prison.

"I had to kill her. I had to," Louis De Paoli told the police after the San Francisco florist was arrested for murder in 1905. He had beaten his sister-in-law, Catherine, to death with a chair. He and his wife believed the woman was bewitching them and their three children. The had bought some pills to combat the spell, and Mrs. De Paoli had tried to beat the evil out of the children, praying to St. Anthony as she did so, but nothing worked.

Louis said later, "I was sorry to do it, but she had a spell on the children, and they were about to die. It was either I killer or five of us die from the spell."

His wife agreed. In broken English, she told the authorities, "Better one die than five, that what he say to me. Then he kill. Katy had spell on us."

Louis spent the rest of his life in an insane asylum.

As most found out, murder and assault were liable to cause the person trying to break a witch's spell to end up in jail, so it's not surprising that most people chose to combat witches at a distance with a different brand of magic.

Some believed you could shoot the image of the witch. Driving a nail into a witch's footprint was another way to harm them. Another technique often used was symbolically beating the witch out of the item or person bewitched. In 1883, Sarah Kocher of Scranton, Pennsylvania, tried to un-bewitch her daughter by beating the baby's cradle with a briar stick. Luckily for the infant, she chose the cradle instead of the alternative.

Milk churns - and even milk - were beaten with hawthorn, hickory, and hazel switches when cows were feared to be bewitched. It was often claimed that the witch would have marks from the beating on her body afterward.

Burning bewitched objects or items associated with the person under the spell was widely practiced, based on the idea that the witch would experience burning pains. Another version of this, practiced by some Germans, was to place a wood chip in the chimney to dry out, with the witch slowly dying in pain as the moisture left the wood chip.

Witch bottles were used to either draw witches to the victims' homes or to force them to remove their spells by causing them great physical torment.

The general recipe was to take a bottle, put some of the bewitched person's urine into it, add some sharp objects such as bent pins, nails, or thorns, and finish it with some of the victim's hair or toenail clippings. Seal the bottle and bury it under the fireplace hearth, put it up a chimney, or boil it in a fire. The bottle was supposed to represent the witch's bladder, and the sharp objects, especially when boiled, were supposed to cause her excruciating pain.

Over the years, witch bottles have been discovered by archaeologists, house restorers, and salvage workers. They have often found bottles hidden away -- especially in the Appalachian region of the country -- still sealed and often containing pins and nails, hair, and other objects. We can only wonder if they served the purpose for which they were created.

Attacking a witch was a good defense, but most believed it was better to prevent a witch from working their magic in the first place.

Salt was the most popular protection from witchcraft - as well as from evil spirits and a lot of other things - in part due to its brilliant white color, symbolic purity, and because of the immense value it once had as a vital substance in preserving food and cleaning wounds. At one time in American history, possessing salt was better than coins or paper cash.

During a slander lawsuit in Pennsylvania in 1915, a plaintiff, Mary Ann Schwartz, complained that the couple who accused her of witchcraft annoyed her by paying someone to scatter salt on the chair and bench in the hat factory where she worked.

In May 1897, a Russian store owner named Isaac Simon complained to the authorities in Hagerstown, Maryland, that a fellow countryman named Solomon Saltzman spread salt on his doorstep and sidewalk every morning to limit his supposed evil influence. Isaac feared that the salt would scare customers away from his business.

Silver was also used as protection from witchcraft. Some believed silver bullets could kill a witch, but the metal also had general anti-witch properties. Some wore dimes around their necks to ward off evil. The practice of depositing or nailing silver dimes to the bottoms of milk churns and buckets were widespread, thanks to the belief that the silver could prevent a witch from bedeviling dairy cows.

There were many other kinds of charms and amulets, too. African American conjure bags and First Nation medicine bundles served this purpose, and the tradition was passed on to cunning men and women in early America.

One important ingredient in each kind of bag was the rabbit's foot. This custom was carried to America from England, where a rabbit's foot was once carried as a remedy against rheumatism or cramps. By the nineteenth century, it was also being used as a charm against witchcraft, but its popularity in England was like nothing it enjoyed in the United States.

In America, the rabbit's foot came into its own, thanks in part to its use in hoodoo and conjure traditions.

In 1884, a Georgia politician named Charles Henry Smith - who wrote newspaper articles using the moniker of Bill Arp - reported that the wearing of rabbit's feet was widespread amongst African Americans of his acquaintance. However, it was only used as protection against witches if it was the hind foot of a rabbit shot in a graveyard during a full moon. The article had been written with tongue implanted firmly in cheek.

A rabbit's foot was a powerful charm for luck and for protection.

"Rabbit Foot Blues," a blues song by Blind Lemon Jefferson, links the rabbit's foot tradition with the bones of the dead.

The rabbit's foot gained popularity among poor whites in the South and elsewhere. When a Chicago civil engineer named E.G. Nourse lost his rabbit's foot, he advertised in the newspapers for its

return. He claimed it had come from the left hind leg of a rabbit shot by a cross-eyed African American as it hopped over the grave of a murderer at midnight.

They didn't come any more powerful than that!

When a black man named Charles Wisdom was in the Missouri State Penitentiary waiting to be hanged for the 1892 murder of a

St. Louis cigar maker, he made one last extraordinary appeal to Governor William J. Stone for clemency.

He mailed Governor Stone a rabbit's foot and a small hoodoo bag in hopes that he could gain power over him through conjure and thereby gain a last-minute reprieve. It didn't work. Wisdom was hanged a few days after the governor received his "spell" in late April 1894.

As mentioned in the last chapter, Bibles were more than just books to conjurers and cunning folk. It was also a powerful protective amulet that could be placed under a pillow at night to prevent the sleeper from being bewitched.

In addition to protecting yourself from an attack by a witch, it was imperative to protect your physical home. A house can be symbolic of the human body, with its entrances open to spiritual and physical assault and intrusion. Thresholds, both physical and symbolic, were weak points, so protective charms were placed in and around doors and windows to keep out unwanted magical intruders, especially witches. Salt, herbs, amulets, and more could be placed at every entry point in a home.

But there was also the chimney, key holes, and window gaps. They had to be protected too, so traditions began of painting or carving protective words and images above the front door, which would - theoretically - protect the entire house. The Pennsylvania Dutch custom of "hex signs" was developed for just the reason, as we'll see in the next chapter.

If you didn't want to figure out symbols and charms, placing a simple cross above your door was also supposed to keep away witches.

In 1866, a Memphis woman named Alvers believed that her child had been bewitched and was instructed by a conjurer to repeat a rhyme while making three crosses in chalk on the door of her home each day. A story from Reading, Pennsylvania, stated that the offices of conjure doctors in town were marked with protective chalk marks of crosses over all the doors and windows.

WITCH VIOLENCE AND VICTIMS

Hunting and persecuting witches - the innocent and not-so-innocent - did not end with Salem. As has been recounted in the previous pages, violence, torture, stabbings, beatings, and even murder continued for decades, even into the twentieth century.

No segment of the American population was immune to the belief in witches or the violence surrounding that belief. It wasn't just religious extremists or uneducated hill folk. Even those who considered themselves the most civilized among us fell victim to the fear of witchcraft.

And fear can lead to not only panic but violence and even murder.

TERROR IN TENNESSEE

Fentress County, Tennessee, can be found in a rugged area in the northeast part of the state. Its population is low, and its greatest claim to fame was the number of saltpeter mines once located here, supplying the main ingredient to gunpowder. Even in the 1880s, a minister and historian named A.B. Wright wrote, "Superstition has a strong grasp on many. It is a popular opinion among some that witches are prevalent and doing a great deal of harm. Some even profess to know how to kill them."

Not much had apparently changed in the previous half-century because, in 1830, a complicated legal case arising from accusations of witchcraft revealed both the depth of emotion about witches in the county and the helplessness of the legal authorities to deal with it at the time.

It started that summer when several young women began suffering from fits and other symptoms that were quickly blamed

on witchcraft. They all recovered after several months except for Rebecca French, who was in her 30s. She was the daughter of a prosperous and respected man named Joseph French, who lived on a 600-acre farm in the county's southwest corner.

With Rebecca still suffering from bewitchment that winter, her parents called in two men who were "celebrated for their skill in putting witches to flight" - Isaac and Pleasant Taylor. Apparently, they did this in their spare time since Pleasant was a blacksmith and Isaac was a well-known surveyor in the area. If that was the case, their reputation as "witch hunters" was overblown since whatever they did for Rebecca didn't work.

In January, an older man named Stout visited the French home. As he walked up the drive, Rebecca was suddenly seized with the telltale signs of violent jerking and convulsing. She demanded that Stout give her the length of rope he was carrying. At first, he refused but reluctantly handed it over, concerned for his safety. When the rope was tied around Rebecca's waist, the symptoms suddenly stopped. In the minds of the people present, this was a sure sign that Stout was the witch responsible for Rebecca's ominous condition. Stout understandably made a hasty retreat from the farm, and Rebecca's torments returned.

An arrest warrant was quickly sworn out for Stout's arrest. With silver bullets in their guns, a constable and five armed men apprehended the suspected witch and roughly hauled him into town, where a crowd of locals waited. They demanded further proof of Stout's guilt and used Rebecca herself to find it. Members of the crowd were told to take hold of Rebecca's hands and speak the words, "May the Great God of Heaven, in the name of the Father, son, and Holy Ghost, bless you."

Several of them went through the process without effect, but her seizures immediately stopped when Stout was forced to do it at gunpoint. The older man was immediately charged with witchcraft.

But Stout pressed charges of his own. He sued everyone involved in his capture for assault, battery, and false arrest.

In the middle of winter, with snow on the ground, the parties involved had to make their way to Jamestown - about 20 miles away - to have the merits of their individual cases heard by county magistrate Joshua Owens. The charge against Stout was considered first, and Owens decided there was reasonable guilt to bring him to trial. His bail was set at the considerable sum of $2,000 to force him to appear before the next county court in February.

But on the date of Stout's trial, Rebecca failed to show up at the courthouse, and the case was postponed. Rebecca was forced to pay the trial costs, and a new date was set before the Tennessee Circuit Court. At the new trial, evidence was given that claimed Stout had been seen exiting houses through keyholes, afflicting local women, and harming horses and livestock with his witchery. However, the state's attorney, John B. McCormick, decided that the prosecution could not be sustained - mainly because it was ridiculous - and refused to proceed with the case.

The decision caused an uproar with the folks from Fentress County because they didn't believe justice was being served by failing to punish the witch.

In May, Stout's attackers were brought to trial. Rebecca's father, Joseph, testified that he had never believed in witchcraft until confronted with his daughter's suffering. No attempt to injure Stout had occurred in his presence - except for one incident when he'd been knocked out of a chair. All the men were found guilty of assaulting Stout, but their lawyer appealed, and they found themselves back in the Tennessee Circuit Court.

The defense stated that the men who attacked Stout truly believed he was a witch. This meant that the rough treatment of Stout was permissible under the English Conjuration and Witchcraft Act of 1604, which had been the law of the land when the United States had been a British colony. The attorney maintained that the act had never been repealed in the state of Tennessee.

It was a stretch, of course, and Judge Abraham Caruthers dismissed the defense, stating that it had never been the law in Tennessee. The county court's decision was upheld, and Stout's attackers went to jail.

What happened to Stout and, more importantly, to Rebecca French remains unknown. Their story has since been lost to history.

THE WITCH OF FAYETTE COUNTY

Often known as the "Witch of the Monongahela," Mary "Moll" Derry was probably the best-known witch of the western half of Pennsylvania. Her legend didn't begin after her death - she was already infamous while still alive.

Born sometime around 1760, Moll Derry came to America with her husband, Valentine, who was believed to be a Hessian mercenary who had been paid to fight for the British during the American Revolution. However, he defected from the military and began fighting for the colonial army. After the war, Valentine and Moll moved across the Appalachians to the Pennsylvania frontier. They initially lived in Bedford County and then moved to Fayette County in the 1790s.

During this time, Moll began to establish a reputation as a woman with supernatural powers - a cunning woman with a skill at healing. She was known for predicting the future, curing ailments, and - unfortunately - placing curses for those who paid for them. Both respected and feared, she had a unique place in the community.

Numerous stories were recorded about Moll - including many in her lifetime - but how many were truth and how many were fiction remains unknown. Some of the stories have minor variations, likely from being told and re-told so many times, but the main elements of the tales remain consistent. Molly lived until 1843 - allowing time for the stories to grow - and her physical appearance has been described in many ways.

She was a woman of mystery - but undoubtedly real.

And one thing that was known for sure was that Moll Derry was not a woman to be crossed. If a neighbor angered her, he would soon find that his animals were sick or his cows didn't give milk. Bread wouldn't rise, chickens laid no eggs, and perhaps his crops would fail.

Or so the stories went.

Once in the 1790s, three men mocked and taunted Moll, claiming her abilities weren't real. Moll supposedly looked at them coldly and announced that all three would hang. Soon, the first man, named McFall, succumbed to Moll's curse. In 1795, he killed a man in a drunken brawl and was arrested, tried, and hanged. The second man, named Doughtery, robbed and killed a peddler passing through the area. He fled to Ohio and committed another murder. He was caught, confessed to both murders, was sentenced to death, and hanged in 1800. The third man, named Flanigan, had heard about the deaths of his two friends and remembered Moll's threat. In despair, he committed suicide by hanging himself.

Another violent incident related to Moll's powers occurred around 1819. A peddler from New Jersey was passing through the town of Smithfield and ran into an old friend who now lived in the area named John Updyke. The peddler told his acquaintance that he'd heard of Molly Derry and wanted to visit her and have his fortune told.

Updyke told his friend he could take him to Molly's home near Haydentown - but he'd lied. Instead, he led the man back to his own cabin, where he met up with an unsavory pal named Ned Cassidy. The pair robbed and murdered the peddler, carried his body through the dark woods, and sank it into a pond. A search took place for the peddler the following day, but only a blood trail was found in the woods. No one linked the crime scene to Updyke or Cassidy.

Even so, Cassidy's conscience soon got the better of him. Unable to sleep and tormented by guilt, Cassidy went to Moll Derry to see if there was anything she could do for him to help him sleep. But Moll's reaction was not what he expected.

She glared at the man and snarled, "Why are you coming to me when your hands are still wet from your dirty work at the mill pond?"

Shocked and frightened, Cassidy walked away - but Updyke was not so lucky.

At the time, Molly was training an apprentice named Hannah Clarke, who lived about one mile from Updyke. One afternoon, not long after the murder, a prominent local man visited Hannah. When he left, he noticed a drawing on the back of her door that vaguely resembled Updyke. The man took notice of a nail that was protruding from the drawing's head. It looked like it had been tapped into the wood once or twice. When he asked Hannah about it, she explained that if she drove the nail all the way into the door, the man in the drawing would die. Instead, she would tap it slowly, a little at a time, so the man would suffer from a crime he had committed.

When the man left Hannah's house, he couldn't shake the drawing's resemblance to John Updyke. He decided to visit the man. Sure enough, Updyke was complaining about a pain in his head. Now believing in Updyke's guilt, the man said nothing and went home.

Over the following weeks, the man checked with Hannah to see if she had driven the nail into the door. Hannah dragged it out, tapping carefully for almost a month until Updyke was in so much pain he was unable to get out of bed. He finally confessed to the murder he'd arranged and committed as he writhed in pain. The next day, Hannah drove the nail the rest of the way through the wood, and Updyke died with a scream on his lips.

MURDER IN NEW YORK

In 1853, the steamship *Edwiner* docked in New York City. On board the vessel were dozens of German immigrants who had traveled from Bavaria to start a new life in New York state. Among those families were a farmer named Pierre Heidt and his wife, Maria; their three sons, Nicholas, 18; Edward, 13; Adam, 4; and a daughter, Caroline, 11. They were one of the thousands of farm families from southwest Germany who had made their way to America in the mid-nineteenth century. They left for many reasons - cheap land, crop failures at home, and extreme poverty - but the Heidts mainly wanted a fresh start. They spent their last cash reserves to purchase land in New York's Sullivan County.

By the time the Heidts arrived in the county, about 2,500 other Germans lived there. They had carved out homes and fields from the woods and hills, many enduring great hardships. One German settler recalled getting lost in the woods trying to reach the settlement of Jeffersonville before a road existed from the south. Worn down and exhausted, he came upon a small settlement of

German settlers came to Sullivan County in the mid-1800s and started large farms that became profitable within a decade or two.

fellow Germans and begged them for food. They were unable to help - they were starving themselves.

By the 1870s, though, farming had started to pay off. Small towns grew, and the German settlers were able to fund the creation of several Catholic, Methodist, and Lutheran churches.

After the first couple of decades in the country, the Heidt family thanked God their immigration to America had been successful. They built a home in what is now Delaware Township, a rural area of small villages in the Catskills. Pierre, who changed his name to Phillip, began farming with the help of his two oldest sons.

One of their neighbors was another German immigrant named George Markert. He and his father worked a small patch of land nearby. The two families got along well. Around 1860, the 26-year-old George married Phillip's daughter, Caroline, and this began a long friendship with his younger brother-in-law, Adam.

In 1869, Adam Heidt married Barbara Ulrich, the American-born daughter of Bavarian immigrants Anton and Ursula Ulrich, who farmed near the town of Bethel. The young couple moved to Rockland, where Adam began working as a carpenter. Their first son, Joseph, was born the following year.

By 1880, the family had returned to Delaware Township, where Adam started a sizable farm at a spot called Swiss Hill, just south of Jeffersonville. Joseph attended school in the winter and worked on the farm in the summer, while Barbara looked after what was now three younger children. Adam became a respected member of the community, acting as an officer for the local fire brigade.

His uncle, George Markert, had by now also bought a small farm of his own for himself and his second wife. Caroline had died a few years earlier. His new place was within "hollering distance" from Adam's farm. George had struggled after Caroline's death. He saved money to buy land by working for a tannery for several years and laboring for other area farmers. In 1888, Adam loaned him $600, so he could pay off some of his most urgent debts.

The Heidt family prospered, but they also went through some difficult times. Adam's brother, Nicholas, was hit by a train, suffered severe injuries, and later died. In 1882, Anton Ulrich fell from a load of hay and broke his neck. In 1888, Adam's mother, Maria, died at the age of 75.

Her death had not been a great shock, but it happened not long after his mother-in-law, Ursula, was murdered at her home in Bethel. A drunk ex-sailor named Jack Allen entered her house, where she lived alone, and shot her to death during a robbery. A neighbor, calling for a jug of cider, found her lying in a pool of her own blood. Allen was hanged at the Monticello jail in July 1888 after adjusting the rope around his neck and telling the hangman, "Let 'er go!" It was the last hanging in Sullivan County.

In addition to these personal misfortunes, there were also problems on the farm. Two of Adam's finest horses had died, and some of his cows dried up. Adam had also been suffering for years from an ailment that no doctors could diagnose or cure. The medicines he was given just made things worse. He had pains in his teeth and limbs, and his stomach "beat like a heart." And then, all at once, he started to improve - until that is, George Markert came to visit after spending some time in Connecticut in 1890.

After shaking hands with his longtime friend, Adam began to experience pain all over his body. He tried some patent medicine, and the first bottle seemed to help. A second bottle, though, made things worse. Pain pills made no difference at all.

Something, Adam believed, was terribly wrong.

One day in the spring, George returned to the Heidt farm, and Adam took him down to the cellar for a glass of cider. As they stood talking, Adam began to experience strange sensations in his eyes. The two men returned upstairs and sat down, and Adam noticed George stroking his beard strangely. He ran his hand down the length of his beard, and at the end of each stroke, he twisted his hand as if he was throwing something at Adam. He did this several times. After George went home, Adam looked at himself in a mirror and noticed his face looked yellow and that he had a blue rim around his eyes. He told his wife that he believed George was a witch and had cast a spell on him. Barbara refused to believe it - Adam and George had been friends for years, and George was a godly man. How could he be a witch? But Adam insisted that he'd done it - and the belief became an obsession.

Adam soon became convinced that George's witchery was the source of all his problems. He started to remember other suspicious words and actions that had seemed innocuous at the time but which he now saw as sinister. He recalled an incident from years before when George had patted him three times on the shoulder and told him, "You're good - a good, right brother-in-law." Why the repetition? And why three times? Clearly, a spell had been placed on him at that moment. He also remembered a time when George had been unusually curious about Adam's health. Had he been concerned about Adam's well-being or the progress of his witchery?

The last time that George came to Adam's house was in December 1890. He wanted Adam to sharpen a saw for him, but Adam refused. The mere sight of the saw had sent sharp pains throughout his body.

He went to a local doctor who prescribed "vapor baths" and a course of medicine. They made him feel even worse. He couldn't eat or sleep and spent two weeks in the hospital. The doctors couldn't find anything physically wrong with him. Released from the hospital and unhappy with the medical profession, he traveled to New York City to consult a well-known fortune-teller. She confirmed his belief that he had been bewitched. She wrote down a charm on a piece of paper, instructing him not to look at it, and told him not to shake hands with any man.

Out of other options, Adam decided to confront George about his spell. He told him that he knew George was a witch and demanded that he take back the words he had spoken to him years before - "You're good - a good, right brother-in-law." George simply laughed at him, and Adam fled the house, angry and embarrassed. His pains became worse after the confrontation.

In November, Adam went to stay with his brother in Bradford, Pennsylvania, for five weeks. During this time, he consulted a quack who called himself a doctor named Clark. Adam didn't tell him that he was bewitched. The doctor gave him two glass bulbs connected by a glass tube that contained liquid. He held the two bulbs in his hands, and the liquid moved from one bulb to the other. From this, the "doctor" diagnosed that he had heart disease, liver disease, kidney disease, and many other ailments. Fortunately, he had a medicine for Adam that would cure them all. But Adam declined. He knew now that he had a problem that was beyond medical help. What he needed was spiritual aid, he thought.

Father Suitbert
Godfrey Mollinger

In Pittsburgh, he went to see the well-known priest, Father Suitbert Godfrey Mollinger, a man who had studied medicine and became known as a healer. Years after his death, a line of "liver pills" would bear his name - although he had nothing to do with them. Father Mollinger offered him a blessing and told him there was no need for him to take any medicine. Adam didn't tell the priest he'd been bewitched but desperately hoped the blessing would counteract George's spell. It didn't work.

Adam frequently talked of the magic George had brought against him with his son, Joseph, and recounted other witchcraft cases to support his belief. Unlike his mother, Joseph became convinced that his father was, indeed, under George's spell.

Adam also told friends and neighbors of his worries. In October 1891, he called at the home of Adam Bernhart and refused to shake his hand, saying that a spell had been laid on him. Another neighbor, Conrad Metzger, tried to convince him he was not bewitched when Adam asked to borrow $10 from him to pay that fortune-teller he went to see in New York. Adam was cautiously seeking support from the community in case action eventually had to be taken against George Markert.

On the evening of January 19, 1892, George left his home and trudged through the falling snow to the Half-Way House, an inn run by Phillip Hembdt on the road out of Jeffersonville. George often spent the evening there with friends. Around 10:00 p.m., he left for home - but never arrived there.

George's family never saw him alive again.

At first, his wife, Catherine, and stepson, John, weren't concerned. He often stayed home late. But by morning, Catherine was worried. She sent John out to ask neighbors if they had seen George, but as the young man reached the farm gate that opened onto the main road, he saw the red stain of blood on the snow.

Two men had also seen blood that morning. One was a local farmer, John Koehler, and a mail carrier, Casper Van Bergen. They found George's hat, jack-knife, and hickory walking stick nearby and followed a trail of blood

The Stone Arch Bridge over Callicoon Creek

and footprints in the snow that led to the Stone Arch Bridge over Callicoon Creek. There had clearly been a struggle between two or three men, and from the tracks in the snow it appeared that a body had been thrown from the bridge.

The two men had gone to notify the local constable, Charles Heidt -- George Markert's nephew. Several boats were taken out into the creek, and the water was dredged with hooks. It didn't take them long to find George's body tangled in fallen trees along the bank. He was dragged onto land, placed on a sled, and taken to the Half-Way House inn. The men who were present had all heard Adam Heidt's accusations against George and decided he was the main suspect in the man's death.

The constable and a doctor examined George's body, but it didn't take much to figure out the cause of death - he'd been shot in the head several times. Two letters were found on him, one in English and one in German. They basically said the same thing:

> *March 19, 1891*
> *George Markert -*
> *You seeming friend and sly enemy. Nothing done so fine but what it will appear in the daytime. God has opened my eyes. You should take your witchcraft back. You know I have a judgment against you. You came to me on a Sunday and got receipt. If you do not take the torture back I will sell the judgment and pay the doctor bill which you have caused. You came to my house and stroked your beard. I was sick all the time. I forbid you my house and my barn, my flesh and blood. In the name of God.*
> *A. Heidt*

For whatever reason, two days passed before a party of local men went to arrest Adam and his son, Joseph. Armed with a search warrant, they found a revolver hidden in a pile of hay and a bloody handkerchief. They were taken to the

The Sullivan County Courthouse, where John's and Adam's trials were held.

Sullivan County Jail while the coroner John Dycker started an investigation.

At the inquest, both Adam and Joseph denied any knowledge of the crime, but the jury decided there was sufficient evidence for them to be indicted for murder. Their case was to be considered by a grand jury in the spring, but both the prosecution and defense requested more time to gather evidence. Of course -- without any of that evidence -- the press had already decided the two men were guilty, and the story of witchcraft and murder was splashed across newspaper pages for weeks.

The murder trials didn't begin until August. Joseph's trial was held first but was short because he eventually confessed to the murder while in jail. He took the blame for the killing, which occurred after an argument when he tried to get his uncle to remove the spell he'd put on his father. They had fought, and George had tried to strike him with his stick, but Joseph knocked it away. Then, George grabbed him and tried stabbing him with his knife. Joseph said he fell and took George down with him. "I drew the revolver and fired for his head," Joseph told the court. "I cannot say how many times. When I regained my footing, I again grabbed him and threw him over the bridge. I then went home. I did not know what I was doing at the time and have had a headache since then."

Joseph's defense attorney told the judge that he was a simple, misled boy who formerly had an excellent reputation. The jury didn't buy it - but they saved him from the hangman by finding him guilty of murder in the second degree. He was sentenced to 30 years behind bars.

The next day, August 18, was Adam's turn in court. After a jury was sworn in, friends and neighbors like Phillip Hembdt, Adam Bernhart, and Conrad Metzger testified about their conversations with Adam about his bewitchment. Oliver Hofer, the justice of the peace, testified about the letters found on George's body. Joseph was called back in to offer more testimony. The trial concluded the following morning, and the jury took only a few minutes to decide that Adam was not guilty of the crime committed by his son - even though his belief in witchcraft had convinced Joseph to take the man's life.

Despite George's death, Adam's health did not recover. His mind deteriorated - or, more likely, deteriorated further. A local newspaper editorial stated that Adam was "not a safe man to be at large." No sane man, the editorial continued, could believe that George Markert possessed the power of witchcraft. It recommended that he be sent to an

The State Lunatic Asylum in Middletown, New York, where Adam was sent after his trial. He remained there until his death in 1897.

asylum - and that's exactly what happened the following June.

At Barbara's request, Adam was examined by two doctors, and he was taken to the State Lunatic Asylum at Middletown. He stayed there until he died in 1897. The cause was "melancholia and inflammation of the spinal marrow," which would explain the nervous symptoms and fatigue he complained about - worsened by the power of his own mind.

Barbara died in September 1901 after being bedridden with stomach cancer.

Joseph was a model inmate at Dannemora prison, and he was paroled in 1913 after serving 21 years of his sentence. He settled in Franklin County and was described in 1914 as an "honest, hard-working man, much respected by the people who know him." He worked in a broom factory for a time, and by 1930, he was working as a laborer and was married with two young daughters.

After that, he disappeared from the historical record, the last survivor of a case of witchcraft and murder that never should have happened at all.

BIG TROUBLE AT BOOGER HOLE

In 1900, Booger Hole was a remote settlement in the wooded hills of Clay County, West Virginia. It was a secluded, isolated spot, and its name advertised it as a spooky and haunted spot.

A "booger" was a menacing supernatural being, like a ghost or monster, seen at night in wild places. Booger Hole was known for a ghostly woman who wandered the woods and fields, dressed all in white, with hair as black as a raven's wing. She was known for wailing and crying in the darkness; no man was ever known to look upon her face.

The locals had deep Irish and Scottish roots and little contact with the outside world. The area had a reputation as a rough, lawless place with a long history of poverty, poor education, and intermarriage. Their stories were filled with tales of haunts and spooks and the very real presence of witches and witchcraft, even during what most would consider the modern world of the early twentieth century.

To the hill folk of the region, bad witches enjoyed stealing milk and preventing butter from churning. They also took the shape of animals and birds and caused illness and death among community members. Locals protected themselves by nailing crosses of hazelwood on their homes and barns to ward off the effects of bad witches. They also hired conjurers to break the witches' spells. They used many techniques, but especially popular was the making of a beeswax image or poppet of the suspected witch, covering it in cloth worn by the suspect, and then burning or driving nails into it.

Or at least that's what someone did with the poppet of Annie Boggs.

Annie was a member of a large extended family that had already been in Booger Hole for several generations. The Boggs - along with the Moore, Cottrell, Lyons, and McCumber families - had been scratching out a living from farming, hunting, and timber harvesting for at least a century. Some had improved themselves to a "respectable" status, while others remained dirt poor. Schooling was deemed unnecessary, and illiteracy was almost a badge of honor.

But it would be the death of Annie Boggs that would curse those families for decades to come.

Annie Boggs returned to Booger Hole to settle in 1899. She was a widow and brought with her two granddaughters, Prudie, 18, and Mabel, who was 2. Annie was given a place to live by a relative, Squire Boggs, one of the more successful men in the area. A few years earlier, he had built a schoolhouse to educate local children, but few parents were interested. It was abandoned by the late 1890s, so Annie and her granddaughters moved in. They put thick blankets over the windows and started a garden of corn, vegetables, and herbs. With help from Squire Boggs, they made it through their first winter and settled into the community.

Unfortunately, Annie made enemies right away. She had planned to offer her services as a healer and conjurer, but her personality made that difficult. She was independent, sharp-tongued, and often hard to get along with - all common personality traits that usually ended with trouble.

By the spring, rumors started to circulate that Mother Boggs was a witch. The rumors seem to have started among members of the Cottrell family, who had heard from relatives in Roane County that Annie had been kicked out of there because of witchcraft.

Local misfortunes began to be blamed on Annie. Among the most vocal of her accusers was Marshall Cottrell, who accused her of riding him at night like a horse. In other words, her spirit was forcing him out of bed and making him run up and down the surrounding hills. As things got more heated, there was talk of lynching Annie. Cooler heads prevailed - at first, anyway - and a conjurer was hired to try and block Annie's spells against community members. A poppet was made, and a pin was driven into the wax figure's back.

And then, on a cold winter's night in 1900, someone pulled aside one of the blankets that covered the window at the schoolhouse, poked a rifle through, and shot Annie Boggs in the back.

A murder investigation was started by Deputy U.S. Marshal Daniel Cunningham, one of the most renowned lawmen in the state. He found the tracks of two people outside Annie's window, and his analysis of the bullet that killed Annie revealed the kind of rifle used to kill her. It turned out that Marshall Cottrell had borrowed just such a rifle from a neighbor a few days before. That was enough to get Cottrell and his nephew - a young man who had been courting Annie's granddaughter, Prudie - arrested on suspicion of murder.

They were taken to the Clay County Courthouse for a hearing, and the courtroom was packed with Cottrell supporters from Booger Hole. They were ordered to leave the guns and rifles they had brought with them outside under guard because the authorities feared a disturbance.

Cottrell and his nephew pleaded not guilty to the murder but couldn't be swayed from the idea that Annie was a witch. The courtroom was filled with outspoken relatives who agreed. Cottrell swore that Annie had ridden him night after night, making him run up Blue Knob, lifting him off the ground, and making him fly.

Cottrell claimed he flew "through the wind and rain and cold, not knowing what minute lightning would hit us."

At this part in his testimony, a woman in the crowd called out, "You can't be stricken by lightning when you're being witch ridden. Lightning don't hit witch horses."

Then another woman yelled, "I wouldn't tell anything about it. It's mighty unwholesome to be talking so much about the witch folk, even if she is dead."

I'm guessing there weren't a lot of courtroom rules in West Virginia in 1900.

Anyway, Cottrell kept talking, describing how Annie had ridden him and how he had woken up every morning with scratches from briars on his feet and burrs stuck in his clothing. He said he'd been ridden 20 or 30 times, and his nephew claimed the same thing.

Under questioning, Cottrell said that he had not tried to kill Annie Boggs. "Don't you know she'd a killed me if I had?" he asked the judge.

Despite his claims of innocence, Cottrell's hostility toward Annie was an obvious motive for murder. The judge had no choice but to indict him and bring him to trial - but in

Jury to Probe Mysteries of Booger Hole

West Virginia Citizens Aroused Over Numerous Killings, Threaten Violence.

'CLAY COUNTY MOB' FORMED

the end, the trial never happened. With no actual proof against Cottrell, the case against him was dropped.

The killer of Annie Boggs was never legally punished for what he did - but the story is not quite over yet.

In February 1905, a neighbor of Annie Boggs was arrested after confessing to Annie's murder. He said he'd done it with the help of two female accomplices - his sister and her friend. Fred Moore was 15 at the time and lived with his sister, Rosa, and her husband, John Lyons. According to Fred, he'd killed Annie because she had threatened to reveal her knowledge of another murder in the community - which she learned because she was a witch.

Apparently, Annie had gotten into a quarrel with Rosa Lyons and, in anger, had threatened Fred's sister by saying, "she could light her pipe and before it burned out, could go to the place where the ashes of Henry Hargus were."

A few days later, she was dead.

The story of Henry Hargus is a little complicated. He was the nephew of a woman named Margaret Moore, whose husband had been a volunteer in the Union Army during the Civil War. Margaret convinced the War Department that her husband had been an officer, not simply a soldier, and received a fraudulent pension of several thousand dollars. Before being arrested and imprisoned for fraud, she gave the money to Henry Hargus, who was murdered for it by John Lyons and Margaret's son, James Moore.

Henry disappeared from his home in Booger Hole in 1883. He was rumored to have been murdered, but no one was arrested, and his body was never found.

Following the arrest of Fred Moore and Rosa Lyons for the murder of Annie Boggs, a detective named A.W. Sell conducted a search and found clear evidence of a grave under Moore's cabin. The body had been burned, but bits of bone, hair, and clothing remained. One button even had Henry Hargus' initials on it.

John Lyons and James Moore were arrested but somehow, lost in the shuffle, Fred and Rosa were set free for Annie's murder. A judge decided the confession didn't hold up.

To make matters worse, Lyons and Moore were also set free. Even though Moore's sister, Caroline, testified that she had seen Henry Hargus' body wrapped up in a sheet before it was burned and buried, the judge decided there was not enough evidence to indict the two men for a murder that happened 20 years earlier.

And the killers of Henry Hargus became as free as the man who may - or may not have - killed Annie Boggs.

So, was Annie murdered because she was a witch? Or was it because she knew too much about a murder that she should have kept her mouth shut? And did she learn about the murder for the reason Fred Moore believed - that she divined it through her conjuring skills?

That will remain as mysterious as the real identity of Annie's killer. Fred Moore may have pulled the trigger, but to many who lived in Booger Hole, a pin shoved through the back of Annie's poppet led to her demise.

THE MICHIGAN WITCH KILLER

In 1905, Frank Lesner managed the dairy department for the Ionia Asylum for the Insane in Michigan, a secure facility for those suffering from both mental illness and criminals changed with insanity. Under normal circumstances, Frank was a reliable and conscientious worker. But things weren't normal that spring. Something was wrong with Frank. He'd seemed nervous and high-strung lately, and his supervisor felt that perhaps a little time away from work would be good for him. Frank accepted the time off. He had something that he needed to do back home in Trenton, Michigan.

Frank Lesner needed to kill a witch.

On May 15, 1905, Josephine Hammernick spent the evening with her husband, Michael, at a friend's home who lived across the street from their own cottage on Third Street in Trenton. They talked, laughed, and shared a few drinks for several hours, but tired, Josephine decided to go home before her husband did. She entered the house, leaving an oil lamp burning on the table for Michael, and got into bed.

Just a little after 10:00 p.m., Michael told his friend goodnight and, while walking across the street, saw a man run out of his house - where Josephine was sleeping. Michael tried to chase him down, but the man was much faster and disappeared from sight. Out of breath, he ran into the house and yelled for his wife. He heard a moan from the bedroom and found her slumped over on the floor, leaning against a wall with a blanket over her.

"Are you sick? What's wrong?" Michael cried, but Josephine continued to moan. She was clearly in pain. Michael knelt, and when he reached out to touch his wife, his hand came away wet. In the light from the oil lamp, he saw that it was blood. Josephine had been shot five times.

Running outside, he began to scream, "Help! Help! My wife's been shot! She's been murdered!"

A doctor was called to the house, but Josephine died before he arrived. She could not tell Michael what had happened or who had shot her. One bullet was lodged in her right arm, three had struck her in the chest, and another had hit her left temple, barely missing her eye. Her skull had been crushed, her nose was broken, and the house was in a state where it was apparent there had been a fierce struggle. None of the neighbors had heard the gunfire, leading the police to believe the shots had been muffled by the feather blanket found on the woman.

After Josephine's body was taken away, Michael was arrested and taken to the police station. With no witnesses to the crime, he was the main suspect, especially since it was obvious he'd been drinking that night. Michael was questioned for several hours, but it soon became clear that he had not killed his wife. He was released, and detectives started looking for Josephine's killer.

He wouldn't be hard to find.

Frank Lesner was in Trenton on the night of the murder. Just before midnight, he had been drinking a glass of water in the Hotel Felder's bar. He wasn't acting strangely at all. He finished his water and then went to his room for a restful sleep.

The following day, he checked out of the hotel and stepped onto the sidewalk. As luck would have it, a police officer was just passing by on the street.

"Excuse me," Frank said to the policeman, "I killed my godmother, Mrs. Hammernick, last night."

Frank then provided the startled officer with every detail of the murder, including where he had disposed of the murder weapon. He said he had killed Josephine because she had bewitched his family, causing them great pain and suffering.

He said he'd killed her simply because she was a witch.

After Frank was arrested, reporters jumped on the story. They took every opportunity given to them to interview Frank in jail. They were perplexed by his crime. He was a boyish-looking young man, well-spoken and nicely dressed. He didn't seem like a killer, yet he readily admitted that he had committed murder. In fact, reporters were shocked at how cold-blooded he seemed about it.

"Frank, would you do it again?" one reporter asked. Frank paused, deep in thought, and then spoke. "Yes, I think I would. I just did what I wanted to do, and I am willing to accept the consequences."

"Then you don't feel sorry?"

Again, he took a moment to answer. "No, I don't believe I do," he said.

"Do you believe in witches?" another reporter called out.

"Certainly, I do," Frank said, this time without hesitation.

When asked to explain his feelings about Josephine Hammernick, he recalled that since he was five years old, his father, John, had been telling stories about Josephine, claiming he knew she was a witch and was the reason for all his family's problems. Frank never thought much of it, though. Josephine was his godmother. As a child, he always called her "Auntie."

But then, recently, Frank received a letter from his sister, Augusta, telling him about a strange affliction experienced by another sister, Rose. She seemed to be suffering from rheumatism, or arthritis and was in pain, which was bizarre for a young girl in her teens. A woman from Toledo examined Rose and concluded that she was "under the influence of a witch." The woman even described where the witch lived, and the family agreed that it perfectly described Josephine's home in Trenton.

"This is what determined me to kill her," Frank admitted.

But that wasn't all. He said that Josephine had also hurt his love life. He claimed that his relationships would be fine, and then the woman would inexplicably "grow cold toward him." As an example, he mentioned his former sweetheart, Isabelle Lazette.

However, when Isabelle heard what Frank said about her, she told reporters that she had not seen him for more than a year and they had never been engaged. She did, however, express shock at hearing Frank had committed murder. She would never have dreamed he was capable of it.

Frank then described the scene when he had snuck into the Hammernick home. He entered through the back door and crept through the dimly lit house to the bedroom. She screamed when she saw him, yelling in German, which Frank referred to as "gibberish."

"I couldn't understand her," he shrugged, "and wouldn't have stopped if I had. She threw the quilts over her head and yelled like a pig. Then I shot and shot until the yelling stopped, and she lay still."

When Frank was told Josephine wasn't dead when he fled the house, he replied with a chill in his voice, "Wasn't she? That's too bad. If I hadn't had enough bullets, I'd have gone out and got more. I'm glad she's gone."

The only family who visited Frank in jail were his two older brothers, Phillip and John. They were horribly disappointed in him but offered to help him hire a lawyer. After they left, Frank finally seemed to show some remorse for the murder, but then added that he wasn't sorry Josephine was dead, "I just wish I had left it for someone else to do."

When Frank's father, John, was asked about the murder, he denied that he believed the family was bewitched, saying that old neighborhood stories about Josephine must have left an "impression" on his children.

But Rose Lesner was convinced she had really been bewitched. Her illness, she insisted, had come out of nowhere. Furthermore, she said her hair had gotten so knotted up that it had to be cut off

The Ionia Asylum for the Insane in Michigan, where Frank Lesner spent time as an employee ~ and as a patient.

- another sign, according to the Toledo woman, that she was bewitched.

Frank never went to trial for the murder. Four doctors declared him insane. After four days in jail, he was brought before a judge for sentencing. Frank was seated at the defendant's table. Michael Hammernick was seated not far behind him, still reeling from the death of his wife.

When the session began, the judge asked Frank to stand. He was asked how he wanted to plead - guilty or not guilty.

"Well, I killed her all right, and pride myself that I made a good job of it, but don't know as I'm guilty of any crime," he shrugged his shoulders at the judge.

The absurdity of the statement sent Michael Hammernick into a rage. He sprang from his seat and charged at Frank. But he was quickly grabbed by an officer. "Let the law deal with him, Mike," the policeman urged him. He helped him back to his seat.

On June 19, 1905, Frank Lesner returned to the Ionia Asylum but not as an employee - he was now a prisoner. No friends or family members showed up to see him off. He was being locked away for life.

He said one last thing when he left Trenton. "I'm glad I did it," he said.

But that was not the end of Frank's story.

On September 12, 1908, Frank and three other inmates escaped from the Ionia Asylum. The men had been planning their escape for months and had carved a key out of a table knife. During routine exercise time, the men used the makeshift key to escape through a basement door. Frank threatened a security guard with a knife, forcing the man to stand out of the way as they fled.

The other three escapees were Hiram McCaffrey, who was charged with larceny; James Swane, an attempted robber; and Fred Clark, a burglar. None of the men had any discernible characteristics, scars, or anything else besides Frank being tall. They were all described as "insane" but capable of carrying on normal and sane conversations - well, as long as no one mentioned witchcraft to Frank Lesner.

After Frank's escape, Trenton was put on high alert. The police believed Frank might try to reach his family or even seek further revenge on the Hammernick family. One local woman said she saw him get off a train, which sent the community into a panic. Was it him? No one knows.

Frank Lesner vanished for good.

6. POW-WOWING
& HEX MURDERS

The history of American folk magic is a fascinating thing. After folk magic was brought to this country by immigrants, it began to change to fit into its new home, becoming uniquely American - especially as it adapted to the various people, places, and ways of life where it was needed.

Not all the folk magic - which I think of as American witchcraft - could be found in Appalachia or among the mountains of the Ozarks. It could also be found in the streets of the big cities, among the African American people of the South, and scattered across the nation's farms, fields, and forests.

It could also be found among the German farming folk of Pennsylvania. That form of folk magic took root around the same time as the witch trials in New England, but in many ways, it was more widely accepted by both ordinary people and the authorities alike. It wouldn't be until the early twentieth century - after a series of so-called "Hex Murders" occurred - that people in the region began to look at their homegrown folk magic differently.

PENNSYLVANIA HEX MAGIC

Pennsylvania hex magic dates to the colony's earliest days, linked mainly to the Pennsylvania German immigrants and their descendants. They are often called "Dutch" since Americans turned the harder-to-say "Deutsch," meaning German, into an easier word. Scores of Germans flocked across the Atlantic to the Pennsylvania colony to take advantage of the economic opportunities and religious freedoms that they could not find in Europe. They soon spread throughout the state, seeking fertile farmland and natural resources.

German settlement was especially dense in the state's southeastern corner, surrounding Philadelphia. The area would eventually become known as "Pennsylvania Dutch Country" and draw legions of tourists in the years to come. The Germans held firmly to their culture and blended customs of the Old and New Worlds to form a distinct identity. Even their language became a unique dialect - different from the German of their homeland and yet indecipherable to the Americans who lived around them.

Though there were a great many religious denominations among the German settlers - Lutherans, Amish, and Mennonites among them - there was a common tradition of folk magic practiced by all, except for the Amish or "Plain Dutch." They rejected the practice much like the Puritans of New England did.

For large numbers of Germans, the belief in folk magic was entwined with their Christian beliefs. Occult practices had always been more accepted in Germany than in England, so there wasn't as much resistance among their communities in the New World.

At one end of the German folk magic scale was the practice of *brauche*, which was more commonly known as "powwowing." It had nothing to do with Native American ceremonial practice, despite the name.

Most powwowers performed folk healing, using gifts they believed came directly from God. But there were also witches among them. At the opposite end of the scale were the *hexerei*, practitioners of black magic who drew their power from the Devil and other unholy sources. Many referred to the hexerei as "hex doctors." The powwowers and hex doctors often worked against one another, with common folk caught in the middle - just as it was with the cunning folk and the witches that bedeviled them.

Powwowers also played an important role among ordinary folk. Before modern medicine, they offered relief from ailments and, perhaps more importantly, a degree of hope. As with all folk magic, powwowing provided a sense of control in a world that was often beyond control. Powwowers provided

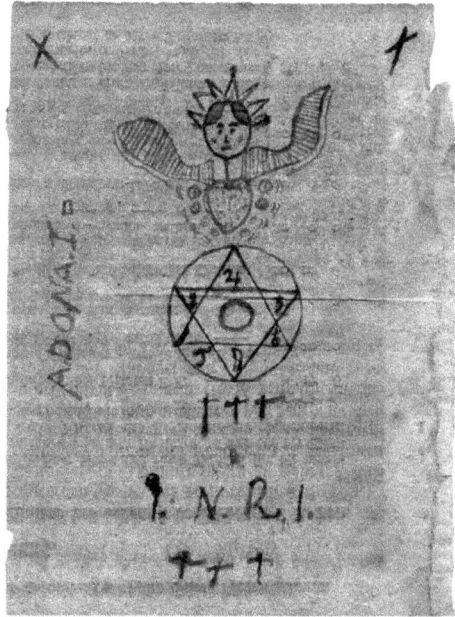

Powwowing provided cures and relief from illnesses, protection from evil, and removal of hexes and curses.

cures and relief from illnesses, protection from evil, and the removal of hexes and curses. They also located lost objects, animals, and people, foretold the future, and provided good luck charms. Those who sought them out were given charms, amulets, prayers, and rituals. It was generally believed that anyone could learn to powwow, but members of some families were more skilled at it. These families passed down their traditions from one generation to the next.

The opposite number of the beneficial powwow was the witch. They used dark magic that was often beyond the skill of the folk healer. They harassed neighbors and committed criminal acts with their supernatural powers.

As mentioned, some witches were also referred to as "hex doctors," but that can be confusing. In some cases, the term was applied to powwowers who were also knowledgeable in the ways of the witch - or hexerei - so they were skilled at battling witches and removing curses. That meant that the hex doctor was sort of in a gray area between a witch and a powwower. They might practice beneficial magic and then cast a hex for someone for a price or for revenge. It was also not uncommon to seek out one hex doctor to remove a curse placed by another.

This meant that for outsiders - and even many Germans - powwowers and witches could not easily be separated into categories. Many believed folk magic was the same as witchcraft, forbidden by their religious beliefs.

Since no one ever bragged about being a witch in centuries past, it's unclear how witches learned the art of the *hexerei*. It was generally assumed they made a deal with the Devil, but there was also a book of spells and incantations associated with hex magic called *The Sixth & Seventh Book of Moses*. The book had a sinister reputation - and we'll come back to it soon - but it was supposed to be in the library of every witch and hex doctor.

Using this book and their own spells, hex doctors targeted their victims in time-honored ways, mostly directing their magic toward livestock and crops. They were always blamed when healthy animals mysteriously died, or harvests failed.

If a large hairball was found in the stomach of a dead animal, it was referred to as a "witch ball," and it might be attributed to the work of a local witch or hex doctor.

In people, they caused illnesses, especially conditions that lingered and caused a person to waste away over time. They could also use spells to launch invisible attacks, causing seizures or fits, the sensation of being pricked, stabbed, choked, or strangled. Witches could also cause a run of bad luck for any individual that they attacked. The witch could even appear in the form of an animal, like a black cat, so that they could move about undetected and harass their victims.

I think it's fair to say that just about any type of misfortune could be blamed on a hex doctor or witch.

HEX MAGIC IN PRACTICE

Powwowers, hex doctors, and witches all used similar techniques, whether healing, hexing, or conjuring. There were many prayers, incantations, and spoken charms. Powwowers frequently invoked God, Jesus, the Holy Ghost, and other religious figures. They generally believed that all their abilities were a gift from God. Witches, of course, did not call on God, but they usually didn't invoke the Devil either. The words, whether spoken loudly or softly, were often accompanied by hand gestures, or placing hands on a person's body.

In addition to spoken words, the written word was also used for magic - not books, in this case, but written charms. Many Germans carried them on their person for protection. The charms might also be concealed around farmyards or homes to protect families and livestock. Sometimes the charms were spells or were verses from the Bible, like the first verse of Psalms 35 - "Plead my cause, O Lord, with them that strive with me: Fight against them that fight against me."

Another common religious charm to ward off witches was to take small strips of paper and write on them in red ink: "†xJxNxRxYx†." This was a variant of the formula INRI or

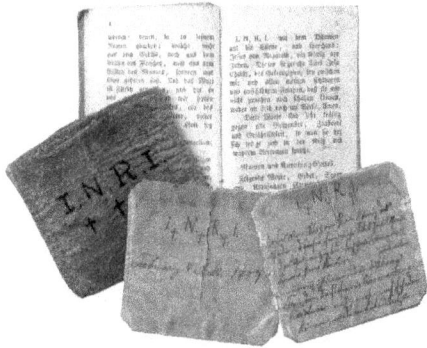

JNRJ, an acronym of "Jesus of Nazareth, King of the Jews," found widely in Christian iconography and used in protective magic.

With other charms, the paper they were written on was usually folded into triangles, which amplified their power. There were dozens of helpful charms that came into common use, like the ancient word square:

```
SATOR
AREPO
TENET
OPERA
ROTAS
```

That one was recommended for bewitched cattle, and the charm was placed into their feed.

The JRNRJ charm was also used to protect households against sickness, while the following charm was written on a white piece of paper, folded into a triangle, and used to protect against "evil spirits and all manner of witchcraft."

```
              I
             NIR
              I
SANCTUS          SPIRITUS
              I
             NIR
              I
```

Another charm that was used "against Bad Men and Evil Spirits, which nightly torment old and young people, to be written and placed on the bedstead" went:

I forbid thee my house and my courtyard; I forbid thee my bedstead so that thou wilt not trot over me into another house; and climb over all mountains and fenceposts and over all waters. In the name of God, the Father, God the Son, and God the Holy Ghost, Amen.

By the way, it had to be written in German - and backward. It could also keep away nightmares.

> **Ein ſehr gutes Mittel für das Herzgeſperr und Anwachſen.**
>
> Herzgeſperr und Ungewächs, weiche von N. Rippen, wie Chriſtus, der Herr, gewichen iſt von ſeiner Krippen.

If charms were not carried in a pocket, placed on a nightstand, or hidden in the house, protection might be hung on the outside of a home or barn.

Folk magic had long used crosses and other signs chalked on the fronts of homes to protect the occupants from evil and to bring good luck. The belief in the anti-witch properties of horseshoes that were hung above doorways has already been documented. Around the mid-nineteenth century, though, German communities in Pennsylvania added another form of magical protection to the mix - the "hex sign."

Or so it seemed.

Painted on barns and outbuildings, the signs included five, six, and eight-pointed stars, rosettes, representations of hearts, birds, tulips, and geometric signs that drew heavily on spiritual symbolism intended to keep away witches and evil spirits. Right?

Hex signs that are often seen painted on barns are not exactly what so many assume they are. They have nothing to do with hex magic at all.

In reality, none of that is true. During the second half of the twentieth century, the "hex signs" began to be interpreted by some scholars and the public as having a magical protective function, but they didn't. It turned out that the designs were just decorative in origin. The investment in paint, artistry, and time was a statement of prosperity and cultural identity - not of anxiety about witches.

"Hex signs" weren't used as a method to chase away witches. The Germans had other more simple, personal, and secretive ways of protecting themselves. They didn't need large paintings on their barns for the entire world to see. The mysterious interpretation of the "hex sign" resulted from some folklorists peddling fanciful tales for the tourists.

The reality of Pennsylvania hex magic has turned out to be much more fascinating than the myths surrounding it.

One of the most unusual ways to avoid curses, hexes, and spells was through the use of ritualized objects. They were usually mundane items that had acquired a special purpose. The objects were used as a surrogate for the afflicted person or even for whatever ailed them, like hardship or an illness.

Much of hex magic depends on the principles of contagion and transference. Basically, the idea is that evil is contagious and can be transferred away from the cursed person and into an object. The object would then be disposed of in a proscribed manner to keep the contagion from spreading.

This is, of course, a traditional kind of "sympathetic magic" - the belief that whatever a person does to a material object will affect equally the person with whom the object was once in contact or as a stand-in for that person or thing. That's a paraphrase of Sir George Frazer from his book of magic, *The Golden Bough*.

It's the same kind of magic that is believed to work with poppets, witch bottles, and anything else that is magically used to represent a person or thing. The most interesting part of it, though, is how often it worked - so long as the person who used it truly believed it would.

Powwowers and hex doctors depended on charms, recipes, and incantations that were passed down through their families. These "recipe" books contained the collective knowledge of a family line of powwowers. By the middle 1800s, these homemade volumes were joined by published volumes that came into common usage. Folk healers had always invoked and used the Bible in their magic, but they increasingly supplemented their knowledge with sources published by other powwowers.

The most famous and widely read of these books was compiled by a powwower named John

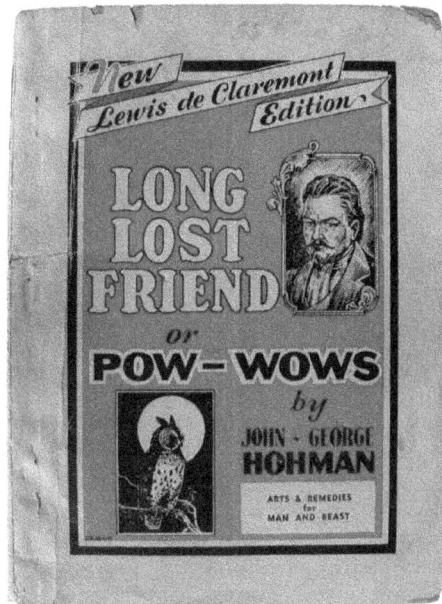

The Long Lost Friend was considered an essential book for any who practiced pow-wow.

George Hohman in 1819. Hohman was a German immigrant who settled on a Berks County, Pennsylvania farm. As a side business, he published broadsides and books about the occult and medicine aimed at the local German population. In time, he published America's most widely read grimoire or book of magic. The compilation of spells, charms, prayers, remedies, and folk medicine was called *Der Lang Verborgene Freund*, which translates to *The Long Lost Friend*. It was the first book of powwow magic to achieve wide circulation. It has been in print in either German or English continuously since 1820.

Aside from being a collection of charms and recipes, the book itself became a talisman. In what was an example of a resoundingly successful early marketing ploy, buyers of the book were told they would be protected from harm merely by carrying it. In the front of each edition was an inscription that read:

> *Whoever carries this book with him, is safe from all enemies, visible and invisible; and whoever has this book with him cannot die without the holy corpse of Jesus Christ, nor drown in any water, nor burn up in any fire, nor can any unjust sentence be passed upon him. So help me. +++*

The bulk of the book consisted of remedies and charms to cure common illnesses, fevers, burns, toothaches, and other ailments. It also contained recipes for beer and molasses and even had a charm for catching fish. Many of the book's charms were meant to protect from physical harm from weapons, fire, thieves, and, of course, witchcraft.

It also provided instructions on how to keep animals from wandering off, healing livestock and cattle, and even curing rabid animals. *The Long Lost Friend* soon became the primary reference for anyone attempting to understand the practice of powwow, and it gained a place of honor on almost every powwower's and hex doctor's shelf.

But as there is light, there is always dark.

In answer to the helpful charms of *The Long Lost Friend* was the far more dangerous book of witchcraft -- *The Sixth & Seventh Book of Moses*.

Drawn from the tradition of European grimoires and ceremonial magic, *The Sixth & Seventh Books of Moses* were purported to have been written by Moses himself and allegedly contain secret knowledge deliberately withheld by Jewish

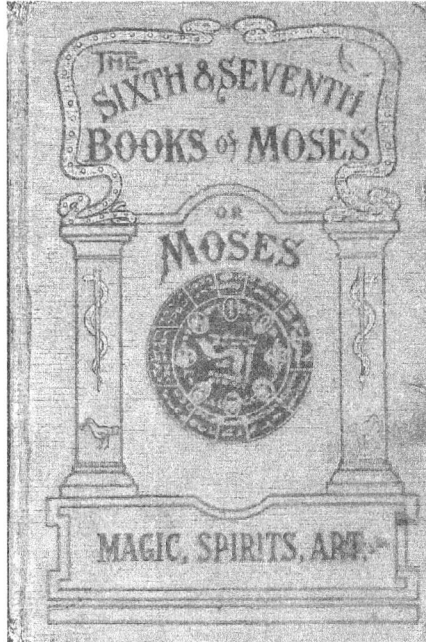

The Sixth and Seventh Book of Moses was considered a dangerous book of witchcraft by pow-wowers.

and Christian authorities when compiling what would be the Torah and Bible.

Described as two separate books, they are almost always published together in one volume, first appearing in Germany in the early 1800s and then in Pennsylvania in 1849. Original copies were in German; an English translation followed in the 1860s.

The book soon gained an evil reputation among the German population and those familiar with its lore. Legends surrounded it, including that the book's original manuscript had been buried for safekeeping in Appalachia's Blue Ridge Mountains. It was also said that some copies had been printed, at least partially, with red ink. A few hand-copied editions that had been written in blood were alleged to exist.

The book's text offered instructions on how to conjure and control spirits and demons. It also contained spells and incantations that were beneficial to the user, as well as spells that would duplicate some of the biblical plagues of Egypt, turn a staff into a serpent, and other miraculous happenings. Much of the volume is made up of reproduced symbols that were allegedly copied from old woodcuts. Biblical verses were also used maliciously, like Psalm 10, which was used to "plague with an unclean, restless, and evil spirit." Psalm 48 was recommended to seek revenge against "an enemy without cause or who hate you out of pure envy."

Though hex doctors frequently acquired the book to enhance their reputations, merely owning the volume was considered dangerous, and if a hex doctor spent too much time reading it - that could be fatal.

Merely opening the pages of the book was believed to attract the attention of the Devil. It might also cause the reader to become so obsessed with the book that they can do nothing but read it. Should such a thing occur, the only way to break the obsession was to read the entire book in reverse, starting at the end and working back to the beginning.

While accounts of hexes, magic books, and incantations might seem hard for some to believe today, they were all common traditions of the Pennsylvania Dutch country of the late nineteenth and early twentieth centuries.

These were all readily accepted ideas and beliefs, which turned out to be the source of troubles and trials in the late 1800s and the most crucial part of the murders that occurred later - those involved truly believed that magic existed. They believed it worked and could ruin their lives if turned against them.

And there would be those who would do anything to stop that from happening.

TROUBLE IN THE KEYSTONE STATE

In the introductory section of this chapter, I hinted at the idea that both ordinary people and the authorities were accepting of folk magic in Pennsylvania. That may have been an overstatement. While there were many followers of hex magic among the German settlers - and the authorities looked the other way compared to groups like the Puritans - those who practiced the craft in the region often found themselves in trouble. At the very least, they were often ridiculed for what some called their "backward, superstitious beliefs."

In the 1880s, a reputation about Pennsylvania began to form across the country, especially its German population, for being a state of rabid witchcraft believers. This reputation was created by a series of newspaper stories about hex doctors and witches that were circulated throughout the United States. Headlines started to appear like "Weird Stories: People in Pennsylvania Said to Believe in Witches." Some of the wilder stories were crafted by editors in distant states, but even the local press was guilty of sensationalism. In January 1891, the *Philadelphia Inquirer* ran a story with the headline "Witches in Berks County: Reading 'Doctors' Minister to the Delusive." From this and other stories, it became clear that the larger cities were targeting only isolated parts of the state as a "hotbed for witchcraft and superstition."

In 1892, another Pennsylvania report called "Queer Witch Stories" circulated in several papers. It sympathized with those who laughed at "the superstitious fears of foolish and immigrant neighbors."

But there was nothing funny about those stories for many people. Pennsylvania's witch belief was becoming seen as a social, moral, and health problem - an embarrassment to the state. There was no sign of it going away, and the problem could not be blamed only on credulous immigrants from Germany either. Yet there was no religious mission to purge Pennsylvania's witches, as there had been in New England.

In Pennsylvania, the medical establishment led the crusade - but they had some help from the newspapers, too.

In December 1899, a doctor in Reading, Pennsylvania, presented a paper to the Berks County Medical Society called "Witch Doctors and Their Deceptions." He'd had many occasions to treat patients who had first consulted a hex doctor and were fed up with their potions and spells. He helped to kick off the backlash against powwowers that followed.

In 1900, a hex doctor became the sensationalistic target of a tough, crusading journalist named Alice Rix. She visited the consulting rooms of a Reading hex doctor named Joseph Hageman, posing as a client seeking help for a sick relative.

Hageman was the prosperous son of German immigrants and had built a large client list over the years. He was listed as a "physician" in the city directory, but his business was pure powwow.

In her article, Alice Rix ripped apart his practice, the treatments he'd recommended, and even his physical appearance. Hageman took affront to the article she wrote about him - not at his unflattering appearance but at how Rix had questioned his medical credentials. His reputation for the "legitimate and scientific practice of medicine" had been assaulted.

Hageman mobilized support, with some of his clients writing to the newspapers in his defense. He also brought a libel suit against the newspaper's wealthy owner - a former U.S. Postmaster General -- John Wanamaker.

This turned out to be a terrible idea.

The trial took place in Philadelphia's Common Pleas Court in March 1903. For six days, a steady stream of Hageman's clients came through the courtroom. Nearly 100 of them took the stand to praise his healing powers.

But when the defense took over, they revealed his methods in slow, agonizing detail. They had some of his potions chemically analyzed, revealing there was no medicine in any of them. For instance, his tonic for "bad blood" was nothing more than grain alcohol that had been sweetened with cherry juice. None of his charms - like the small canvas bag that was supposed to keep away witches - had been proven to work. They brought their own witnesses into court - unhappy former clients of Hageman.

Hageman sat nervously, fidgeting in his seat as the days passed. He knew he'd made a huge mistake. On the stand, he was torn apart by the defendant's attorney, ex-Judge James Gay Gordon. Hageman, who had no medical license or formal training, was made to admit that he knew nothing of the circulation of blood, was unfamiliar with the word "pathology," could not define what "hygiene" was, and was ignorant of the chemical name for common salt.

His "medical competence" claims were shredded, and the case was dismissed.

In 1904, the journal *American Medicine* announced that the Pennsylvania State Medical Board placed to start a campaign to wipe out hex doctors and powwowers. The increased attention to them was partly due to the Hageman trial and partly to claims from coroners claiming a link between hex doctors and high infant mortality rates - claims that turned out to be questionable at best.

In September 1900, a Reading doctor was filling out a death certificate for an infant in his care when he learned that the baby had been unsuccessfully treated by a hex doctor before coming to his office. He blamed the death on powwowing and not his own inadequate skills.

A few years later, a coroner in Reading dealt with the infant son of Frederick Carl, who had died from malnutrition. A hex doctor who had visited the Carl home with a charm written in red ink had attempted a cure for the child. It was placed in a muslin bag and hung from the head of the baby's cradle. Whatever was written on the paper didn't work.

York County Coroner L.V. Zach claimed that powwowers had caused the deaths of five children in the previous two years. The children's parents had taken them to healers instead of "real doctors," and they had died. When questioned about his evidence, though, Zach had to admit that none of the cases had been formally investigated - he'd heard about them secondhand - but they were "common knowledge." The New York Times featured the coroner's allegations in an article with a headline that read "Death of Five Babies Laid to Witch Cult."

Not exactly subtle - and definitely not true.

The story went on to quote several unnamed "officials" from the York County Medical Society, who said that the coroner's count of deaths attributed to witchcraft was much too low. Hex doctors, they hinted, were running wild.

By the end of the summer of 1909, Reading coroner Robert Strasser reached his limits. He stated that in a single day, he had investigated six infant deaths that involved treatment by hex doctors. He made a public statement, blaming all the powwowers - and those who believed in them - for the deaths of all the children.

Other doctors joined the crusade against hex doctors the following year and were joined by a branch of the Visiting Nurse Association. The association had been founded in America, starting around 1880, inspired by charitable nursing organizations started by Florence Nightingale in England. They had a strong presence in Pennsylvania. Charitable donations paid for nurses to go into the homes of the poor to improve sanitary conditions, instruct mothers on childcare, and care for the sick. They were at the frontline of healthcare in neighborhoods all over the country.

A supervisor for the Visiting Nurse Association, Anna Barlow, released a statement denouncing the activities of local hex doctors. Barlow said that her nurses had saved the lives of numerous children and adults that powwowers had maltreated. She explained that finding the hex doctors to confront them was difficult because "they were an exclusive set of men and women and their workings are secret." Even so, she was sure they were guilty of not providing the correct medicines for her patients.

Legal authorities finally started to listen to the criticism from doctors and nurses. In 1911, they passed the Medical Practices Act. After that, no one in the state could call themselves a doctor or treat diseases using medicine without obtaining a license from the new Bureau of Medical Education and Literature.

No one cared. It was an empty gesture to pacify the complaining doctors and nurses. No hex doctor was going to stop practicing, and they certainly weren't going to apply for a license they didn't believe they needed. In addition, the new act was toothless. No one enforced it or had the resources to monitor anything that was going on.

All the publicity - negative or not - helped the local hex doctors. Their practices thrived, although many of them didn't deserve to remain successful.

After the death of Martha Adams of Harrisburg in 1915, her will stated that she left the bulk of her $12,000 estate to a hex doctor named Harrison Seiferd. His primary occupation was as a bricklayer in a local furnace works, but he had been treating Martha and her late husband with magic for several years. She had complete faith in his ability to communicate with her dead husband, provide her with protection spells, and put hexes on others. She was, in short, enthralled with the man. His principal treatment of her had consisted of "force bags" that have the possessor power over others. He sold them to others, too - for prices ranging from $1 to $1,000, depending on the client's wealth.

One of the bags owned by Martha Adams was opened and found to contain only a toenail and a written charm.

Her extended family contested the will, but, in the end, Seiferd ended up with the money.

HECKMANS PAY $17,690.56 FOR THE HEX DOCTORING

Conclusion of Middle Ages Case is Finally Reached

The final episode of the sensational and picturesque Kriner-Heckman case, which began in the local courts in the fall of 1919 and terminated several weeks ago when state supreme court refused a petition for re-instatement of the appeal by counsel for Heckman, was completed within the past few days when the total verdicts and costs—amounting to $17,690.56—were paid.

The total of the verdicts, recovered by W. H. Kriner against John Keckler, hex doctor, and the Heckmans, amounted to $16,884.33. The costs $806.23.

The case, which attracted state-wide attention, was bitterly fought in the county courts. The first trial in the case was that of John Keckler, whose superstitions practices in ridding livestock on the Heckman and Kriner farms of ailments have been termed worthy of the Middle Ages. Keckler was sentenced to a long term in the Eastern penitentiary. Mr. Kriner then instituted litigation to recover for damages to his two daughters, used immorally by Keckler in effecting his cures. The verdict for one daughter amounted to $9,786.17 and for the other $7,148.16.

The sordid practices of another powwower and bricklayer, John Keckler, were exposed during a long-running legal drama that stretched from 1918 to 1921. Keckler, who was married and had several children, abused his magical reputation by coercing his clients into having sex with him.

Keckler was eventually arrested after the rapes of Ada and Grace Kriner, the 12 and 15-year-old daughters of a farmer who had summoned Keckler to his home in Franklin County in 1915. When Keckler arrived, he announced plans to lay a number of sigils around the property to protect it against witchcraft. But then he realized that wouldn't be enough. Keckler told the farmer that a malignant influence had been cursing the place for at least 30 years, but he reckoned he could fix it, even though the sigils would not be enough. He would need to involve Ada and Grace in the rituals to remove the hex on the family.

The two young girls were brought to a neighbor's house, the Heckmans, to spend the night. In that house, on several occasions between 1915 and May 1917, Keckler had sex with the two girls. He told the Heckmans that the girls had to "touch the hem of his garment as part of his secret magic ritual." On one occasion, he drew a circle around one of them and uttered an incantation. Grace later testified at his trial that Keckler would be waiting for them in bed, and after performing some ceremonies - including painting sigils on their naked bodies - he would force himself on them. They were sworn to secrecy with the threat that telling anyone would "do no good."

After Keckler was convicted and sent to prison, Kriner filed a $20,000 lawsuit against Keckler and the Heckmans -- $10,00 for the rape of each of his daughters. The suit was dragged through the courts until April 1912, when Kriner was finally awarded $17,690.50

The hex doctor problem slipped into the background for the next few years. America was dealing with other things - including the aftermath of the Great War and Prohibition and the lawlessness that came with it.

But it would soon explode into the national consciousness again in 1928 when the burned and battered body of a York County farmer and hex doctor was found.

Suddenly, Pennsylvania's pow-wow problem was making headlines again.

THE REHMEYER "HEX MURDER"

What many would refer to as the "Pennsylvania Hex Murders" were bookended by two violent, headline-grabbing homicides - with a lot of nonsense and sensationalism in between.

The first - and most famous - of the murders managed to captivate the people of the region and would be splashed across the front pages of newspapers all over America.

The story began with a third-generation powwower named John Blymire. Born in 1895, John was poorly educated but had a good reputation as a healer in York County. He started providing remedies and cures to folks when he was seven years old. Despite this early success, though, by the time he was in his 20s, he began to believe a dark shadow was hanging over his life.

There was an incident that cemented John's idea that trouble was ahead.

One day, he was leaving the cigar factory where he worked, and an apparently rabid dog ran toward John and some of his co-workers, barking, snarling, and spraying white foam from its jaws. John knew the spell to handle such things. He carefully approached the dog, held out one hand, and spoke a string of words. Instantly, the dog calmed down. Its mouth stopped foaming, and it became quiet and subdued. John patted the dog's head, and it happily followed him as he walked down the street.

The other men were amazed by John's magical skills, but for John, the rabid dog was a dire omen, and soon after the encounter, his luck turned bad. His hair began falling out, he lost hearing in one ear, and he became so sick that he couldn't work, which resulted in him getting laid off from his job. He couldn't eat, couldn't sleep, and was unable to pow-wow. He tried to use charms to remove the hex he believed had been placed on him, but he

John Blymire, the third generation powwower who believed he was living under a curse. His belief became an obsession.

couldn't. It was difficult to remove a hex if one did not know the identity of the witch who placed it.

Then one night, as he lay in his bed trying to sleep, the answer came to him. Just as the clock struck midnight, an owl outside his window hooted seven times. John suddenly realized that he had been hexed by the spirit of his great-grandfather, Jacob, a powerful powwower who had been the seventh son of a seventh son.

Unable to fight back against a spirit, John decided to move away from his family home and from the cemetery out back where his great-grandfather was buried. He believed this would break the hex - and he was right. Soon, John's luck improved - at least for a little while.

After losing his job at the cigar factory, John earned a living through pow-wow clients and by performing various odd jobs. While painting a house one day, he met a young woman named Lily, and they were married. They had a happy life together - until Lily became pregnant with their first child. The baby was born but only lived for three days. Lily miscarried before their second child could be born.

These two tragedies quickly convinced John that another hex had been placed on him. Unable to determine the source of this new hex, he turned to other powwowers for help. One of them was a man named Andrew Lenhart, who told him that the person that had hexed him was someone he knew well.

John immediately became suspicious of everyone around him, even his wife. Lily had reason to fear for her safety. For starters, John was irrational regarding his belief that he had been hexed. Secondly, one of Andrew Lenhart's other clients had actually murdered her husband after receiving similar information from him. That client, Sallie Jane Heagy, had hired Lenhart to "drive the witches" from her home but didn't believe his spell had worked. In terrible pain, she snapped one day and shot her husband, Irving, while he was sleeping. She believed he had invited the witchcraft into their home. Away from Lenhart's influence, Sallie Jane regained her senses in jail and, in a fit of regret, committed suicide.

Lilly was determined not to let John start thinking she was to blame for his troubles. She consulted with a lawyer and got a judge to commit John to an insane asylum for treatment. When he arrived, doctors determined he was obsessed with hexes and magic and booked him for a lengthy stay.

But it wouldn't work out that way.

Soon after the asylum doors were locked behind her husband, Lilly filed for divorce. It was quickly granted.

And that was likely a good thing because John didn't stay locked up for long. Just 48 days after he was committed, he simply walked out the door one day and vanished. No one even bothered to look for him.

John disappeared for a while, but by 1928, he was back to work at the cigar factory where he'd been previously employed. His obsession with hexes returned after he met two co-workers who also believed they were suffering because they had been hexed.

One of them, 14-year-old John Curry, was trapped in an abusive household and felt that a malevolent force was causing the trouble at home.

The other man was a farmer named Milton Hess. He and his wife, Alice, had been successful and prosperous until 1926 when a series of unfortunate events began at their farm. Crops failed, cows stopped producing milk, and they lost a large amount of money. The entire family believed that someone had hexed them, but they didn't know who it could be.

The discussion of hexes and hardships reinforced John's belief that he had also been hexed, and he became increasingly terrified that someone was out to get him. He once again consulted with other powwowers, trying to discover the source of the hex that had plagued him for so long.

John sought out a woman named Nellie Noll - who was known as the "River Witch of Marietta" - and she identified the source of the hex as someone from a local family named Rehmeyer. When John asked which of them it had been, Nellie placed a dollar bill in his hand and then removed it. When John looked at his hand, he saw an image appear - the face of a man named Nelson Rehmeyer, a skilled powwower that John had known most of his life. In fact,

Nelson Rehmeyer, the well-known powwower who John Blymire believed had placed a hex on him.

when he was only five years old, he became seriously ill, and his grandfather, unable to cure him, took him to Nelson, who healed him.

John questioned Nellie, asking why Nelson would want to hurt him, but she would only say that she was sure he was the one who had done it - and he'd also hexed his friends John and Milton.

After telling his friends what he'd learned, John assured them he knew how to end the hexes placed on them. They needed to take Nelson's copy of *The Long Lost Friend* and a lock of his hair and bury them both six feet underground.

On November 26, John and his friend, John Curry, visited Nelson at his home in Rehmeyer's Hollow. They were driven there by Clayton Hess, Milton's oldest son.

They stopped first at the home of Nelson's former wife, Alice, who gave them directions to Nelson's home, about a mile deeper

The house in Rehmeyer's Hollow, where John and his friends went to confront Nelson about the hex ~ a confrontation that would lead to his brutal murder.

into the hollow. When they arrived at the house, John went to the door and was greeted by Nelson, a stocky, older man with blondish hair. John asked to speak with him briefly about powwowing, and Nelson allowed the three young men inside.

John later said that Nelson was much "larger and meaner-looking" then he remembered. However, he was pleasant to the trio, offering them chairs in his parlor and cups of tea. John chattered away, reminding Nelson of mutual friends and distant cousins they shared. He did not, of course, mention the real reason for the visit.

After talking for a while, the three young men noticed it had gotten dark outside. Time had passed, and they had been unable to look for Nelson's hex book. They would have to return on another day. But as they got up to leave, Nelson insisted they stay the night. He'd feed them supper, and they could sleep downstairs. John, seeing his chance, hastily agreed.

That night, while Nelson was sleeping, he looked everywhere he could think of for the older man's book. It was nowhere to be found. They debated about whether to try and get a lock of Nelson's hair but finally decided against it. Nelson was too big for them to try and hold down while they cut his hair.

They left the next morning but would return and bring more help.

The following day, John told Milton Hess he needed a family member

Wilbert Hess and John Curry were Blymire's accomplices in the murder.

to help him subdue Nelson Rehmeyer. Clayton hadn't been willing to help if things turned violent. Milton and Alice then offered the assistance of their 18-year-old son Wilbert. He was a rough and tumble young man who'd always been good in a fight.

That evening, November 27, they returned to Nelson's home, and he let them inside. Before Nelson could ask why they'd come back, Clayton attacked him. Nelson's back was turned, and the boy hit him across the mid-section. As he tumbled over, John Blymire and John Curry piled on. All of them crashed to the floor. While Clayton pinned him down, John Blymire struggled to tie up the fallen man with a rope they'd brought with them.

And things turned uglier from there.

What happened next depends on which of the three men told the story, but Nelson was beaten and strangled to death during the struggle.

When they realized Nelson was dead, they took all the money in the house, hoping to make it look like a robbery - but left the

FAMILY, VICTIM AND SLAYERS IN WITCH

Witch Slayer Suspected in Girl's Murder

CHICAGO DAILY TRIBUNE: SATURDAY

Diamond

BURN HERMIT FOR CASTING SPELL ON FARMER'S FAMILY

Powwow Doctor, 2 Boys Held for Murder.

York, Pa., Nov.

THE KNICKERBOCKER

WITNESS INJECTS WITCHCRAFT INTO TRIAL OF 'DOCTOR'

Brother of One of Defend-
ants Referred to Mur-
dered Man as 'Witch'

THEFT ALLEGED MOTIVE

John H. Blymyer, Accused
'Pow-wow' Healer,
Faces Jury at York,

YORK, Pa., Jan. 7. (AP)—Efforts
of the prosecution to keep the trial

Newspapers all across America quickly spread the news of the "Hex Murder" after the three young men were arrested and placed on trial.

hex book and the lock of the dead man's hair behind. John believed that since he was dead, the hex had been lifted.

If that was true, though, none of their luck improved. It became worse - much worse.

The three assailants doused Nelson's body with kerosene and lit it on fire, sure that the flames would spread through the house and burn the entire place down, destroying the evidence of the crime. Nelson's body was engulfed in flames when they hurried out the door. They ran to the car and drove off.

And moments later, the flames were mysteriously snuffed out, leaving behind a slightly charred body, a ransacked home, and bloodstains.

Some believe that Nelson wasn't quite dead when he was set on fire and that he moved enough to put out the flames but was too badly burned to survive. Others believe that Nelson's magic was so strong that, even after death, he could leave clues to his killer's identities behind.

Regardless of what happened, things were just about to get very bad for the three young men who'd killed him.

Two days later, a client discovered Nelson's body. The shocking crime stunned the community, but the immediate shock was nothing compared to what emerged at the trial.

The police investigation into the murder didn't take long. Alice Rehmeyer informed the police of John's visit, and he, John Curry, and Clayton Hess were soon arrested.

As details of the events emerged, the entire country became riveted by the newspaper headlines. Every strange part of John's hex-obsessed life was described for the public, and when the three went to trial, there were daily reports of the proceedings.

All were found guilty by the jury. Clayton Hess received a sentence of 10 years in prison, but John Blymire and John Curry both received life sentences for murder. All were eventually paroled, and Blymire and Hess vanished into history. John Curry, the youngest of the three, served in the military during World War II and became a talented artist.

HEXES GONE WILD

The Rehmeyer" Hex Murder" received wide coverage. While the local authorities didn't launch an official assault on folk magic in the area, the press and authorities in other parts of the state eventually would.

The sensationalistic newspaper coverage of the case again brought intense scrutiny to powwowing, just as it had a decade or more before. Folk magic practitioners and hex doctors alike began

VERNA DELP

to be maligned, even those who practiced the most benign types of healing. Lurid - and mostly inaccurate -- descriptions of magic and strange beliefs filled the newspapers and shocked Americans who were unaware that such things were still taking place in the modern world of the twentieth century.

Law enforcement officials, doctors, and educators began working together to put an end to what they considered superstitious and dangerous practices. Soon, any death that was even vaguely connected to a powwower - or, more accurately, was rumored to have a connection - was labeled a "hex murder."

In March 1929, the body of a 21-year-old woman named Verna Delp was discovered in some woods near Allentown. On her body were three pieces of paper with magical charms written on them, supposedly to protect her from murder and theft. A coroner's report identified three poisons in her body.

Verna's adoptive father, August Derhammer, told the police that he'd recently learned that Verna was being treated by a powwower named Charles T. Belles and that she was supposed to have met with him on the day she died. Belles was quickly arrested. The police were sure they had another "hex murder" on their hands. He had obviously poisoned the young woman.

At first, Belles denied treating Verna but admitted that he had given her a salve for her eczema and some written charms - but that was all. He didn't know anything about any poison. The police didn't believe him, and even though they had no evidence to link him to the crime, they continued to hold him in jail.

Soon, though, the investigation took another turn. It was discovered that Verna was pregnant, and she had not seen her boyfriend, a truck driver named Masters, for several months, so he was not the father. She had not yet told her family of her predicament, and friends said she had been looking for a way to end her pregnancy.

Had Belles been responsible for her death? Had he given her some lethal drug to cause a miscarriage that had killed her? Again, there was no evidence of this, and Belle continued to deny that he had given her anything that would have killed her. Finally, charges against him were dropped in mid-April, and he was released.

What really happened to Verna Delp remains a mystery. The case turned cold while the police were distracted by hexes, charms, and magical potions.

The press jumped on another case of "murder by powwow" in January 1930. Mrs. Harry McDonald, a 34-year-old housewife from Reading, died after receiving severe burns at home. She had apparently been given some sort of ointment from a hex doctor with instructions to rub it on her skin. At some point in the night, her body went up in flames when she got too close to her stove. She was seriously injured, and when her husband, who worked the night shift, found her in the morning, she was on the verge of death and could not be saved.

The woman's brother told reporters that he believed the lotion she was using was flammable and caught fire, killing his sister. He had no evidence of this, but the press latched onto this theory and kept the story alive with "occult" connections for weeks.

Another "hex panic" murder occurred on January 20, 1932, when the body of a Philadelphia man named Norman Bechtel was discovered in Germantown. The accountant and Mennonite Church worker had been robbed and stabbed nine times.

Norman's car was later discovered six miles away, and from the bloodstains in the automobile, it was clear that he had known his attacker well enough to let them into his car.

The case gave all the appearances of a robbery gone bad - except for the stab wounds and the cuts all over his face, which detectives surmised might have "special occult significance." According to reporters, some of the stab wounds appeared to form the shape of a circle around his heart. There was also a crescent-shaped cut on each side of his forehead, and a vertical slash ran from his hairline to his nose.

When it was learned that Norman had grown up on a farm near Boyertown -- where powwow was common -- the police immediately searched for evidence of another "hex murder."

Captain Harry Heanly, the chief investigator, had the victim's apartment searched for any possible connection with hex magic, but all they found were Mennonite religious books and pamphlets. After following a few more leads, the police still had no answers, so the press began calling the "mystery" a "hex murder."

Then in April 1937, a blackmailer named William Jordan confessed that he and four others had killed Norman Bechtel. He'd been paying Jordan and the others to keep his wife from learning about several different women with whom he'd been having affairs.

Norman wasn't such a god-fearing, mild-mannered accounted after all, and the case certainly had nothing to do with hex magic.

If these cases had been the only ones tied to powwow in Pennsylvania in the first half of the twentieth century, it's likely that the "hex scare" would have died out sooner, and the public would have lost interest.

That was not meant to be, though, for another actual "hex murder" occurred in 1934, and this one gave hex magic a black eye for decades to come.

THE SHINKSKY "HEX MURDER"

The last true "hex murder" in Pennsylvania occurred in Pottsville, in Schuylkill County, on Saturday, March 17, 1934, when a shotgun blast ended the life of Mrs. Susan Mummey as it tore through her living room window.

At that time, few residents in the area had electricity or modern plumbing, and telephones were largely nonexistent. Susan lived in a fairly primitive farmhouse with her adopted daughter, Tovillia.

Susan was a powwower and had earned her reputation years before. Back in 1910, she'd had a premonition that told her that on July 5, 1910, her husband, Henry, would die if he went to the local powder mill where he worked. Although Susan begged him to stay home that day, he laughed, dismissed her fears, and went to work as usual.

You can likely guess what happened next - Henry was killed that very day when an explosion occurred at the mill. His death

Susan Mummey's primitive farmhouse near Pottsville.

earned Susan little sympathy, though. It just made people afraid of her.

On the night she was killed, Susan was tending to the injured foot of a boarder, Jacob Rice. He was seated in front of her, and her daughter was standing next to her, holding an oil lamp so that Susan could see to tend to Jacob's wound.

And then the window behind Susan exploded.

She was killed instantly while Jacob and Tovillia scrambled for cover. They stayed hidden in the darkened room all night, not knowing if the assassin still lurked outside. Finally, as morning approached, Jacob decided to make the three-mile walk to Ringtown to report the crime.

Although the victim had led a quiet, reclusive life, the police soon learned there was no shortage of people who might have wished Susan dead. She was a quarrelsome woman who had feuded with most of her neighbors - which enhanced her already sinister reputation. She was believed to have turned an "evil eye" on one of her enemies and "hexed" many others. A great sigh of relief was expressed in the community when it was learned she was finally dead.

VOL. XLIX—NO. 119. POTTSVILLE, PA., THURS

WITCH LORE MOTIVE I

Shenandoah Youth Says He Shot Aged Woman Because She Hexed Him

Solved Murder Mystery

SCENE OF "HEX" LOCATED IN | EARLIEST

Born of Strength by "Spell" Cast Upon Him Seven Years Ago He Planned to Kill Mrs. Susan Mummey

Held for Killing

Carbines Old Strain of Early Settler Witchcraft Found by Incentives in North Union

DETECTIVE RECONS

ALBERT SHINSKY

Albert Shinsky quickly confessed to the murder but claimed that it was self-defense because Susan had hexed him years before and his life had become unbearable ~ until he killed her.

This left the police with a lot of possible suspects for her murder.

Soon, though, their attention was focused on one man. Three days after the murder, some local boys told the detective in charge of the case that on the night Susan was shot, they'd seen a car parked on the road that led through the woods to Susan's house. No one was in the car then, but they had immediately recognized it as belonging to a 23-year-old man named Albert Shinsky.

Albert quickly confessed to the killing - but claimed it was self-defense. He said that Susan had placed a hex on him seven years earlier while he was working in a field across the road from the Mummey farm. There had been a dispute between Susan and the man that he worked for about property lines, and one day, Susan came over the fence and stared at Albert for a very long time. He claimed that he felt cold sweat come over him and felt hands gripping his throat.

From that day on, he said, he felt a "constant physical and mental torment" that sapped him of all his strength. Susan, he told investigators, had placed a hex on him.

Albert described how he constantly felt invisible hands on his shoulders. Pins were stuck into him. A black cat would come down from the sky and attack him while he slept. It would creep slowly across the room and jump onto the bed. The cat's appearance made him so cold, he claimed, that he had to get up and run around the room to get warm again.

He tried going to doctors and priests, but they were no help. In desperation, he consulted other powwowers, who gave him amulets and spells, but they provided only temporary relief. The harassment - and the cat - always returned.

Finally, a "spirit" came to him, explaining that he could only be free of the hex if he killed the conjurer who had placed it on him. So, on the night of March 17, he borrowed a shotgun, loaded it with a "magic bullet" guaranteed to kill witches, and went to Susan's farm.

He told the police that he didn't enjoy committing the murder, but it had worked. At the moment Susan died, he claimed, he felt the curse lift from his shoulders.

After his arrest, Albert became something of a local hero. Other men went to the police, alleging that Susan had cast spells on them as well - hexes that were only broken by her death. People in the community raised a legal defense fund for Albert, who was now in jail. He was behind bars feeling happy and unconcerned. Even the thought of facing the electric chair didn't seem to faze him. He was just so happy the hex had been broken.

The judge at his trial hardly knew what to make of him. The story he told was deeply, utterly crazy, but aside from that, Albert appeared calm and rational. He indignantly rejected any suggestion of an insanity defense.

Psychiatrists who interviewed him thought otherwise, however. They recommended he be sent to the Fairview State Hospital for the criminally insane. The judge agreed. He remained at the hospital until 1976. He lived for seven more years after he was released.

He was, apparently, never bothered by Susan's hex again.

To the authorities and the press, the murder of Susan Mummey confirmed that witchcraft was a menace to society. Newspapers once again warned of the danger of strange beliefs and the practice of pow-wow.

But the healers and hex doctors still had a few defenders and plenty of clients. It's just that the tide of public opinion was turning against them - again.

Thanks to the two high-profile murder cases - and the many silly cases that were inflated by the newspapers - war was declared on the belief in hexes, pow-wow, and witchcraft in general. Modern medicine, educational authorities, and the scientific community would erase the superstitions that plagued the country - or so it was thought.

Pennsylvania officials also launched their own campaign against powwowers, arresting and prosecuting them for practicing medicine without a license.

Of course, doctors, reporters, and officials had tried this before, and it hadn't worked any better than in the 1930s. Powwowers just went underground - again.

Most of those who continued to practice avoided the public spotlight and downplayed their work to non-believers. However, they continued to provide services to those who sought them out.

As time passed, fewer members of the younger generations showed interest in learning about the old ways of healing and hexes, but the practice refused to die out completely. Many powwowers still exist today, and German folk magic - like every other kind - remains alive and well, although practitioners today are far less likely to be driven to murder.

7. THE ROOTS & BONES OF MAGIC
AMERICAN VOODOO
& HOODOO

It began not in America but in Africa when entire nations of people created a system of beliefs, lore, stories, and customs designed to help them blend into a world filled with plants, animals, elements, and an array of gods and spirits.

When those same people began to be kidnapped, placed in chains, and sold into slavery, the physical bond with their home was broken, but like seeds carried on the wind, their beliefs found fertile lands far away.

Those beliefs took root in the Americas in different ways. They began to thrive in coastal Brazil, the Dominican Republic, and Cuba as Santeria, and in Haiti and Louisiana as Voodoo. In the southern United States, Hoodoo took root in Alabama, Mississippi, Georgia, Florida, and the Carolinas. Hoodoo was established during the years of slavery using wisdom gathered from Native Americans.

With immigration and migrations of formerly enslaved people, the African-based religions spread from earlier cultural centers to cities like New York, Miami, Los Angeles, Chicago, and beyond. Some of the traditional practices were transformed, incorporating Catholicism, and blending Western and non-Western religious rituals, ceremonies, prayers, invocations, and blessings, but also opening up to the darker side of the spiritual world with curses and hexes.

Over time, both Louisiana-based Voodoo and Southern-based Hoodoo have become distinctly American versions of folk magic. They have often been mixed together, even though each tradition has its own unique system of beliefs and practices.

VOODOO COMES TO NEW ORLEANS

Ask any tourist - or anyone who watched a season of *American Horror Story* - and they can tell you that Marie Laveau is the undisputed Queen of Voodoo in New Orleans. Voodoo is as big a part of New Orleans as jazz, gumbo, and Mardi Gras. Even after seeing the Voodoo shops in the French Quarter, most tourists assume that Voodoo is a thing of the past - but they couldn't be more wrong. The religious faith is very much alive today, and it's taken just as seriously now as it was in the days of Marie Laveau.

Voodoo came to New Orleans from Africa, primarily by way of the Caribbean islands. Enslaved people in Louisiana began arriving in 1719. Most enslaved Africans that found their way to New Orleans came directly from West Africa, bringing their language and religious beliefs, which were rooted in spirit and ancestor worship. In the Fon language of West Africa, "Vodun" means spirit - an invisible and mysterious force that can intervene in human affairs.

One reason Voodoo developed in New Orleans more than in other parts of America is largely because the French - then the Spanish, then the French again - colonized Louisiana. They were far more tolerant of the practices and the faiths of the slave population than were the British, who, as you'll recall, were the people who came to America for religious freedom and then suppressed the faiths of anyone who disagreed with them.

Another reason was because of the sheer numbers. Thousands of enslaved people were brought to Louisiana. In fact, according to the census of 1732, the ratio of enslaved people to French

Early New Orleans was a melting pot of various cultures ~ French settlers, Native Americans, and Africans who arrived via the islands of the Caribbean. They brought a variety of beliefs with them.

settlers was two to one. The white minority would have had difficulty suppressing the Voodoo faith, so they mostly didn't bother.

However, some worries popped up here and there. The first reference to Voodoo in official documents appeared in 1782 when the Spanish were in charge of New Orleans. A document about imports to the colony shows a terse line regarding enslaved Black people from the island of Martinique. Governor Galvez wrote: "These Negroes are too much given to voodooism and make the lives of the citizens unsafe."

But I think the governor was less worried about Voodoo and more concerned about rebellious enslaved people. A series of slave revolts had rocked Haiti and other islands in the Caribbean, and each time, French colonists were driven from those lands and ended up in New Orleans. When they arrived, they brought their

The enslaved people of New Orleans practiced Voodoo openly, later incorporating the Catholic saints into their practices.

slaves with them - enslaved people who not only practiced Voodoo but also may have been recently involved in uprisings.

Voodoo was always based on oral traditions, beliefs, and practices passed down from generation to generation. American Voodoo is also eclectic - as we'll soon see - collecting pieces of other things to further round out the faith. There is no one Voodoo, and it is a personal religion. However, all versions of it have things in common. There is a God who is seen as good - often known by the Haitian name *Bondye* - that is all-seeing and all-knowing but unable for humans to understand. Aloof and distant, there is no way to reach him through prayer.

The intermediaries between God and humans are spirits, called *loa*, and many of them exist. From the sea to the sky, there are spirits who represent everything in nature. The spirits also represent the dead and ancestors who have passed on. Just as there are thousands of Catholic saints, there are thousands of *loa* in Voodoo.

Voodoo in New Orleans began to blend with the Catholicism of the white residents of the city. Many saints became stand-ins for Voodoo deities ~ like St. Peter for Papa Legba, the guardian of the spirit world.

New Orleans-style Voodoo evolved just like New Orleans's food: a blend of different cultures. One of the most important cultures was Catholicism. Some believe those who practiced Voodoo started using Catholic saints, holy water, and the Lord's Prayer in their ceremonies to hide Voodoo in plain sight. It's been suggested that enslaved people were forbidden to practice their religion, so they used Catholic saints and icons as stand-ins for important Voodoo deities.

But this may not be true. Some believe it was a conscious decision to integrate Catholicism into voodoo because the white man's magic did seem to have some power - you know since the white man had a better life as an enslaver instead of an enslaved person.

For others, blending voodoo and Catholicism was simply a natural course of events. After many years and generations away from their homeland, enslaved people slowly lost their old beliefs, and the predominant Catholicism of New Orleans bled into their practices.

Voodoo altars were used to hold gifts and offerings for the gods. These items, which can include money, coins, cigars, rum, or anything else that the gods enjoy, are given in exchange for wishes and blessings.

Regardless, go into an authentic voodoo shop today. In addition to charms, roots, potions, and powders, you'll find icons of Catholic saints, statues, and prayer candles, all of which are used in the ceremonies and practices of the faith because the power of the spirits has been transferred to these symbols.

The seven African Powers are the primary spirits - Legba, Obatala, Yemaya, Oya, Oshun, Chango, and Ogun. There are a lot of different regional spellings, but they are all identified with Catholic saints. Papa Legba is the guardian of the spirit world, recognized as St. Peter holding the key to heaven. St. Patrick drove the snakes out of Ireland, so he is the place holder for the serpent spirit Damballah. Agwe is the patron spirit of fishermen, so he is personified by the fish-carrying St. Ulrich. The evil spirit

Kalfu is often considered like a demon, so he corresponds to the Christian Devil.

Like any other faith, Voodoo has light and dark sides. There are many bad spirits, and most were criminals in their former incarnation, like Baron Kriminel, who was believed to have been a murderer. These evil spirits are called upon for assistance with malevolent spells. Some spirits reflect the brutal and tragic history of slavery, like Dinclinsin, feared for his cruelty and was portrayed as a white enslaver with a whip.

Unlike the unreachable God, the spirits communicate with humans all the time and are believed to affect the day-to-day lives of followers. Good spirits advise and assist, offer protection, bring good luck, and perform healings. Specific spirits can be called on to resolve financial problems, find love, or cure disease. Such favors are only usually performed in exchange for gifts, however. The spirits haven't lost their taste for earthly things, and based on what food and objects a spirit is associated with decides what kind of offering is brought to their altars. Papa Legba, for instance, loves a bottle of rum and a good cigar.

Gris-gris bags are cloth bags used to bring good luck or protect the owner from evil.

Other kinds of offerings may be demanded, too. Animal sacrifice - goats, chickens, etc. - is often performed in healing rituals or when the spirits are asked for large favors.

Magical objects are also an essential part of Voodoo. Amulets are carried for protection from harm, such as an item of jewelry or an object like a black cat's tooth.

Gris-gris, mojo, and conjure bags are among the most important objects used for protection in New Orleans-based

Voodoo. It grew to be quite different from what was practiced in Haiti and elsewhere. The evolution of the faith in New Orleans created many new practices that most of us associate with some of the basics of Voodoo, including Voodoo dolls and gris-gris bags.

These small fabric bags were filled with magic items to bring good luck or to protect the wearer from evil spells. Items include beads, buttons, bones, stones, coins, crystals, handwritten spells, herbs, roots, and powders.

If you think this sounds like the charms and spells used by cunning folk in Appalachia and hex doctors in Pennsylvania, you'd be right.

A large part of Voodoo is the ceremonies and rituals its followers perform. The rituals are used to petition the spirits, and these requests are made via spells. Voodoo spells are used just as spells are within other kinds of magical practices - for protection, fertility, and luck, to attract love, sex, marriage, money, health, and beauty. They might also be used to keep a partner from cheating, recover from heartbreak, persuade a former lover to forget you, or maybe the other way around. Alternatively, spells might be malicious, for revenge, to place a curse, remove a curse, seek retribution, break up a relationship, injure someone, or cause sickness or even death.

Spells might follow a specific recipe or involve incantations with ritual objects like oils, candles, herbs, roots, and spices. In many cases, Catholic prayers, novenas, psalms, Hail Marys, and the Lord's Prayer are interwoven into spells. Holy water, communion bread, rosary beads, and crosses become ritual objects.

Candles are very important tools in Voodoo. They're burned to honor spirits or to petition the spirits for certain things. A St. Joseph candle is burned to help buy or sell a home. A St. Jude candle is burned for anything situation that seems hopeless, and St. Expeditus candles were used for fast assistance in any matter.

Some candles were burned according to their color - red for love and passion and green for money.

To appeal to the spirits, candles are decorated with fabric, ribbons, and glitter - for benevolent spells, that is. Malicious spells used candles with images of snakes, skulls, and crossbones. The candles are "fixed," which means they are rolled in oils and herbs to enhance their power. Many different oils are used, depending on the intent of the spell, and incense is often burned to entice the spirits to communicate and dispel misfortune.

Voodoo dolls are another facet of New Orleans Voodoo that is not used elsewhere. But they're nothing like what you may have seen in movies, pulp stories, or magazines. Similar to the cloth poppets used in folk magic, these figures are usually made from wax, sticks, clay, wood, rope, and other materials. They are used to attract luck and cure illness but can also be used to harm others. They're not really jabbed with pins, but they are commonly used as effigies.

As with any kind of folk magic, practitioners of Voodoo believe that performing magic on the representation of a person will result in a real-life effect on that person. Personal possessions - like clothing, bodily fluids, hair, fingernails, etc. -- are used as an extension of that person's body. They hold the person's energy and solidify the connection between the person and the figure. It is, as we have discussed before, "sympathetic magic," which works when the victim of the magic believes that it does.

A lot of Voodoo seems to be about asking for favors, but even the spirits get tired of someone who only calls when they want something. For this reason, worship is another integral part of the faith.

Altars are sacred spaces dedicated to a spirit. They are used for both creating spells and for private devotion. They display ritual objects, including candles, incense, and statues of saints. Offerings are left for the spirits, like flowers, alcohol, money, food, cigars, and anything else associated with the particular spirit the altar was built for. These gifts are used to repay favors, not usually as a way of requesting more.

Voodoo rituals aren't always private affairs; they're often performed in groups. These ceremonies occur for healing, ending bad luck, and at birth, marriage, and death. If a specific spirit is being celebrated, they are invoked using prayer, chants, feasting, fire, and traditional music involving drums and bells.

The ceremonies involved frenzied dancing, singing, convulsions, and fainting. They build in intensity until someone goes into a trance-like state because a spirit has possessed them. Possession is a good thing in Voodoo. The spirits no longer have earthy bodies, so they must "borrow" one. A person is "mounted" by a spirit and "ridden" like a horse. They actually *become* that spirit and begin behaving like the spirit that now inhabits them. For example, those ridden by Pape Guede drink a mixture of rum and habanero peppers. Those inhabited by Damballah may slither on the ground like a snake. They have no memory of what occurs while possessed.

I WALKED WITH A ZOMBIE

Even though zombies are not part of traditional American Voodoo, I have to at least mention them here because they aren't anything like what you may have seen in films like *Night of the Living Dead* or television shows like *The Walking Dead*.

The idea of zombies first came to America in the early twentieth century when author William Seabrook wrote about encountering zombies in a book about Haiti called *The Magic island* in 1929. They soon became the subject of pulp magazines and horror films like *White Zombie,* and *I Walked with A Zombie* in the early 1930s.

You see, a traditional zombie is not the flesh-eating, reanimated dead man from popular culture - it's a fact, not fiction.

Zombies are the creation of a *bokor*, an evil sorcerer. Using a poison, the victim is taken to the brink of death and even buried by a grieving family before being revived by the *bokor* as a submissive slave.

In Haiti, the belief in zombies has been widespread for generations. Turning someone into a zombie was seen as an act of revenge, and it was so feared that it was common practice for family members to stand guard over a loved one's tomb for weeks to protect the corpse. They might also place charms and poisons with the body to frighten off a *bokor* or even decapitate a body before burial. There is even a law under the Haitian Penal Code that makes zombification a criminal offense.

But that doesn't always stop those who wish to do harm.

On May 2, 1962, a Haitian man named Clairvius Narcisse died of a mysterious illness - or so it seemed at the time. A little over 18 years later, his sister, Angelina, was shopping in a local market and saw a terrifying, vacant-eyed man lurching toward her. Angelina couldn't help but scream - the man was her dead brother, Clairvius.

It seemed impossible. She had been at his funeral nearly two decades earlier. It was soon discovered, though, that her brother had been turned into a zombie.

In the spring of 1962, Clairvius had checked into the Albert Schweitzer Hospital complaining of a fever and body aches. Two physicians treated him – one from America, the other American-trained – who diagnosed Clairvius with hypertension, heart failure, a respiratory issue, and other ailments. With each passing day, his condition got worse. Clairvius reported a tingling sensation that was felt throughout his body. His skin grew pale, and his lips turned blue. Then, finally, on May 2, he was pronounced dead.

Clavius Narcisse became a real-life zombie in 1962.

His sisters, Angelina and Marie Claire, were at his deathbed when he passed. Angelina was inconsolable, so Marie Claire "signed" the death certificate with her thumbprint. Clairvius was buried in the local cemetery the next day.

That should have been the end of the story, but it was just getting started.

No matter what the doctors and the death certificate stated, Clairvius did not die that day at the hospital. According to his own account, he was aware of everything that happened on the day he "died," but he could not move or speak. He felt the sheet being pulled up over his face and - worst of all - was awake when he was sealed into his casket and buried. He was later able to show a scar that he said came from a coffin nail that missed its mark and punctured his skin.

Shortly after his family left the cemetery, Clairvius was disinterred by a *bokor* who partially revived him from his catatonic state and forced him to work as a slave on a sugar plantation for the next two years. During this time, Clairvius was fed a steady mixture of poisons that kept him in a functioning stupor, able to walk and follow orders but unable to think or act independently.

Clairvius Narcisse had been turned into a zombie.

After his two years of slavery, the *bokor* died, and Clairvius slowly became himself again. But 16 more years would pass before he returned to his family. He discovered that it had been his own brother who had sold him to the sorcerer, arranging for Clairvius to be poisoned and turned into a zombie because of a land dispute between them. He remained in hiding until his brother died and then tried to find his sisters.

Shortly after his seemingly miraculous return, his family verified his identity. Clairvius used a childhood nickname for Angelina on the day that he found her in the market - one only he would know. In addition, researchers from the Centre de Psychologie et Neurologie Mars-Kline in Port-au-Prince confirmed that the man who appeared at the market was indeed the same man who had been buried 18 years before.

His story got the attention of a graduate student in anthropology and ethnobotany at Harvard University named Wade Davis. He came to Haiti to investigate the story and wrote two books about his experiences. The first, *The Serpent and the Rainbow* became a bestseller and later inspired a horror film that loosely follows the book.

While in Haiti, Davis acquired a sample of the "zombie powder" - the same poison *bokor*s used to turn people into zombies. The powder turned out to include a variety of ingredients, including human bones and toxins from toads, plants, and pufferfish. When people were given this powder, they slipped into a death-like state that caused them to be declared dead by doctors and buried by family members. Soon after, they were dug up by *bokors* and given an antidote, but a constant injection of drugs kept them in a trance for days, months, and even years.

Mixed with a belief in Voodoo - and sympathetic magic - bokors could keep their victims under their spells and provoke fear in everyone who knew that zombies were real.

As for Clairvius Narcisse, he lived for another 14 years after his dramatic reappearance in the marketplace. I would guess that when he died for a second time, the doctors made doubly sure that he was really dead.

VOODOO DOCTORS AND QUEENS

Another difference between traditional Voodoo and New Orleans-style Voodoo is the prominence of Voodoo queens in Louisiana. In Africa, Voodoo was a male-dominated faith, but it was the opposite in New Orleans. The enslaved people credited a female spirit, Aida Wedo, for allowing them to survive the ocean crossing to the New World. This was the beginning of women being central to New Orleans Voodoo.

Marie Laveau is, of course, the most famous Voodoo queen in the city's history, but she was not the first. Sanite Dede was an early voodoo practitioner in the city. She was a young woman from Haiti who held rituals in her courtyard at Dumaine and Chartres Street, just a few blocks from the St. Louis Cathedral. The local newspaper printed sensational stories about her rituals, describing "wild, uncontrolled orgies" and "serpent worship."

But it wasn't the newspaper stories that first upset the white residents. Whether it was the drums that could be heard during Mass at the church or the supposed orgies, the Catholic leaders managed to push through an ordinance in 1817 that stated that Catholicism was the only recognized faith in New Orleans - making it illegal to practice any others. This demonstrates the power of the Church at the time since this was after Louisiana had

become part of the United States, and the city wasn't filled with only French and Spanish settlers anymore.

Soon after the short-lived ordinance was passed, the police arrested 400 women for allegedly dancing naked in Sanite's courtyard. The charges were later dropped for lack of evidence - which turned out to be almost as bad as if they had been sent to jail. Rumors spread that voodoo spells had either erased the evidence or clouded the minds of the judges and prosecutors.

White residents feared that the religion - practiced by enslaved people and free people of color - was so powerful that it could entice followers to commit any crime or deed. Supernatural powers and secret drugs made Voodoo a force to be reckoned with. Enslavers began to fear poison in their food. Men and women were convinced they could be forced to fall in love with anyone just because of a sprinkle of magic powder.

The message became clear -- Voodoo was not welcome in New Orleans. To avoid harassment in the city, Voodoo practitioners moved outside the city limits to the swamp of Bayou St. John - near what is now the City Park.

But the fears and prejudices of the city's white residents did not drive voodoo out of New Orleans altogether. Trying to push Voodoo out of the city was as much a reaction to the fear of the faith as it was to the terror of large groups of African Americans gathering together. White leaders feared rebellion more than magic.

Some Voodoo practitioners protested the ordinances, like Betsey Toledano, described in the newspaper as a "stout, intelligent, free woman of color." Articles that appeared in local papers like the *Times-Picayune* reported that Voodoo queens like Betsey carried on "in secret, bringing slaves in contact with disorderly free negroes and mischievous whites to promote discontent, inflame passions, and indispose them to the performance of their duties to their masters."

Stories with headlines like "African Barbarians," "The Rites of Voodoo," and "Voodoo-ism Unveiled" were published, stating that a group of African American women had been arrested for "performing the barbarous ceremonies and mysteries of Voodoo-ism." In other words, Betsey and a few others were charged with gathering enslaved people at her home to engage in "heathen rites."

After her arrest, Betsey appeared before the authorities to plead her case and defend her right to practice Voodoo, which she believed was her religion. She was not intimidated, nor was she silent about her beliefs. Instead of denying the accusations against her, she admitted to frequently having meetings for women to ding songs and discuss the religion that had been passed down to her by her grandmother.

The arresting officers were forced to admit that they had broken into her home after hearing singing inside, which they believed was evidence of criminal behavior. They described the scene of the "crime" and stated that they had confiscated "Voodoo paraphernalia" like "shells, horsehair, curious aprons, colored stones, etc."

When Betsey was asked what the objects were used for, she explained them, saying that she used stones to keep the house from being struck by lightning. They were placed in bowls of water during a storm, which, according to African custom, offered protection. The shells were turned into necklaces. When worn, they could be used to cause it to rain. Other items, though, were secret, and she refused to discuss them.

After reviewing the case, she was charged not with practicing Voodoo but for "an unlawful assemblage of free people and slaves." Another hearing to decide her fine was scheduled, but there is no record of how it turned out.

Artist's rendition of Dr. John, the first Voodoo leader of New Orleans and mentor to Marie Laveau.

The first real leader of Voodoo in the city was John Montenee, a heavily tattooed Voodoo priest known better as Dr. John. He was a well-respected free person of color who sometimes claimed to have once been an African prince. He had many beautiful wives and mistresses, with whom he had over 50 children. In addition to what must have been a busy love life, he was also famous for predicting the future, casting spells, making the first gris-gris bags, and reading minds.

And if his name sounds familiar, it's likely because you've heard his music. Well, not the original Dr. John, but the music of Mac Rebennack, who took the stage name of Dr. John as an homage to the nineteenth-century Voodoo man.

He was the first in New Orleans to use Voodoo for profit. He charged fees to mix potions and make gris-gris bags and was happy to sell them to whoever wanted to pay - black or white. Dr. John was the mentor and teacher; some even say the power behind Marie Laveau. She eventually decided to break away from Dr. John and set up her own practice.

Not much is known about Dr. John's life, primarily because he invented and changed his biography many times during his life. He was born in 1815, likely from Senegal, and died in 1885. Most of what we know about him comes from travel writer Lafcadio Hearn, who, as we'll learn soon, was not the most reliable biographer. But he did write an obituary about Dr. John that appeared in *Harper's* magazine in 1885.

According to Hearn, Dr. John had been kidnapped by Spanish slavers from Africa in 1839. He was sold in Cuba, and while enslaved, his master took a liking to him and taught him to be an exceptional cook. His owner decided to free him, and soon after, John got a job as a cook on a Spanish ship, traveling all over the world. He eventually settled in New Orleans, where he worked as a cotton roller.

John's size, intelligence, and facial tattoos made him an imposing presence, but there was more to him than that. He seemed to possess what some described as an "occult presence," which he put to good use. He gained a reputation for telling fortunes and soon had many black and white customers who sought him out and paid him for his services. This allowed him to buy property on Bayou Road and build a large home. He became accepted in New Orleans, even by the highest echelons of Creole society.

Prominent men like John Slidell, the politician and eventual Confederate envoy to France, and General Pierre Beauregard, consulted him regularly. The *Daily Republican* newspaper reported, "When ignorant people came, he used cards and crystals, but with the higher classes, he employed his 'second sight' gift, making at times, it is said, startling revelations."

What is known about Dr. John's Voodoo practice also comes from Lafcadio Hearn., who described his office:

His office furniture consisted of a table, a chair, a picture of the Virgin Mary, an elephant's tusk, some shells that he said were African shells that enabled him to read the future, and a pack of cards in each of which a small hole had been burned. About his person he always carried two small bones wrapped around with a black string, which bones he appeared to revere as fetishes. Wax candles were burned during his performances; and as he bought a whole box of them every few days during "flush times," one can imagine how large the number of his clients must have been. They poured money into his hands so generously that he became worth at least $50,000.

Some of Dr. John's received notoriety that might make some approach his magical working with caution - especially when it comes to spells for love.

One of those infamous clients was an enslaved person named Pauline, who was the property of a man named Peter Redeck. She became the first person hanged at the Parish Prison. She had purchased a love spell from Dr. John in 1844 to charm her master. She wanted him to fall in love with her, not merely use her for sex, as he had been doing. Unfortunately, she misunderstood the directions for the potion she had to make and drank it herself instead of giving it to Redeck. She became obsessed with him, beat his wife and three children while he was traveling on business, and locked them in a cabinet for six weeks. She refused them food and water and taunted Mrs. Redeck with stories about her affair with the woman's husband.

In January 1845, Mayor Edgar Montegut received an anonymous letter that claimed a white woman and her children were being held captive. The police were dispatched to the Redeck home and found the family alive but in terrible condition.

Pauline was arrested, imprisoned, and sentenced to death by hanging. Her execution was delayed, though, because she was

This modern location is said to have been the home and office of Dr. John.

pregnant. Once she gave birth, she was put to death as planned. Her only excuse for her actions was that the love spell had gone awry.

But in addition to love spells and gris-gris bags, Dr. John was also known for his healing abilities. During a yellow fever epidemic in 1878, he nearly lost two of his children to the disease. "I have no money," he said, "but I can cure my children." He did so by harvesting, preparing, and administering an herbal concoction containing Chinaberry. According to witnesses, the children were playing outside the very next day.

His reputation was so great that people from all races came to see him for help. Many of them paid hefty fees for his cures, while some were charged nothing at all.

There is a story about a wealthy family, the Krawlens, whose baby had fallen ill. They consulted with several doctors, but none of them could ease the child's sickness or even diagnose what was wrong with her. Finally, their African American nurse suggested that the baby was under a Voodoo spell and that only a Voodoo doctor could save her. The nurse sent for Dr. John.

He spent about a half hour with the baby, practicing "mysterious mummery" as the *Times-Democrat* newspaper called it, and agreed that the child was under a Voodoo spell. He cut open the child's pillow, reached inside, and pulled out a small coffin-shaped piece of canvas. He smelled it and realized that it had been dosed with some kind of poison. The fetish that had been tucked into the pillow was the reason the baby was still sick. After Dr. John removed it, the child almost immediately began to improve and was perfectly healthy again within a few days.

Dr. John charged the Krawlens family nothing for the cure. He was ashamed that another Voodoo worker had targeted an innocent child. However, most of his clients paid as much as $10 and $20 for cures, medicines, gris-gris, and advice. This was a substantial amount of money in those days. One time he was paid $50 for a single potion. He told a friend, "It was water with some common herbs boiled into it. I hurt nobody, but if folks want to give me $50, I'll take $50 every time."

As you might imagine, John was a successful businessman. He made a lot of money and owned several properties. He earned a living from his practice but also from real estate, a café he owned, a grocery store, and rumor has it, from a brothel he owned and operated. He had no faith in banks, so he buried his money. When he needed some of it, he'd dig it up at night by the light of the moon.

However, he always tried to keep his business transactions simple because John could not read. This put him at a disadvantage on many occasions. He didn't understand the terms of loans and often fell behind on payments, causing some of his properties to be seized. Eventually, he asked a business associate to help him learn to read.

As it turned out, he asked the wrong man.

After agreeing to help, he first taught John to sign his name. One day, he put a blank sheet of paper in front of him and asked him to sign it, which he did. Unbeknownst to John, he had just signed away all of his real estate holdings.

He had plenty of cash to buy others, but I can't imagine this deed went unpunished.

Regardless, John did eventually end up financially ruined. It was not because of real estate holdings but because of how he "desperately invested in lottery tickets," folklore author Lyle Saxon wrote. Apparently, no matter what kind of a conjurer he was, John couldn't pick the winning numbers.

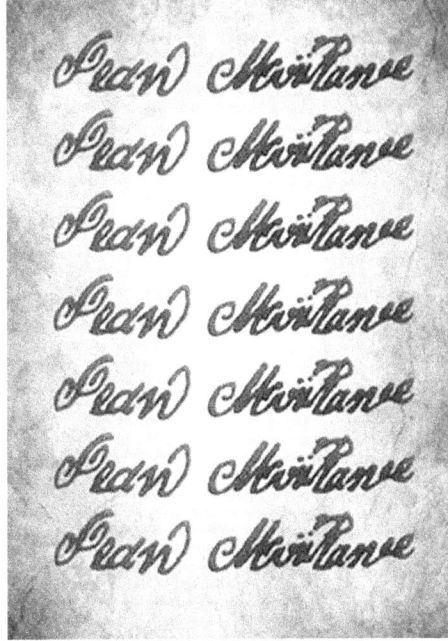

Dr. John learned to sign his name ~ a skill that he would eventually regret.

His Voodoo practice sustained him for the remainder of his life, and he maintained a great reputation until the end of his days. He died from Bright's Disease in 1885 and was laid to rest at St. Roch's Cemetery. His body was placed in a wall vault, but its location has been lost over time. The wall deteriorated, was torn down, and replaced after Hurricane Katrina. There's no way of knowing if his bones are still there or if they were washed away in the storm.

For just this reason, the grave of an unknown man in St. Louis Cemetery No. 1 has been designated as a place to honor and commune with Dr. John. The tomb is behind the conspicuous white pyramid belonging to actor Nicholas Cage, and for years, root doctors and Voodoo practitioners conjured there. Some even slept at the grave as a rite of passage.

Today, such things are much harder to do in the cemetery since it's not always open because of vandalism. But if you find the tomb - and you have some water with you - pour a little water on it and leave something with your sweat or saliva behind as an offering.

MARIE LAVEAU

Over the years, Marie Laveau has become for Voodoo what Louis Armstrong became for jazz. By that, I mean many people claim to have invented jazz, from Buddy Bolden to Jelly Roll Morton - but Louis Armstrong made it internationally famous. Marie Laveau may have come later than Sanite Dede and Dr. John, but she was the one who made it notorious and the reason that we still talk about it today.

Although no one knows for sure what Marie Laveau looked like, this is a widely accepted artist's rendition of her, created in the nineteenth century.

Marie was born a free woman of color in New Orleans - or maybe in Haiti - in 1794, or maybe 1801, or perhaps neither. Her father was a white plantation owner, and her mother was one of his slaves. The first official record of her appears in 1819 when she married Jacque

Paris, another free person of color. She was soon abandoned or maybe widowed. No one knows.

At some point in 1825, she began a second, common-law marriage to Louis Christophe Dominique Dominy de Glapion, a white man, possibly from French nobility, with whom she would have seven children between 1827 and 1835, although only two of them survived to adulthood. One of the two daughters - Marie Heloise Euchariste or Marie Philomene - may have taken her mother's place when she passed away. This would give the illusion that Marie lived an extraordinarily long life.

While she would become most famous for her role as the Voodoo Queen of New Orleans, she was also beloved in the city for her charity work. She lived during the yellow fever epidemics that plagued the city for 67 summers in a row and worked tirelessly to comfort and heal the sick.

But, of course, she is best known for her magic. Marie worked as a hairdresser. She learned all the latest styles and cared for the affluent ladies of New Orleans. This allowed her access to the most fashionable homes in the city, gathering gossip and information during every appointment. Her clients talked to her about anything and everything, from childbirths to scandals, and she created a network of intelligence by recruiting cooks, maids, and domestic workers as her informants.

In this way, when she told fortunes, she was remarkably well-informed, presenting information that she couldn't possibly know - or so it seemed to her clients.

Her reputation became well-known throughout the city. Visiting Marie for a reading became the latest craze. Politicians paid her as much as $1,000 for help in winning elections. The cost of her love potions soared to $10. As a lifelong and devout Catholic, she has been credited for introducing the Virgin Mary as a central Voodoo worship figure, attracting even more followers. She dealt in spells and charms for white and black customers and produced cures for their ailments. Marie was a clever and astute businesswoman who knew how to use her beliefs -- and the beliefs and fears of others -- to the advantage of herself and her clients.

One tale of Marie Laveau has reached legendary status. A young man from a wealthy family was arrested and charged with a series of crimes. While the young man was innocent, the actual perpetrators had been several of his friends, who had let the blame fall upon their unlucky companion. His grief-stricken father sought Marie's assistance and explained the case's circumstances to her. He promised a handsome reward if she would use her powers to obtain his son's release.

St. Louis Cathedral in Place de Armes, which is now known as Jackson Square.

When the day of the trial arrived, Marie placed three peppers into her mouth and went into the St. Louis Cathedral to pray. She remained at the altar for some time and then managed to get into the courtroom where the trial was going to be held. Before the proceedings could start, she took the three peppers from her mouth and put them under the judge's chair. None of the spectators could see them - but there was no way that the judge could miss them as he walked to his chair. We can only imagine what he must have thought after seeing the peppers and then looking out and seeing Marie Laveau sitting behind the defendant in his courtroom.

The trial began, and the prosecutor presented hours of unfavorable evidence against the young man. But after a lengthy deliberation, the judge returned to the courtroom and pronounced the young man "not guilty."

Magic? Probably not. More likely, it was the power of suggestion and the worries of the judge about what might happen to him if the young man went to prison. Marie possessed the secrets of the most influential people in the city - probably including the judge.

The young man's father was thrilled with the verdict, and in return for her help, he gave Marie the deed to a cottage at 1020 St. Anne Street, between Rampart and Burgundy. It remained her home until her death many years later.

Above and beyond her network of spies and her potions and charms, Marie had great showmanship. She knew how to take money from the white man's pockets so that he could watch her rituals. Men and women danced wildly after drinking rum and became possessed by various spirits. Seated on her throne, Marie directed the action, or she danced with a large snake in honor of Damballah.

Once each year, Marie presided over the ritual of St. John's Eve, beginning at dusk on June 23 and ending at dawn the next day. St. John's Day is the most sacred of holy days in the Voodoo faith. Hundreds attended each year, including reporters and curious white onlookers, each of whom was charged a sizable admission. Drum beating, bonfires, animal sacrifice, and nude women dancing were all part of the all-night ritual - creating lurid stories for newspapers and magazines nationwide.

But Marie knew what she was doing. In addition to being a mother, voodoo queen, and hairdresser, she also probably should have started New Orleans's first tourism bureau.

One of the reporters who attended Marie's rituals was writer Lafcadio Hearn. The quiet, scrawny, bug-eyed, weak-chinned, bird-legged writer was a reporter in Cincinnati before moving to New Orleans in 1877. He'd been fired from his job at a Cincinnati newspaper because he'd married an African American woman, which was against Ohio law at the time. He spent the next ten years in New Orleans, writing pieces about the city for national magazines like *Scribner's* and *Harper's*. His articles created the popular reputation of New Orleans as a place that was more like Europe or the Caribbean than like the rest of the United States. Essentially, he put the city of New Orleans on the tourist map.

He also wrote a lot about Voodoo. While not entirely accurate in his reporting, he certainly made it seem like something every adventurous traveler of the nineteenth century should see. Most of his articles portrayed voodoo rituals as snake handling, bourbon drinking, nude dancing, and chicken killing affairs that ended with people sticking pins into dolls.

It's a reputation that has endured for a century and a half - all thanks to Lafcadio Hearn and, by extension, the showmanship of Marie Laveau, the Voodoo queen who laughed all the way to the bank.

But make no mistake; she also helped many people along the way. She has become a woman known for two identities. She was feared by some and beloved by others. While she charged uptown ladies and politicians hefty fees, she provided many services for free when she cared for the sick, ministered to jail inmates, or helped those in need who had no money.

Marie died in June 1881 - maybe - but whenever it was, many people didn't realize she was gone. The second Marie Laveau - her daughter - stepped in, took her place, and continued her traditions for some time to come.

One thing we do know, of course, is that St. Louis Cemetery No. 1 is the final resting place of Voodoo queen Marie Laveau.

Or do we? Like Marie herself, there is a lot of controversy about what may - or may not - be her final resting place.

DEATH OF MARIE LAVEAU.

A Woman with a Wonderful History, Almost a Century Old, Carried to the Tomb Yesterday Evening.

Those who have passed by the quaint old house on St. Ann, between Rampart and Burgundy streets, with the high, frail looking fence in front over which a tree or two is visible, have, till within the last few years, noticed through the open gateway a decrepid old lady with snow white hair, and a smile of peace and contentment lighting up her golden features. For a few years past she has been missed from her accustomed place. The feeble old lady lay upon her bed with her daughter and grandchildren around her ministering to her wants.

Marie Laveau likely died in June 1881, but she was replaced by one of her daughters, so many people didn't realize she was dead.

Most believe the tomb, which bears the name Glapion, holds the remains of Marie and her daughter, the second Marie, but many others disagree. There is also a "Marie Laveau Tomb" in St. Louis Cemetery No. 2. It is located at the rear of the cemetery, and the slab over the crypt is always covered with literally hundreds of red crosses inscribed with pieces of brick. Some tales claim Marie is buried somewhere else altogether.

It's believed that the confusion started after the body that was originally interred in the tomb was allegedly moved. Marie was said to be first entombed in St. Louis Cemetery No. 1, but her spirit "refused to behave." People became so scared that they refused to go near the cemetery, so another priestess, and some relatives, moved Marie to Holt Cemetery. She was placed in an unmarked crypt so her name would not be remembered.

But most don't agree with this tale. New Orleans tradition states that Marie is buried in St. Louis Cemetery No. 1, and thousands have come here searching for her crypt. The tomb looks like so many others in the cemetery until you notice all the stuff that has been left behind in front of it. You'll find coins, pieces of herb, bottles of rum, beans, bones, bags, flowers, tokens, and just about anything else you can imagine left behind as an offering for the good luck and blessings of the Voodoo Queen.

If you visit the tomb and don't leave anything, legend has it that your teeth will fall out. I don't know if this is true, but don't say I didn't warn you.

In addition to the offerings, you will also find thousands of markings and Xs covering the tomb. The tomb is often repainted, but the marks come back. There's nothing supernatural about this - it's done by stupid people. The origins of what some claim is a Voodoo practice are unclear, but, despite what some people may claim, it's not an old tradition. The Xs found on the tomb have been left by tour groups, and uneducated guides, who instruct the tourists to leave three Xs inscribed on the tomb in hopes of good luck.

If visiting St. Louis Cemetery No. 1, think twice before leaving your own Xs on the tomb. The Glapion family -- who owns the tomb -- does not consider this voodoo but vandalism. If you are hoping to get on the good side of Marie Laveau, leave an offering instead.

Marie's ghost has been seen many times in the cemetery, along with the ghost of her large black snake. Legends say she has

The generally accepted location of where Marie Laveau is entombed at St. Louis Cemetery No. 1.

sometimes been seen walking the cemetery's narrow paths. One man even claimed to have been slapped by her spirit after making a disparaging remark at her tomb one day.

Bad things happen to you when you cross Marie Laveau.

In late 2013, someone climbed over the cemetery wall at night and painted Marie's famous vault with pink latex paint. Latex paint, which traps moisture and does not breathe, can ruin brick-and-mortar tombs. It required months of work and over $10,000 to repair. I don't know if anything bad happened to this person, but I have to say - I hope it did.

VOODOO LIVES!

The "golden age of Voodoo" in New Orleans began in the late nineteenth century when Lafcadio Hearn started spreading stories of the rituals he and numerous tourists had witnessed in the city.

But that "golden age" was not destined to last. By the 1930s, tourism had become the foundation of the city's economy. City leaders didn't want to frighten away visitors who might think they'd see the sensationalized version of Voodoo that Hollywood movies like White Zombie and best-selling books like The Magic Island had created. Most of the publications about voodoo in New Orleans or Marie Laveau printed in the 1930s, '40s, and '50s are always sensationalized and usually -- surprise, surprise -- inherently racist.

Voodoo today is making something of a comeback in New Orleans. There's the touristy voodoo rebirth -- which means you'll find about a dozen shops selling gris-gris bags and pin dolls in the French Quarter - and then there's the real embrace of the religion. People today are hungry for spiritual fulfillment, and Voodoo offers a direct experience that appeals to people. What's happening is very apparent in New Orleans, which has always been the center of these beliefs.

The main focus of voodoo today is to serve others and to influence the outcome of life events through a connection with nature, spirits, and ancestors. Most rituals are held behind closed doors since public shows are considered disrespectful to the spirits. Voodoo practices include readings, prayer, and personal ceremony and is often used to cure depression, loneliness, anxiety, depression, and other ailments. It also tried to help the poor, the hungry, and the sick, just as Marie Laveau once did.

But attitudes are slow to change. There is still fear among many people as to what Voodoo is and how it works. They dismiss it as superstitious nonsense, but there's no denying they are afraid of it.

It's impossible to deny the fear and racism that lurks behind statements made by people like evangelist Pat Robertson, who, after the massive earthquake that occurred in Haiti a few years ago, stated that the Haitians deserved the death and destruction because, in following Voodoo, "they made a pact with the Devil."

You won't find the Devil mixed up in Voodoo. You can't say the same for fundamentalist Christianity, though.

What should we be more afraid of?

HOODOO ROOTS AND BONES

Over the years, Voodoo and Hoodoo have been confused with one another over and over again. I even hesitated to include them in the same chapter because I didn't want to add to the confusion. In the end, though, I relented. They share many traditions and styles, but the same could be said of folk magic in general because Hoodoo - like New Orleans Voodoo, conjure, and hex magic - is purely American and purely the magic of the common folk.

Hoodoo came to America based on the African religions that arrived with the enslaved people. It began in the South and soon became a multicultural tradition that linked Native Americans, immigrants of various religious faiths, and enslaved people, mainly from West Africa. It became mostly a healing practice that involved using herbs, plants, roots, trees, animals, magnets, minerals, and natural waters combined with amulets, chants, ceremonies, rituals, and what were called "handmade power objects." These kinds of objects empower the practitioner to take control of their fate rather than place that power in the hands of various gods or religious figures.

Interestingly, the name "Hoodoo" has rarely been used by African Americans who practice it. They have always seen it as a reminder of slavery. Plus, it's a term of dubious origin that likely came about as a variation on "Voodoo." It was a name rarely spoken in African American homes, even if it was a part of daily life.

The term "Hoodoo" is often avoided by African Americans because it's a reminder of slavery, where this kind of folk magic originated. The illustration here is just one of many racist drawings that portrayed the enslaved people of the mid-nineteenth century.

We'll use it here the way that it's most commonly used - as a colorful way of describing the folk magic of a wide range of believers that historically included the Gullah people of Georgia and the Carolinas, African Americans in major cities, white people of the Appalachians, and Native Americans.

Since Hoodoo is not a religion, it has always been practiced by a wide range of people, regardless of their faith or skin color. Its attraction has always been because it is natural, practical, and requires no religious background. Primary concerns of Hoodoo include blessing the home and keeping life peaceful and free of unwanted intrusions, like bad vibes from humans or spirits. Other concerns are finding a faithful partner; general health and happiness; predicting the future; controlling others when necessary; and freeing yourself or others from unwanted control, hexing and un-hexing, drawing good luck, wealth, love, and happiness.

The methods used to achieve these desired situations are called "laying of tricks" or "fixing tricks," which is basic folk magic. As with Voodoo and hex magic, herbal bundles are created that are called "a bag of tricks," gris-gris, or most commonly, mojo bags.

The term "mojo" appears in the lyrics of many traditional blues songs, which got their start, like Hoodoo, in the South. In the songs, though, the lyrics are misinterpreted to mean that "mojo" has something to do with sexual prowess. A "trick bag" becomes a metaphor for bad behavior. They are, of course, the same thing when it comes to Hoodoo - a bag of charms that serves as an amulet for purposes ranging from attracting love to drawing luck and money. The bags are carried close to a person, usually on the thigh, in a woman's bra, or hanging around the neck. If someone "steals your mojo," it's not for any reason that's in a blues song. It's because they have stolen something that holds your hopes and dreams. A mojo carries someone's personal power, which is why it's believed that it can be dangerous - maybe even fatal - if it falls into the hands of another, especially if that person is a conjurer or witch.

In addition to mojos, Hoodoo involves a lot of magical oils and incense. Oils can be applied to a person, diffused in the air, set out in certain places in the home, and used with candles. Oils can often be found with names like "Black Cat Oil," "Fast Luck Oil," "Bend Over Oil," and others. Incense is burned while chanting, singing, and praying.

As with other types of folk magic, salt is a primary component of Hoodoo. Salts have been used for cleansing and healing for thousands of years. In Hoodoo, it is usually placed on the floor ort in corners during spiritual cleansing and used during bathing for curative and restorative purposes.

Hoodoo practitioners also use sweet waters for bathing and place them in bowls to keep away - or attract, depending on the situation - people and spirits.

Divination is important to Hoodoo. It's achieved using natural materials like crystals, tea leaves, coffee grounds, animal bones, water, seashells, and more. Many practitioners dream of the future, interpret dreams, and control their nocturnal visions through lucid dreaming.

And like other types of American folk magic, Hoodoo invokes spirits of all kinds, from natural to ancestral, and requests protection, healing, curses, and blessings.

But let's start at the beginning and look at how it took root in America at the same time that Voodoo did but became something very different to those who believed in it.

THE ROOTS OF HOODOO

While both blacks and whites use Hoodoo, its roots began - like Voodoo - with the African Americans who were brought to America in chains, starting in 1619. They brought their traditions, faiths, and religions with them, and when mixed into the melting pot of the various cultures found here, it became something different. As mentioned earlier, Hoodoo is not a religion, which is why so many different kinds of people have embraced it.

The magic behind Hoodoo began with the conversion of many Africans to Christianity, which was then mixed with the traditions carried from home. Both enslaved and free Africans also learned some regional botanical knowledge from Native Americans and from white immigrants who settled in the mountain regions of the South. They had also learned of the herbs and healing roots of the region from the native people. All of this combined into Hoodoo.

The extent to which it could be practiced varied by region and the temperament of enslavers and the authorities. For example, the Gullah people of the coastal areas enjoyed an isolation and relative freedom that allowed them to retain many traditional West African practices. In places like the Mississippi Delta, though, root work was practiced in secrecy by free people of color and enslaved people alike. They practiced their magic in isolated areas, like the woods and graveyards, and created methods to decrease noise to keep nearby whites from hearing them. Using sticks, a wash pot would be turned upside down and raised about a foot off the ground. That way, the noise from prayers or chants went into the pots.

A documented history of Hoodoo dates to America's colonial days. A slave revolt that occurred in New York in 1712 was led by a conjurer named Peter the Doctor. He made a magical powder for the enslaved people to rub on their bodies and clothing for protection and empowerment. The powder likely contained graveyard dirt, which would conjure the ancestors of the enslaved people for help.

In the early nineteenth century, mojo bags began to be used as a resistance to slavery. William Webb helped the enslaved people on a plantation in Kentucky resist their oppressors by instructing them to gather roots into the bags and then "march around the cabins several times and point the bags toward the master's house every morning." Legends say their treatment markedly improved after the enslaved people did what Webb instructed them.

Formerly enslaved person and abolitionist William Wells Brown wrote about the lives of enslaved people in St. Louis, Missouri, in a book published in 1880. He discussed the conjure practices of the people and how Hoodoo was practiced in "invisible churches." These were secret churches where Hoodoo was combined with Christianity. Enslaved and free black ministers preached resistance to slavery, and Hoodoo rituals were practiced that were intended to free the people from bondage.

Another enslaved man, known as Dinkie King, used "goofer dust" - an unknown mixture of powders - to resist a cruel overseer on a farm near St. Louis. Dinkie was an enslaved person on the farm but never worked as the other enslaved people did. He was feared and respected by blacks and white alike. He was known to carry a dried snake with him all the time, along with goofer dust

Advertisements for mojo bags became common after Hoodoo started to reach mainstream and commercial audiences.

made from the skins of frogs and lizards. He would sprinkle the dust on himself and conjure up the spirit of the snake to threaten the overseer.

Henry Clay Bruce, a black abolitionist and writer recorded an incident involving enslaved people on a Virginia plantation who hired a Hoodoo conjurer to prevent their owner from selling them to a plantation in the deep South.

Louis Hughes, an enslaved man who lived on plantations in Tennessee and Mississippi, carried a mojo bag that he claimed kept his owners from whipping him.

Formerly enslaved person and abolitionist Henry Bibb wrote that he sought the help of several Hoodoo doctors when he was enslaved. Bibb went to the conjurers in hopes that charms provided to him would prevent beatings and whippings. He was given a conjure powder to sprinkle around his owner's bed and put in the man's shoes. He was also instructed to always carry a bitter root and other charms with him.

In Alabama slave narratives, it was documented that formerly enslaved people used graveyard dirt to escape slavery on the Underground Railroad. They would rub the graveyard dirt on their feet or sprinkle it behind them on the trail to keep slave catcher's dogs from picking up their scent.

Former slave Ruby Tartt from Alabama said a conjurer could "Hoodoo the dogs" using charms that would confuse the hounds used to catch runaway slaves.

A story from a formerly enslaved person named Mary Middleton, a Gullah woman from the South Carolina coast, told of an incident when an enslaver was physically weakened from Hoodoo. The men had beaten one of his slaves badly. The enslaved person then went to a conjurer, who allegedly created a spell that broke the white man's health.

Another story told of an enslaved woman known only as Old Julie. She was a Hoodoo woman known among the enslaved people on the plantation for her ability to conjure death. She did it so often that the owner eventually sold her to keep her from killing anyone else. She was placed on a steamboat that would take her to a new owner, but, according to the stories, Old Julie used her powers to turn the boat around and forced the original owner to cancel the sale and keep her.

Needless to say, Hoodoo conjurers were seen as a threat by white enslavers before the Civil War. The enslaved people received charms and spells - for protection and revenge - from the conjurers, and there seemed to be no way to stop them.

There's no way of knowing how many people succumbed to poisons during this era, but the number is undoubtedly high. That was seen by many, of course, as the price of keeping another man in chains.

Hoodoo spread throughout the United States as African Americas left the South during what became known as the Great Migration. Just as Delta blues singers went north to Memphis, St. Louis, and Chicago and traded their acoustic guitars for electric

As Hoodoo went north with the
"Great Migration," it became more
commercialized and began to be
marketed in magazines and
newspapers ~ often by white drug
store owners.

Hoodoo also became a staple in
blues music, although the term
"mojo" was misunderstood.

instruments, conjurers took Hoodoo with them to communities in the North.

For many who practiced Hoodoo, providing conjure services in the black community for people to obtain love, money, employment, and protection was a way to help blacks during the Jim Crow era in the United States. They needed jobs to support their families and protection from the unjust laws that segregated the country.

When they came north, Hoodoo rituals were modified because there weren't many rural country areas to perform rituals in the woods or near rivers. Rituals were improvised inside their homes or in secluded areas of the city. The needed herbs and roots couldn't be gathered in nature, so they were forced to buy them in neighborhood stores that sold botanicals and books that became essential to modern Hoodoo.

And many of those stores were owned by whites.

White pharmacists opened their shops in African American communities and began offering items both requested by their customers and things they thought would be useful. They stocked colored wax candles in glass jars labeled for things like "Fast Luck" or "Love Drawing."

These pharmacists - along with white-owned mail-order companies - changed the culture of Hoodoo. Even though white mountain folk and indigenous people had long been a part of traditional Hoodoo, the "Hoodoo" of the early twentieth century was something altogether different. You might recall that most African American families rarely used the word "Hoodoo," even though they practice the traditions - well, this is why.

Hoodoo began to be marketed and commercialized, changing it in many ways. Merchants replaced authentic methods with fabricated practices and tools, reducing them to "tricks." It became all about hexing people and casting candle spells for love and money.

For example, in African American folk stories, High John the Conqueror was an enslaved black man whose spirit resides in the root, a common part of Hoodoo. But drugstore owners began putting an image of a white man on their High John the Conqueror Root labels. As a result, many African Americans eventually forgot that John was actually a black man.

They also introduced the *Sixth and Seventh Books of Moses* into the Hoodoo tradition. It was easily found at a time when it was all the rage in Pennsylvania hex magic, so why not include it with their Hoodoo goods, as well? It was quickly accepted because African Americans connected to the story of Moses freeing the Israelites from slavery in Egypt and also because of the magical powers he used against the Egyptians. He was soon being referred to as "the finest Hoodoo man in the world," even though he'd never previously been part of the traditions.

Although Hoodoo was commercialized and trivialized in the first half of the twentieth century, a resurgence has occurred recently. It is a unique form of magic that allows users to add personal and cultural touches to fixing tricks and creating mojo bags. You'll find it in the city and rural areas, in the northern and southern states, and gaining popularity among many different walks of life.

THE STICKS, STONES, ROOTS, AND BONES OF IT ALL

Nature is, of course, the essential source of power for Hoodoo. And all the things mentioned above are the basic ingredients for any good mojo bag. But why?

Sticks - along with tree bark, tree branches, and their leaves and flowers - represent the relationship between the living and the dead. Sticks are essential because they are used as the activating motion performed on poppets or dolls, representing the people toward whom the magic is directed.

Stones are often taken for granted in any kind of folk magic, but not in Hoodoo. While they seem inert, they actually store history and energy within their form. Each type of stone is believed to have its own frequency and ability to aid in conjuring. They are used in mojo bags, potions, rituals, and tricks.

There are several different ways to charge a rock. Some people bury and dig them up repeatedly to feel the change in the stone's energy. Others simply place them in the sun for three to seven days or soak them in salt water. After a stone is charged, it's wrapped in a piece of silk and kept close so that its energy can be felt.

Hoodoo is another form of American "root work," so understanding herbs, roots, and indigenous wisdom is a vital tool for traditional conjurers. Roots are believed to contain powerful medicine and can be found in just about every kind of Hoodoo working.

High John the Conqueror root, angelica root, Queen Elizabeth root, and Adam and Eve root are central ingredients in the conjurer's medicine bag. Often, to use the roots sparingly, small amounts are crushed into powder or turned into an oil.

In the earliest days of Hoodoo, bones and animal parts were widely used in every kind of trick. Animals were plentiful at the time. People hunted regularly and used every part of the animal for food, shelter, warmth, medicine, and magic. Today, only rural Hoodoo conjurers use bones as widely as in the past. Bones are not as easily accessible as they once were, although it's not uncommon to find bones from rabbits, raccoons, and other small animals for sale - providing ample supplies for love potions and a lucky rabbit foot. There are also parts of the country where snakeskins, animal horns, and skulls can easily be found.

Many conjurers who shy away from bones have replaced them with metal in their practice, which has also become important in Hoodoo. Many abide by the words of author Scott Cunningham, who stated, "Metals are the flesh of the gods and goddesses, the bones of the Earth, manifestations of universal powers."

Silver is used for intuitive work, fertility, and love. A silver ring on the left hand's third finger is considered a spirit power conduit.

Copper is a healing metal that can transfer healing from the spirits. It works especially well when combined with quartz crystals. Copper pennies were long revered as good luck charms in Hoodoo.

Iron - used for cooking in skillets - has long been treasured for its strength. The use of nails, rust, and metal filings are often used in mojo bags.

Lead is used for its ability to hold and deliver intent, while lodestone is central to love, luck, and prosperity charms. It's a stone made from magnetite. Similarly, fool's gold is used in drawing magic, mojos, and on altars.

MOJO WORKING

And those are just the basics. There are so many other elements to Hoodoo that differ from other forms of folk magic - and, of course, those that remain eerily the same.

The mojo bag is an excellent example of this. Much like the charms of the Pennsylvania hex doctors, they are - as already explained - small bags that contain items that vary in their intent, from protection to love and success.

The origins of mojo bags begin in Africa and begins with *ashe*, the invisible power of nature. The created charms incorporated many kinds of nature, from bones to fur, claws, dirt from an elephant's footprint, crocodile teeth, scales, things touched by lightning, human flesh, nail clippings, hair, and more. All sorts of items were used to hold the charms created, including shells, baskets, pots, bottles, and leather bags.

The bags were then used to address various ills, express power as warriors, fight off supernatural threats, and foil evil intentions.

When the enslaved people arrived in America, mojo bags changed with the traditions and the customs of the people who created them. The objects within the bags guide the spirits to understand the reason why their help is being sought.

Materials with especially close connections to nature - like dirt from human or animal footprints - are placed in a flannel bag. Other materials include things associated with dead ancestors, like coffin nails, bones, or graveyard dirt. The objects - whether sticks, stones, roots, or bones - have a corresponding spirit and particular medicine connected to them. Many recipes are known to conjurers as to how to mix all the parts correctly and activate the energies for which the mojo bag is intended.

THE BROOM IN HOODOO

Hoodoo offers every kind of working imaginable. There are detailed methods of cleansing the spirits, creating altars, finding peace and prosperity, good luck, getting pregnant, having children, 0and death and dying. Horseshoes, iron nails, and other items were used for good luck. Bad things happened when graveyards weren't respected property.

But the most fascinating aspects of Hoodoo will be familiar to those interested in other kinds of magic - it's the importance of the seemingly innocuous broom.

The humble broom holds an essential place in Hoodoo folklore and magical practices. For African Americans, "jumping the broom" has a prominent role in traditional weddings, but its history goes back further than that, as far back as Africa.

Magically, brooms are often thought of in regard to the form of witchcraft that was brought to America from Europe - wild rides under the full moon and sexually charged sabbat rituals.

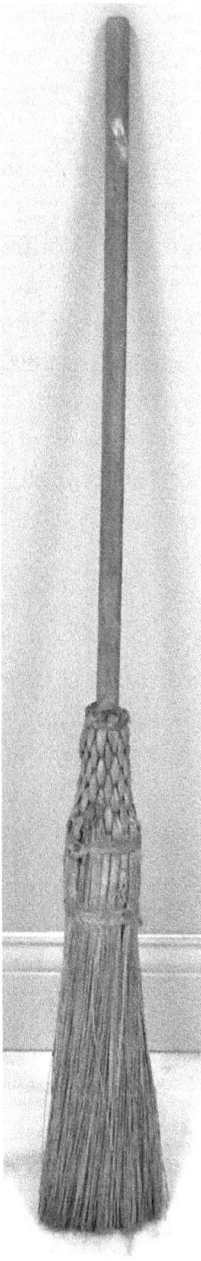

Broom-making was common in Europe as far back as the Middle Ages. However, broom corn itself originated in Africa as sorghum, the stiff grass that was used extensively in the production of molasses - which plays a key role in not only soul food cooking but in Hoodoo, as well.

Thanks to this, grass, straw, and brooms became part of African rituals and, eventually, a part of Hoodoo rituals. In America, broom straw became known for its healing powers. According to folklore, placing broom straw over a wart in the shape of a cross could encourage the wart to heal.

Other customs and cautions about brooms became well-known, too, like resting a broom in the wrong way, which could cause injury, pain, or loss. Resting a broom on a bed was believed to cause the last person who slept there to die. Broom straws had to be stored facing upward because leaving them with the straws on the floor would bring bad luck.

Even approaching a broom was the subject of lore. If you stepped over a broom or if it fells over as you started to leave, death might follow. Carrying a broom inside a house was a sign that death was coming for the family.

Proper handling of a broom, though, would bring luck, happiness, and prosperity. If you went looking for a home to rent or buy, you might be told to carry a broom under your arm or even throw it into a window so that it entered the house before you did. Holding a broom was also a barrier against arguments. If arguments or fights occurred, a person would be told to go outside with it tucked under their arm and throw it inside the door. The first thing to enter a new home was always supposed to be a broom.

If someone swept the house while company was present, it would send bad luck to the guests. Sweeping was a sign of bad manners and meant you wanted your guests to leave. Sweeping after dark meant sorrow, bad luck, and poverty. Sweeping dirt out the front door wasn't advised. Dirt must be swept out the back door, discarded in running water, or buried. A person struck by a broom might be arrested or have other kinds of bad luck. A broom that fell across a doorway was a sign that a person would be entering an unknown or unfamiliar time of life. When the accidental fall of a broom occurred, it was advised to walk backward to pick it up. Sweeping was not advised on Mondays or Fridays. Bad luck is guaranteed for the next year if someone was foolish enough to sweep on New Year's Day.

In light of all this, the tradition of "jumping the broom" makes a lot of sense. Jumping the broom is like taking a leap from being single into a new, settled life of domesticity. The broom serves as the symbolic boundary between opposite lives.

HOODOO LOVE MAGIC

To get to the point where you are "jumping the broom," though, you might need a bit of love magic. Hoodoo is famous for its various rituals to draw luck and prosperity for the client or the conjurer, but perhaps its best known for the love spells that have been linked to this kind of magic over the decades.

Magnetic stones play a big part in love magic - for obvious reasons. In 1600, William Gilbert described the act of magnetic stones being attracted to each other as being "in the act of coitus." You must admit that's pretty accurate. This way of thinking is

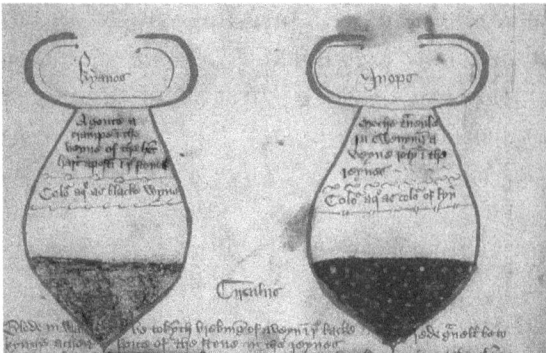

deeply embedded in the uses of such stones in Hoodoo. The male and female stones are so attracted to each other that they seem to be locked into a state of ongoing intercourse. A conjurer capitalizes on that by using two such stones in a mojo bag, drawing love and luck for the people the stones represent.

Animal magnetism is also mimicked in Hoodoo love spells. Folklorist Ruth Bass described a mojo bag that was assembled for a female client by a conjurer in Mississippi as containing dirt from the tracks of her man's right foot, gunpowder, and a blue stone that would keep him faithful. There was also snail water - because of how slowly snails moved, meaning fidelity. It was, the conjurer said, the perfect recipe for keeping a loved one close.

Other Hoodoo ingredients for love incorporated animal parts - or behavior - into the tricks. Carrying a raccoon's penis was a symbol of male virility. Urine was widely used in traditional love formulas. It was used to wash a doorway or a bedroom floor to keep a lover faithful. Urine might also be boiled with a loved one's hair to bind them.

And urine isn't the only human substance used in Hoodoo love spells. Bodily fluids are sometimes added to the potential lover's drink, food, and morning coffee. They can include vaginal fluid, saliva, blood, menstrual blood, or semen.

This should serve as a warning to always keep an eye on your drink.

Hair and knots are also used in love magic. Since hair comes from the top of the head (usually), it's from the "seat of thought," so it observes vibrations. A lock of hair was typically included in any mojo charm.

Certain herbs named for animals were also used. Deer's tongue smells like vanilla and was often placed in a mojo bag, on a person, or in their purse, shoes, or pockets. It is also considered an aphrodisiac so it could be sprinkled on or under a bed. Daffodils, which are also known as Goose Leeks, are love, fertility, and luck charms. The flowers bear a resemblance to male sex organs - with the bulbs as the testicles, the stem as the penis, and the flower representing ejaculation. Wearing a daffodil or placing a bouquet in a bedroom was supposed to inspire intense passion.

Photographs may also be used for some types of love magic. To attract a lover, a photograph was charmed by its owner. A wish was written to the ancestors and the spirits, and this wish was placed under the potential lover's photograph. A red or pink candle - sometimes coated with one of the oils named for ancient goddesses -- was then burned on top of the photo. As the candle burned, the intended became the focus of wishes for love and a long life together.

Often, a conjurer might be called in to help release the grip of someone the client had fallen out of love with. A photograph was also used for this. It would be submerged in turpentine, liquor, or perhaps even plain water. The conjurer would then focus on rubbing the rejected person out of the client's life as they swirl the photograph around in the liquid. Of course, the person doesn't die but will find love elsewhere after completing the trick.

Love spells rarely lead to death, but other aspects of Hoodoo can. Curses, hexes, and harmful spells exist in Hoodoo, just as in other folk magic. Sometimes, though, death isn't caused by magic - although it might occur *because* of magic.

That's what likely occurred in this story of a Hoodoo-related murder that happened in 1929. Of course, we'll never know that for sure because, to this day, this bloody and violent massacre has never been solved.

THE EVANGELIST MURDERS

On July 3, 1929, police officers entered a house at 3587 St. Aubin Street in Detroit, Michigan. Inside, they found a man named Benny Evangelist seated behind his desk. His hands were neatly folded in his lap as though in prayer.

His head was at his feet, lying on the floor.

Upstairs they found his wife, Santina, and their children -- Mario, 18 months; Angelina, 7; Margaret, 5; and Jeanne, 4. Santina was on the bed with baby Mario. She had also been beheaded, and Mario's skull was crushed. Across the hall, the other children had been slaughtered in their beds.

The story of the Evangelist murders is one of the strangest stories in American crime. It's a dark tale of Hoodoo, murder, and a clever and enterprising man who came to Detroit with big plans and used the opportunities he found in a city that was bursting at the seams.

It was the time of the Great Migration when African Americans from the rural South flocked to northern cities in search of work and hoping to escape the racist Jim Crow laws back home. It was also a time when immigrants from all over the world were settling in the same cities with the same dreams of prosperity and freedom.

Sadly, both of those groups found their slice of the American dream working in factories, doing back-breaking labor, and living in overcrowded tenement buildings and ramshackle homes. They had come to Detroit hoping for a better life - but the future still seemed just out of reach.

But all hope wasn't lost. There was always someone who could offer something better- a pathway to a brighter existence, a little love, a little luck, and some good fortune - for a price.

One of those best known for offering such things in Detroit's black and immigrant neighborhoods was Benny Evangelist.

And that may have gotten him killed.

Benjamino Evangelista was an Italian immigrant who changed his name to Benny Evangelist before embarking on a career as a mystic and Hoodoo doctor in the early 1900s.

Born in Naples, Italy, in 1885, Benjamino Evangelista came to America in 1904 and settled in Philadelphia with his brother, Antonio. But the two eventually had a falling out. By his own accounts, Antonio disowned Benjamino when he began dabbling in Hoodoo and magic, which was very much against their strict Catholic upbringing.

Benjamino moved to York, Pennsylvania, and started a job for a railroad construction crew. One of the friends he made on the crew was a fellow immigrant from Naples named Aurelius Angelino. He began to share Benjamino's passion for magic, and the two began dabbling in spells and hexes. One day, though, something snapped in Aurelius, and in 1919, he attacked his family with an ax and killed two of his children. He was sent to a prison for the criminally insane, and Benjamino, unsettled by what had occurred, moved to the bustling city of Detroit.

The Evangelist family in 1929.

He first went to work as a carpenter, married another Italian immigrant, and invested his savings in real estate, soon becoming a prosperous realtor and landlord. With his newfound success, he decided to change his name and began calling himself "Benny Evangelist," dropping the vowels from the ends of his names to Americanize them, as it was referred to at the time.

On the side, he supplemented his income with a drug store that also sold Hoodoo remedies, hexes, herbs, and roots. He had many clients and earned a lot of money with the tricks he sold to them. He performed rituals and psychic healings for fees that sometimes were as high as $10, equivalent to two days of pay on a factory assembly line.

But his clients happily paid it, and soon he was making as much money selling love spells and hexes to his African American customers and protection from the "evil eye" to the immigrant ones as he was with real estate deals. His clients began calling him the "Hex Doctor of Detroit."

Doing so well for himself, Benny purchased a house at the corner of St. Aubin and Mack Avenues and moved his wife and children into it. It was a large, comfortable home - the nicest in the neighborhood. It was painted green and had a wide front porch. Benny began meeting many clients there, escorting them down to the basement, where he kept all his conjuring tools.

It was said that someone passing by the house could catch a glimpse through one of the basement windows and see what Benny called his "Great Celestial Planet Exhibition" hanging from the ceiling. It was a paper-mâché, wire, and wood model of the solar system. The sun was represented by an electric eye in the center of the model.

The rest of Benny's conjure kitchen wasn't as easy to see. There, he mixed up his potions and spells, wrote down hexes, and sewed together mojo bags. The shelves around his work table were filled with jars that contained herbs, roots, dirt, dried animal parts, and anything else he might need. An assortment of knives and daggers was hanging on a wall rack within easy reach.

Copies of Benny's self-published book, *The Oldest History of the World Discovered by Occult Science in Detroit, Michigan*, were stacked around the room. Benny claimed to have produced the book by going into nightly trances. He planned for it to be the first in a series of four books that would reveal previously unknown information relayed to him by God.

But, of course, the series would never be finished. God, or fate, or someone, had other plans for Benny Evangelist.

On the bright and sunny morning of July 3, a client of Benny's named Vincent Elias arrived at the house on St. Aubin Street. He had made an appointment to meet Benny that morning, so it seemed strange to him when no one answered when he rang the bell. But then Vincent noticed that the door was cracked open an inch or so - and he saw the smear of what seemed to be blood on the doorknob.

Fearing something terrible may have happened, he pushed the door open and went inside. He only got as far as Benny's office, located next to the parlor, before he saw the headless body of Benny Evangelist sitting in a chair behind the desk.

Vincent fled the house in terror and immediately notified the police.

Officers were soon on the scene, including most of Detroit's homicide detectives. Word had spread about the gruesome discovery in the house, and everyone, including many of the neighbors, wanted a look. They had started gathering outside as the detectives arrived to search the place, making notes featured in newspaper reports later that day.

In addition to Benny's headless body, another strange discovery was made in his office. Surrounding his severed head were three framed photographs of a deceased child in a coffin. There were resting around it, the edges of the frames soaked with blood. The dead child was later determined to be Benny's son, who had passed away several years before. There was no explanation as to what message the photographs were supposed to send.

According to a newspaper article, "Several pieces of women's undergarments, each tagged with the name its owner, police point out, revealed the so-called 'mystic' indulged in practices of 'voodooism' or devil worship. Such garments, 'voodooism' has it, can lead to finding a missing person when they are properly handled by one versed in the mystic arts of that belief."

While untrue, the police had little knowledge to work with. The discovery of women's undergarments - along with all of the workings that Benny kept in the basement - certainly seemed strange and exotic to white police detectives, newspaper reporters, and most of the paper's readers. However, they were likely used for love spells that Benny was making for his clients. In the racist era of the 1920s, though, "voodooism or devil worship" was a term to imply that the victims had been either African American or immigrants. It wasn't long before rumors spread that Benny's Hoodoo business was responsible for the murders of the family.

Unfortunately, the crime scene was poorly secured by the police. They failed to keep out the reporters and the morbidly

SIX VICTIMS OF DETROIT AX MURDERER

Here are Paul Evangelist, said to have been the head of an Italian religious cult at Detroit, and his wife and four children who were brutally slain by an ax man as they slept. Evangelist is shown at the left with his oldest daughter, Angeline; while below them are Jeanne and Margaret. At the right is Mrs. Satin Evangelist, the wife, holding Mario, their youngest child.

curious neighbors, and they quickly contaminated the scene, gawking at the bodies, picking up souvenirs, and possibly destroying clues. Only one clue managed to survive the invasion - the bloody fingerprint on the front doorknob. Detectives believed that it had been made by a thumb. It was well-preserved, though, and if a suspect were found - and could be matched to the print - they'd have their killer.

More problems arose when detectives canvassed the neighborhood and tried to get assistance from the Evangelist family's neighbors. Most were Italian immigrants who had no interest in providing information to the police. Detectives encountered the same problem when interviewing those on Benny's client list. His African American customers wouldn't talk to the police either.

Benny's records proved that hundreds of people had come to him for his services, but only a handful of those on the list admitted they knew him, and even fewer still offered anything useful to the detectives.

Thousands of people came out for the funerals of the Evangelist family while the police were still investigating the murders.

The police used what little information they had to form three very different theories about the massacre. One of them revolved around some threatening letters Benny had in his desk that suggested he had once crossed paths with the "Black Hand," a loose criminal group known for extorting wealthy Italian immigrants. The most recent letter was over six months old and warned, "This is your last chance."

The problem with the Black Hand theory was that, by 1929, it was an outdated, defunct enterprise that had long since evolved into organized crime. Crude extortion schemes were a thing of the past, dating back to the years before Prohibition turned common criminals into bootleggers who amassed their own wealth.

It's unlikely that Benny took the notes seriously. They never explicitly said they came from the Black Hand, and whoever had written the crude, misspelled letters had likely been an amateur looking for an easy score. It wasn't someone who would have carried out the grisly murders of an entire family.

The second theory suggested that someone from Benny's past may have killed the family - notably his old friend, Aurelius Angelo, who attacked his own family and killed two children. Aurelius had been sent to a hospital for the criminally insane, but in 1923, he escaped and was never seen again. Could he have traveled to Detroit, intent on some kind of revenge against Benny?

The third theory seemed the most plausible. One of Benny's clients was a 42-year-old man named Umberto Tecchio, and he had visited the Evangelist home on the night of the murders. That was no secret. Tecchio had owed Benny money for a hex he'd made for him and had stopped by the house with a friend, Angelo Depoli, to pay his bill.

The police brought both men in for questioning on July 5 after an ax, a "keen-edged" knife, and a pair of suspiciously clean work boots were found in the barn behind the boarding house where Tecchio lived.

The two men claimed to know nothing about the murders. They stated that nothing unusual had occurred during their brief visit. After Benny was given his money, they went out drinking. Tecchio said he hadn't even thought about Benny again until he saw the story about the murders in the newspapers.

But the fact that two Italians had been brought in for questioning was something that the newspapers could sensationalize. Stoking prejudice against immigrants, reporters started digging and brought up that, just three months earlier, Tecchio had stabbed his brother-in-law to death during an argument. He had been released when it was judged self-defense, but this was enough to turn him into the prime suspect for the murders. When his fingerprints were compared to the print left behind on the doorknob, the police were forced to let him go. The prints didn't match Tecchio or his friend. Tecchio died a few years later, in 1934.

The police also briefly suspected one of Benny's tenants, who was posthumously accused of the murders by his vicious ex-wife, but the dead man's thumbprint didn't match the one left on the door either.

And with that, the investigation began to grow cold, and it eventually fizzled out altogether. There was nowhere left to go without witness statements and physical evidence, and the murders remain unsolved to this day.

Looking back at this crime many years later, only two answers might fit what happened. The first was that Aurelius Angelino murdered Benny and his family. This was a man who had slaughtered his children while attempting to kill his entire family. It's not that far from what occurred in the Evangelist home. It wouldn't be impossible for him to have made his way west to Detroit from Pennsylvania and to have tracked down a man who had made quite a name for himself in the immigrant community.

Perhaps he came looking for an old friend, who he believed would help him make a new life for himself. Maybe he found Benny and was turned away for one of several reasons - fear, disgust, or even disinterest. Perhaps Aurelius looked around Benny's luxurious home and saw how happy he was with his wife, his children, and his prosperous business and became enraged. He thought about the horrors he'd endured over the last nine years and felt anger boil up inside him.

It isn't hard to imagine the escaped madman slithering in an open window while Benny sat at his desk during the early morning hours of July 3. And once inside the house, how difficult would it have been for him to murder the family of the man who had left him behind to rot in the insane asylum while he practiced his magic and grew rich selling spells and potions?

It's not hard to imagine at all.

And yet, after Angelino's escape from the state of Pennsylvania's custody in 1923, no record of his existence can be found in Detroit or anywhere else. Could a family of six be slaughtered so easily, and the killer simply disappear? It's certainly possible, as history has proven time and time again.

It is also possible that a disgruntled client of Benny's murdered the Evangelists. Hundreds of people had come to him during his years in Detroit looking for hexes, potions, and cures. And this also meant there were a lot of people in the city who might have been victims of the hexes and curses that Benny had created for his clients. Perhaps someone's life had been ruined by a trick that Benny had conjured, or perhaps it was as simple as an unhinged man who had come to Benny for a love spell had then been denied by the object of his intentions. Would those people have sought out such an act of extreme revenge?

It's impossible to know what anyone would or wouldn't do under the right circumstances. The blood-stained pages of history certainly prove this to be the case.

In the end, it doesn't matter. The murder of the Evangelist family was never solved. All we know for sure is that someone entered the house on St. Aubin Street that night, exacted some sort of punishment on its inhabitants, and then vanished into the hot July night, leaving a bloody thumbprint on a doorknob - and nothing else.

8. THE MODERN "WITCH HUNTS"

We had a lot on our minds in America in the 1950s.

Americans were dying in Korea during the conflict that had started there. The Russians had gone from allies to enemies after World War II, and the Cold War was beginning to heat up. Racial segregation was still deeply entrenched in the nation, and the Civil Rights movement was reaching new heights with the influence of the Nation of Islam. And Senator Joseph McCarthy was pursuing his dangerous "witch hunts" against real and imaginary communists that were burrowed into all levels of the government.

And all the while, *real* witch hunts still took place in some parts of the country.

In 1950, a woman named Helen Evans was charged with witchcraft in Wilmington, Delaware. She wasn't the first, by any means, and even as recently as 1892, a couple of fortune tellers had also been hauled to jail under the same outdated Delaware law. The penalty for being a witch in Delaware meant one year in prison and a $100 fine.

Helen Evans was a 23-year-old "character reader" who was arrested on March 13 after the police received a complaint from one of her female clients with a case of nerves. After analyzing her handwriting, Helen told the woman she had been cursed. She gave the woman some bread and sugar wrapped in a handkerchief, saying that it might help, and told her to return in a few days, and for $10 Helen could remove the curse. The woman called the police and told them that Helen had been the one who put the curse on her in the first place.

Helen was arrested and charged by Detective Lieutenant George Keinburger with "practicing the art of witchcraft."

The newspapers pounced on the story, and Helen was interviewed and quoted as saying, "Do they mean I'm one of those things that fly around on broomsticks? If that's what they mean, then I should have a big black cauldron and be stirring things up in it, shouldn't I? Why should I even have black cats running around!?"

A reporter traced Delaware's anti-witchcraft law back to before the state was even a British colony - the English Witchcraft and Conjuration Act of 1604. The state's attorney general, Albert W. James, said that he was unfamiliar with the statute and was at a loss to explain what the "art of witchcraft" entailed.

Helen's case was presided over by Judge Thomas Herlihy, Jr. He had been elected to the bench four years earlier on a promise to clean up and modernize the municipal court. One of his first acts was the end racial segregation in the courtroom and formalized the practice of informing defendants of their rights. Dealing with an offense of witchcraft in 1950 was clearly something he wouldn't tolerate. He first postponed the case to allow the lawyers to work things out on their own - and to get it out of the media spotlight - but that didn't work.

The press had a field day mocking the state with editorials encouraging the end of witchcraft laws. "It doesn't speak much for the modernity of the state of Delaware," one wrote.

In early May, Judge Herlihy ruled that Helen would only stand trial on charges of fortune-telling, which was just as ridiculous. Racist "fortune-telling laws" had once been popular nationwide to use against so-called "gypsies" when officials wanted to run them out of town. Actual fortune-telling caused no threat to anyone and was as antiquated as witchcraft laws.

However, it did the trick in Helen's case. She paid a fine, and the story vanished from the headlines. A year later, the Delaware legislature removed several "obsolete statutes" from the books and changed the wording to prosecute only for "fortune telling and dealing with spirits."

Witchcraft was now legal, but apparently, ghosts were still a problem in Delaware.

A lot of people had been laughing about the case of Helen Evans in 1950, but no one found humor in another incident that occurred on August 15 that year.

Carl Walters, a 40-year-old resident of Rogersville, Tennessee, walked into a local store where Alberta Gibbons and her mother, Alta Woods, were drinking soda pop and shouted at them, "This has gone far enough!"

He drew a pistol and shot Alberta in the head while she was holding her baby in her arms.

Alta pleaded with him, "Please, don't kill me!" But Carl fired three bullets into her anyway.

He then got into his car and drove to Kingsport, which was about 20 miles away, arrived at the police station, and walked inside. He went to the desk and calmly said to the officer on duty, "I have just shot two women in Hawkins County. I am tired of being bewitched."

Carl's family had seen more than its share of heartache. His wife, Ruby - the sister of Alta Woods, by the way - had recently fallen down a flight of stairs and had broken her hip. One of their children had died not long before, and Carl himself had been suffering from a strange complaint.

In April and May 1949, he had been to see Dr. Herbert Pope in Knoxville. He confided in the physician that ever since he was 13, people had been "against him, and told him a story of an 11-year-old boy that he knew who hanged himself under a witch's hex. On one occasion, he brought his 11-year-old daughter, Sylvia, to see Dr. Pope and said she was also bewitched. Dr. Pope administered electro-shock therapy to Carl and recommended that he go to a clinic. Carl agreed and spent two weeks at St. Alban's psychiatric hospital in Radford, Virginia.

Evidently, though, it didn't help.

When he came home from the hospital, he started telling people that he and his family had been bewitched. His tales became more feverish, and he eventually shot Alberta and Alta in the Rogersville store.

While Carl was locked up in the jail in Rogersville, the area's residents organized a lynch mob of about 75 men. They assembled around midnight and marched on the jail - armed to the teeth. When they arrived, they demanded that Carl be released to them. Sheriff Bradley Blair - a cousin of Ruby and Alta - refused to open the doors. Shots rang out. Bullets pounded into the walls, windows, and doors of the jail. Sheriff Blair and one of his deputies managed to shoot two members of the lynch mob, and the rest of them fled the scene.

This was not the last attempt to try and hang Carl before his trial. Sheriff Blair got wind of another plan to form a mob but threatened the ring leaders and managed to get that one called off.

In December, Carl went to trial. More than two dozen friends and neighbors took the stand and stated they had heard him complain about troubles with witchcraft. Most testified that they believed he was sane. A separate mental health jury also found him sane, despite the testimony of three psychiatrists who believed that he suffered from delusions.

Carl was at the defense table, calmly chewing gum when the jury returned with a guilty verdict. He was sentenced to die in the electric chair, but his attorneys launched an immediate appeal, and in May, he was taken to Nashville for more psychiatric tests. They proved convincing, and he avoided the chair, instead spending the rest of his days in a hospital for the criminally insane.

Just a year later, in Knoxville, Tennessee, an African American woman named Alberta Jefferson went on trial for the shooting of a Hoodoo doctor, Obie Lee Roddie. Alberta claimed the man had put a "death hex" on her and her husband. Hoping to break the curse, she had killed him.

The police searched Roddie's home and found herbs, powders, and a little black book containing spells and recipes written in green ink. It included one spell for "laying a burden on your enemy's heart" - which he had placed on Alberta.

In 1952, the Tennessee Supreme Court ruled that Alberta's belief in witchcraft did not mitigate her crime, but nevertheless, she was given a lenient three-year sentence.

Later in 1952, a Mission, Texas, man named Alfredo Medrano shot waitress Maria Acevedo in the chest with a .22-caliber pistol. Fortunately, Maria was not seriously hurt by the small gun - and perhaps Alfredo had some second thoughts because he and Maria had once been friends. But when he began to suffer from crippling headaches and his family became sick, he concluded that she had paid a witch to put a hex on him.

That same year, a 42-year-old Arizona rancher named Joe Chavez shot another witch - although, in this case, the witch died.

Joe ran a cattle ranch and alfalfa farm about 30 miles east of Phoenix, near the Superstition Mountains. Around 1942, his wife, Josie, started going blind and experiencing terrible back pain. Joe took his wife to doctors in the United States and Mexico, but no one could help her or even diagnose the ailment. He soon turned to traditional healers - *brujas* - who offered many spells and cures, but nothing worked. Finally, one of them told Joe that she believed his wife had been hexed. Through gossip, Joe heard that one of his female relatives had paid a witch named Miranda to put a spell on Josie.

The 41-year-old bruja, Maria Estrella Miranda, lived with her husband, Antonio, in Guadalupe, southeast of Phoenix. The local sheriff, L.C. Boies, noted, "Everyone in Guadalupe who suffered any kind of disease blamed Mrs. Miranda. Lots of people thought they had reason to kill her." But just as many people considered Maria to be a devoutly religious woman.

Most likely, she was both.

A neighbor told Joe Chavez that he had seen pictures of Joe and his wife in Marias's home, and "she probably used them to work her spells." Chavez wrote to Maria and begged her to remove the spell from Josie, even offering her as much as $9,000 to do so. She replied dismissively that he should try and take her to court.

Finally, on September 12, 1952, Joe decided to go to Maria's home and demand the return of the photographs.

He took his pistol with him.

According to his version of events, Maria refused and ordered him to leave. He stepped forward toward a box of photos on a table, and Maria reached for a shotgun. Joe then took out his pistol and shot her four times. She was dead before her body hit the floor. Joe was arrested five days later.

When the police searched Maria's home, they found a small Catholic shrine on which there were about 100 photos. Among them, curiously, were three Democratic politicians who were defeated in that year's elections. Someone had paid Maria for their misfortunes.

Joe's trial - postponed while the court searched for Spanish translators for most of the witnesses - began in April 1853. His attorneys put together a case for temporary insanity and self-defense. From the stand, six of Maria's neighbors testified that she was a witch.

The jury wasn't having anything to do with witchcraft, and neither was the judge. Joe was convicted of second-degree murder, which the judge called "more than merciful." He sentenced him to spend the next 25 years in prison.

After this witch murder, disputes over witchcraft began to be covered less and less in the newspapers, although the age-old neighborly suspicions and accusations still occasionally popped up.

In 1960, for instance, 83-year-old Minnie Gilland of Detroit suspected an elderly neighbor, Mary Donaldson, 75, of witching her much younger husband away from her. Hence, she painted a "hex sign" of tar and chicken feathers on Mary's house. Mary sued her for damages, saying removing the sign would cost at least $75. "I had to do something. Afterward, I felt better," Minnie told a reporter.

By then, though, the abuse and assault of suspected witches had primarily become a thing of the past. Of course, that didn't mean that a belief in witchcraft had disappeared - it's just that fewer people complained about being victims of it.

Hex doctors continued to ply their trade. John Jerrigan, Chief Deputy Prosecutor of Little Rock, Arkansas, issued a stack of summons against African American conjure doctors after he had been visited on several occasions by a man who claimed that a local Hoodoo doctor named "Dr. Snake" had put a spell on him. Dr. Snake and several others were charged with practicing medicine without a license.

And then there was the baffling story of Calvin Tuck of Talladega, Alabama, in 1958.

Fire Captain S.H. Joiner of Talladega realized that he had a serious problem on his hands. His concerns revolved around a four-room rental house where, by August 28, there had been 22 fires reported - 17 of them breaking out on the same day. So far, he had not been able to deduce a cause for the blazes. "It's really a mystery," he told one newspaper.

The house was occupied by an African American man named Calvin Tuck, his wife, Lillie Bell, and their six children, which ranged in age from three months to nine years. The fires had gotten so bad that they had been forced to move out. They were now homeless, broke, and hungry.

The fires began three days earlier, on August 25. It caught fire three times, and then, the next morning, two more fires started. The family managed to put out the fires until there were just too many, and the fire department was called. Firefighter Glover Williams was the first on the scene, and he later said that Calvin's story was so fantastic that he summoned Captain Joiner to the house.

Each of the fires had started near the ceiling, except for one blaze that ignited on a mattress. The house had a metal roof and no electricity. There seemed to be no reasonable cause for the fires, but there was no denying that they were happening.

A local contractor named Ortis Horton visited the house on August 27, hoping to help with the investigation, and reported a fire that started literally before his eyes. It burned in an exact circle. He said that fires started about every 15 minutes while he was at the Tuck home, and he had no explanation for how they occurred.

News of the mysterious fires made the local newspapers and spread throughout the community. More than 200 people showed

Mystery Fires Cause Negro To Move Again

TALLADEGA (AP)—Mysterious fires have caused Calvin Tuck to move again.

The Negro and his wife left his father's house near Talladega Sunday after another outbreak of strange fires.

Deputy Sheriff Pat Cooper said they told no one where they were going. They took one of their six children with them, leaving the others with Tuck's father, Otis Tuck.

Calvin Tuck and his family moved from two other homes and finally into that of his father several weeks ago as a series of unsolved fires plagued him.

For nearly two weeks no fires were reported at the residence of Otis Tuck. But a few days ago the fires began breaking out a-gain. Furniture, walls and various

up at the Tuck home to watch the excitement, but most pitched in, water buckets in hand when new fires broke out.

After the first rental house was destroyed, the Tucks moved into another location nearby. Almost immediately, four fires occurred.

The Tucks moved again, taking shelter with Calvin's brother-in-law, Darnell Suttle - who must have been a brave and loyal man. He wasn't rewarded for either. As soon as the family arrived, five more mysterious fires occurred.

On Labor Day, two police officers - Lieutenant Ben Cooley and Officer John Childers - visited the Suttle house. They found buckets and tubs of water placed throughout the house as a precaution. Lillie Bell showed them a newspaper and a window frame that had caught fire just minutes before they arrived.

The Suttle house was understandably in an uproar, with clothing and furniture scattered all over the yard and all the children playing amongst it. Lieutenant Cooley saw a quilt hanging on a tree, and - as he was watching it - it suddenly started to burn. The fire only lasted a few moments, and then it was gone, leaving the quilt blackened and smoking. "I saw it, but I wouldn't have believed it myself if I hadn't seen it," he later said.

Things soon became more challenging for the Tuck family. Darnell, who needed to protect his own home and family, was forced to ask them to move out. Calvin's father came to help them move and offered to let them stay at his house. They moved into their fourth home in eight days, and once again, buckets of water were placed in each room, and even the family washing machine was left filled, just in case.

Calvin had now come to believe that a hex was responsible for the trouble happening to the family. He visited a Hoodoo doctor to try and find out who was responsible. The doctor couldn't tell him but assured him that a spell had been cast. He could remove it, he told Calvin, for a price. Calvin promptly paid. The doctor then instructed him to bury a bottle containing a half-pint of vinegar, two gourd seeds, two six-penny nails, three straight pins, and a mule biscuit upside-down at a 45-degree angle. He also gave Calvin some herbs that he and his family were supposed to chew for the next three days. Then they were to take another gourd seed, cut it in half, and Calvin and Lillie Bell were each to swallow one of the halves.

The best thing to say about the Hoodoo doctor's medicine was that it didn't work.

The fires continued, occurring five or more times each day. A fireman and a newspaper reporter each witnessed a fire start spontaneously in the kitchen and burn some clothing.

As the fires continued, more people came to the house to see them, numbering as many as 2,000 people each day. Dozens were present when the fires occurred and could not explain how they started.

The Tucks fled from Calvin's father's home to Anniston, a town about 20 miles from Talladega. A friend named Troy Caldwell offered to let them stay at his home, but they could not escape the fires. They started all over again, but the police in Anniston didn't waste time investigating them - they simply arrested Calvin on a vagrancy charge and put him in jail "for his own protection."

Attempts made to solve the mystery of the fire were met with frustration. The police were sure an arsonist was at work, but fire officials, reporters, and witnesses couldn't see how this was possible. More and more people were starting to agree with Calvin - that the fires resulted from a Hoodoo trick.

Needless to say, the Anniston police didn't believe in witchcraft. They wanted to find a flesh and blood culprit, so they did - nine-year-old Calvin Tuck, Jr. They claimed he had been setting the fires with matches when no one was looking. Little Calvin quickly confessed --mystery solved!

Of course, the cops forgot to mention how they managed to get the boy to confess. They told him that a Hoodoo man was after his daddy and would get him if he didn't admit to what he'd done.

After the boy was taken into custody, Judge Henry O. Hurst immediately returned him to his parents, saying that the police had insufficient evidence to hold him.

Police officers from Talladega, fire officials, and reporters all agreed - none of them believed the boy's confession. They had seen the fires appear and knew he hadn't caused them by "playing with matches." Fire Marshal Frank Craven stated that the case would remain open until a reasonable explanation was found.

As far as I know, it's still open today.

Stories like this one - or anything to do with magic and witchcraft - began to be relegated to the back pages of newspapers, if they were reported on at all.

It's possible that the rise of the Cold War and the fear of communists infiltrating American politics and society somehow replaced the public's concern about witches. There are parallels, as Arthur Miller noted when his play *The Crucible* dramatized the Salem witch trials as an allegory of McCarthyism. Propaganda such as a U.S. Army pamphlet issued in 1954 explained how one could identify communists by how they talked, the terms they used, and the people they associated with, which certainly fed into the deep-seated fears of those among us who were "different."

But parallel lines don't cross one another.

The communist boogeyman was an abstract threat to America's national security, not a threat to a person's well-being on a day-to-day level. Communists didn't replace our fears of a neighbor who bewitched our animals, caused our crops to die, or made babies be born deformed. Witchcraft accusations declined because they became less relevant as our personal well-being became more secure in the modern age. At the same time, Americans' sense of insecurity regarding a threat outside our homes grew to epic proportions during the Cold War.

The belief in witchcraft became more private. Those who considered themselves bewitched no longer felt confident discussing their suspicions with friends and neighbors. Communities no longer fueled gossip about the outsiders among them. Twentieth-century medical advances like penicillin and painkillers played their role, too, offering cures that had once been the domain of the hex doctor or the folk healer.

Creating safety nets like welfare, social security, and unemployment began assisting the poor and the disabled. Many witchcraft accusations had been born of necessity, the inability to understand or cope with misfortune. Creating national and state welfare programs made explaining those misfortunes less necessary. A child got sick, and cows died, but witchcraft was no longer required as a diagnosis leading to a solution, and consequently, witches didn't need to be identified anymore.

A survey conducted in 1986 revealed that 22 percent of those who responded believed in witchcraft. A more extensive poll in 2007 showed that 31 percent believed in witches, which was even higher in 2009. The population of the United States was over 308 million in 2010, which made some 70 million people believers in witchcraft.

A more recent poll revealed that 41 percent of respondents thought books on witchcraft and magic should not be available in school libraries. It's probably an even higher number at the time of this writing.

That means the concern over witchcraft has not gone away over the years. Is it less worrisome in our daily lives? Yes, but it's still there, lurking in the shadows.

But the question must be asked - did the people responding to the polls understand the terms "witch" and "witchcraft?"

9. REINVENTING WITCHCRAFT

By the late 1940s, a new era of witchcraft was brewing as a former civil servant in England set started a turn toward a new revival of the old religions.

Based on a knowledge of folklore, occultism, Spiritualism, and Freemasonry, the new tradition of Wicca claimed to be a direct, surviving descendant of an ancient fertility cult that had worshipped a goddess and a horned god. It had allegedly survived the persecutions of the Middle Ages and had been preserved by covens in England. This claim fit nicely with published books by American author Charles Leland and British Egyptologist Margaret Murray - who were widely accepted at the time.

This idea has been challenged since then, but initially, the revival of the old religion struck a chord with many, including Gerald Gardner, who would become the founder of modern-day Wicca.

Gardner was born into a wealthy family from Liverpool, England, in 1884. He lived most of his life abroad, running rubber plantations in the Far East, then working for the British authorities in the customs service in Malaysia.

Although he had no university education, he did have a passion for archaeology, folklore, history, and anthropology. He was also fascinated with religion, magic, and the occult.

When he retired from service abroad in 1936, he returned to England and settled in a rural area called New Forest in the

Gerald Gardner, the man who created the Wicca movement.

southern part of the country. It was there that Gardner would later claim to have discovered the existence of the old witch religion among a coven he met there. He was initiated into the coven in 1939 - just before World War II began.

He later told a story that described a meeting of witch covens from around the country in New Forest in 1940 when Britain feared an invasion by Germany. The group cast a great circle and raised a cone of power toward Hitler and the Nazis, pushing them away from an invasion. The exertion was said to have been so great that several elderly witches died the following day.

Incidentally, a similar event in England occurred with witches casting spells against the invading Spanish Armada in 1588, which was defeated at sea with the help of freakish weather conditions.

Soon after the end of the war, Gardner met Aleister Crowley, a powerful character with many followers within the world of magic. He had a reputation for being the "Wickedest Man in the World" - a reputation largely created by his own publicity.

Regardless, Crowley, although quite old by this time, was still the head of the Ordo Templi Orientis. This society had been influenced by Freemasonry, the occult, and various ancient traditions. The meetings between the two men encouraged Gardner to revive the work of the society in England, but it didn't last long after Crowley's death in 1947.

But Crowley did have an influence on Gardner, and his writings helped inspire Gardner's collection of rituals and beliefs that would become known as *The Book of Shadows*, a combination

Doreen Valiente, Gardner's first High Priestess. The two would have a falling out, which would allow Doreen to take Wicca in other directions.

of ceremonial magic, paganism, and witchcraft that helped to create the Wicca movement.

It couldn't have come at a better time. In 1951, England repealed the last remaining anti-witchcraft laws in the country, allowing people to practice witchcraft effectively without fear of prosecution.

Gardner soon began appearing in newspapers and in the media discussing the presence of witchcraft in the country and the desire of modern witches to do good works.

In 1954, he published his book *Witchcraft Today*, in which he announced that the religion of witchcraft was alive and well and had survived from ancient times. He began calling it Wicca - although he initially spelled it with only one C - which referred to witches in Old English.

The modern concept of witchcraft was finally born - it had been re-invented for a new generation.

But there would be dissension within the Wicca community and within Gardner's own coven. His first High Priestess, Doreen Valiente, did a lot of rewriting of his material and introduced the new version of the "Charge of the Goddess," which remains to this day one of the central parts of Wiccan belief and spirituality as a poetic incantation by the Goddess through her intermediary, the High Priestess of the coven.

Eventually, Doreen and Gardner had a falling out over the kind of publicity that Wicca was receiving. She started a series of other covens as Wicca spread and grew in popularity.

By the time Gardner died in 1964, Wicca - the new "old religion" - had evolved and become a movement that embraced paganism, the historical concept of the witch, and the folk traditions of cunning men and women.

Gardner's tradition incorporated both the Horned God and, more importantly, the Goddess as the heart of the faith. Wiccan rituals emphasized the importance of the two in nature, as well as their symbolic union.

He championed the role of women in rituals, and the High Priestess always had the senior position in the coven. The action of the Priestess in "Drawing Down the Moon" -- which means becoming, in effect, the goddess herself, is a central part of Wiccan belief.

Modern Wiccans typically associate more closely with the Goddess or "Triple Goddess," who is presented as the phases of the moon -- the maiden, the mother, and the crone.

The same goes for the Wiccan God—the young man, the middle-aged man, and the older man. The symbolic union between them is crucial, but the Goddess is of greater importance. She is typically more associated with the moon, fertility, beauty, and rebirth. The masculine version is more associated with the sun, hunting of the forests, nature, and death.

Another key element was the acknowledgment of "north" in rituals, which was associated with darkness, and because of this, was rejected by traditions that were associated with Christianity. Gardner felt that the north and its darkness were not something to be feared but to be embraced as an essential part of the universe.

Wicca also acknowledges the Gods of other faiths, believing that none are wrong, but they do not believe in the Devil or Hell - which are purely Christian constructs.

Alex Sanders, the controversial champion of ceremonial magic, took over the moniker of "King of the Witches" after the death of Gerald Gardner.

The loose development of Gardner's movement in the 1950s and early 1960s made room for rival traditions - the earliest of which was created by Alex Sanders, a flamboyant character who put himself in the limelight after Gardner's death.

Sanders, who took over the moniker of "King of the Witches," attracted a lot of attention and notoriety in the 1960s. Though Sanders was responsible for a lot of lurid publicity for witchcraft and alienated many people in the community, he was a powerful personality who emphasized ceremonial magic more than Gardner did.

Sanders championed the ideas of practical magic, steering away from the traditional, pagan-style Wiccan movement.

His brand of modern witchcraft is less popular today than it was in the 1960s, but the continued success of Wicca shows that

Gerald Gardner recreated something new and important that has never gone away.

Raymond Buckland

The origin of the Wicca movement in America comes, like in Britain, from the work of one man - Raymond Buckland. Born in England, he met and corresponded with Gerald Gardner, thanks to his deep interest in witchcraft and history. He and his wife, Rosemary, were initiated into the movement in Scotland and then moved to the United States with Gardner's *Book of Shadows* in hand. They founded the first coven on Long Island in 1964, officially bringing Wicca to America.

Growth and conflict followed, and eventually, the Bucklands stepped down from their leadership roles, and their marriage ended in 1973. Raymond left the coven altogether but continued to play an important role in American witchcraft, publishing books like *A Pocket Guide to the Supernatural* and *Witchcraft from the Inside.* He also created an offshoot of Wicca that is based heavily on Saxon heritage.

He died in 2017, but The Buckland Museum of Witchcraft and Magick continues to operate in Cleveland, Ohio, offering a look back at how magic and witchcraft shaped America.

It turned out that 1964 was an important year for American witchcraft. It was the year that Gerald Gardner died, the year that the Bucklands founded the first Wicca coven in New York, and it was also the year that the comedy *Bewitched* began airing on television sets across the country. The half-hour show, starring

Elizabeth Montgomery, presented a kind of witchcraft that Americans had never seen before - funny, down-to-earth, and as relatable as your next-door neighbor.

It was also in 1964 that a flamboyant Englishwoman named Sybil Leek truly brought Wicca to the consciousness of the American public. She might not have been the first to do so - but she was the one who made it famous.

While the writings of Gardner and Buckland

In 1964, Elizabeth Montgomery began appearing on television as Samantha Stephens in the comedy, *Bewitched.*

were not unknown in the U.S., the idea of witchcraft as a religion was a new concept to most of the country at a time when the old traditional fears about witches were waning but not yet forgotten. America was now introduced to witches who formed covens and met for sabbats, just like in the old stories, but who were followers of an ancient pagan fertility cult, motivated by good intentions and celebrating the power of nature. They weren't killing livestock, stealing babies, and putting curses on people.

It was a tough sell for many people - especially since it was barely a decade after a few people had been shot for being witches.

Still, America was not exactly virgin territory regarding esoteric groups who mixed magic and ancient wisdom. The

country had been home to many prophets, cults, masonic orders, and occults from the Rosicrucians to the Hermetic Order of the Golden Dawn - even Aleister Crowley himself had set up lodges of the Ordo Templi Orientis In California and Chicago in the 1930s.

But none of the nineteenth and early twentieth-century American occult groups had linked themselves with witchcraft. So, early American Wiccans began the work of rebranding the persecuted witches of the past into their benign pagan ancestors, hoping to overcome centuries of engrained prejudice about witchcraft.

This occasionally involved some well-meaning myth-making by adherents of the Wiccan craft, and Sybil Leek was no exception. She claimed that her family had been witches since 1134 and that she descended from Molly Leigh, a legendary eighteenth-century witch from Staffordshire. She said she had been brought up on an English estate and the French Riviera, where she was first initiated into a witch coven. Aleister Crowley was a highly unlikely family guest during the 1920s. At 16, she married a famous but unnamed pianist who died two years later. Back in England, she spent time living with "gypsies," learning their secret lore, and was initiated into the ancient coven at New Forest.

Creative, but well, not exactly accurate.

According to actual records, she was born in September 1917 near the dirty pottery town of Stoke-on-Trent in Staffordshire. Her father was Christopher Fawcett, and her mother's maiden name was Booth. They did not, in fact, own a country estate or spend summers on the French Riviera.

In 1944, Sybil Fawcett married John Delves, a butcher's son. He died during World War II. In 1952, she married again to an antique dealer named Reginald Leek in Hampshire.

In the early 1960s, Sybil was living in the village of Burley, in New Forest, running an antique store, and starting her campaign to educate the world about the new witch religion. A feature in the *News of the World* in October 1963 called her "Britain's No. 1 Witch" and reported on her intentions to start a school of witchcraft. In early 1964, she was involved in creating the Witchcraft Research Association. Sybil was briefly its first president but quickly irritated her fellow founders.

By late 1963, Sybil was starting to make news in the United States, while at the same time, she was being evicted from her home and her antique shop because of accusations that she was involved in orgies and black magic. Over the previous months, churches and

The English witch who would achieve her greatest fame in America ~ Sybil Leek.

churchyards had been vandalized and desecrated in ways that suggested ritual activity. The press ate it up, and the police didn't help by claiming it was done by Satanists. There was no evidence that the desecrations had been done by witches or Satanists, though. The culprits were more likely teenagers influenced by Dennis Wheatley novels and the recent film version of one of them - *The Devil Rides Out.* However, Sybil's public expression of interest in the cases harmed her reputation. Even though she condemned the incidents, neighbors turned against her. "It's heartless," she told a newspaper. "They are taking away my livelihood. I'm a white witch. My witchcraft does nothing but good."

In the spring of 1964, Sybil finally made it to America, but not as a witch. She was promoting a book about her experiences in the antique business, *A Shop on the High Street*. But once the press learned about her "side business" as a witch, she started appearing on the long-running, syndicated talk show, the *Mike Douglas Show*. It became the first of hundreds of television appearances over the next decade.

In June 1964, Sybil returned to England and announced that she was emigrating to the United States to escape continued persecution. She resigned from the Witchcraft Research Association, claiming she was forced out because her colleagues frowned on her interest in black magic. True or not, she did have issues with her fellow witches, especially regarding the nudity involved in Wiccan rituals. "I can get enough power for occult healing with six fur coats on," she once said. "All I need is my mind to generate power."

She moved to America and began drumming up interest in herself, taking part in dozens of interviews and always being patient with the endless joke that asked if she had arrived by broomstick. She was always ready with a soundbite or a wild claim. No Halloween passed without a quote from Sybil Leek. In 1966, she claimed American witches had more power than the Mafia. That same year, she told *Sports Illustrated* that she would use her psychic powers to pick the winners in the Kentucky Derby. It was claimed that she foresaw the assassinations of President John F. Kennedy and his brother, Robert. *Playboy* claimed that she was consulted by the military on several occasions.

And yet, somehow, her magic powers failed to prevent the burglary of her hotel room in St. Louis in July 1966. Several items went missing, including a purse that she said was given to her by Ian Fleming, the creator of James Bond, $450, and three magic rings, one of which she warned would "have a disastrous effect on anyone who wears it." Sybil was so angry that she announced she was conjuring a hex on the thief. She said that it had been 20 years since she had cast a spell that was so terrible she wouldn't even tell anyone about it. She was later tempted to whip another spell for a female journalist who called her a "jolly little pudding of a woman."

By 1968, Britain's former "No. 1 Witch" was being described as "America's Most Famous Resident Witch." However, she preferred her description to be a little longer than that --- "astrologer, entrepreneur, lecturer, publisher, radio, and television producer and personality, mother, and manufacturer of sailboats and jewelry." Oh... and she also claimed to have once been a scriptwriter for the BBC.

Sybil enjoyed a flamboyant career until the mid-1970s when she seemed to lose the energy she'd once shown for self-promotion. In truth, she may already have been sick. She died of cancer at her home in Melbourne, Florida, in October 1982 after leaving an indelible mark on the culture of modern witchcraft in America.

LOOKING FOR WITCHES

Sybil Leek sparked the interest of Americans in the new version of witchcraft, and soon it started to be found everywhere.

The earliest investigations into the modern witch religion started in an unusual place. In the summer of 1964, Don Shepherd of Channel 6 Philadelphia researched witchcraft in connection with the premiere of the series *Bewitched*. This led him to former actress Mary Manners Hammerstein, the former wife of Reginal Hammerstein, brother of the famous song lyricist Oscar. Mary, who was best known by her nickname "Hexie," described herself as a "white witch" who made "witch brooms" for children, invented cooking utensils, and marketed a pie-making kit. She'd made news before. A few months earlier, it was reported that her hilltop home

in Upper Black Eddy, Pennsylvania, was haunted. She had invited Philadelphia television presenter Bill Hart to the house, where he had hoped to record spirit activity for his afternoon show. He didn't, but it was a good show.

Don Shepherd passed Hexie's name along to other media contacts, including Bob Feldman from television station WHYN, but what most of them were looking for was a real witch. Bob had been having trouble finding one, and a newspaper columnist that he knew named Brian King suggested that he try Sybil Leek.

Bob said he'd thought about it but wanted a witch who was located in western Pennsylvania, where the station was. A few weeks later, he told Brian that his "results had been good," although he hadn't found a witch who was willing to identify themselves publicly as such. He'd received telephone calls from people who claimed to be witches and a few letters, but most of them seemed "vague, and what they had to say didn't ring true." Bob ended the investigation still looking for an American witch to interview - not knowing then that they'd start turning up in huge numbers within a few years.

Sam Tate of Edison, New Jersey, had a day job as a buyer of baby clothes for a major department store but, in his spare time, was a writer with an interest in witchcraft. In 1965, he attracted a lot of press attention when he placed an advertisement in the *New York Times*: "Author wishes to interview witches for completion of a serious book on Witchcraft Religion. Legitimate replies only."

He was not exactly overwhelmed by responses. Most of the calls and letters came from newspaper journalists looking for a story. He also heard from "a couple of researchers, two sweet little old ladies, three drunks, and a man looking for an apartment."

Based on what research he was able to do, he came to believe that the Old Religion was legitimate but had gotten a lot of bad press "since that messy business in Salem." He estimated there were no more than 50 or so witches in the U.S. at the time but was willing to meet with all of them. Unfortunately, the book he planned to write never made it into print.

Throughout the later years of the twentieth century, Wicca - and America's witches - began to change and evolve. It started to develop in distinctive ways through its embrace by the counterculture movements of the time. One of its main influences was the feminist movement. Interest in feminism and ecology were pathways into Wicca. It became the spiritual dimension of feminism, while feminism strengthened Wicca's social and political identity. The combination of the two transformed the nature of modern witchcraft.

Attention began to be drawn to the women of the Middle Ages who had been accused of witchcraft by the male-dominated society and then persecuted and killed. It resonated powerfully in the modern feminist movement and within the Wiccan movement as a symbol of the crushing misogyny of the past that had yet to be eradicated from western society.

The new adherents to Wicca began pushing the idea of the "Burning Times," a name coined by Gerald Gardner to describe the historical persecution of the witches he had adopted as pagan ancestors. Since most of those executed as witches in the past were women, the idea became important in feminist circles. Unfortunately, much of the information being put out at the time contained exaggerated numbers of witches who had been killed,

Leo Martello

hurting the legitimacy of the "Burning Times" with critics. Even so, we do know there were at least 50,000 witches burned to death during the European witch trials - with hundreds more hanged in America - so the numbers are tragic no matter what they turned out to be.

In an era of protest and activism, it would be surprising if Wicca didn't develop a radical wing. Leading it from New York was Leo Martello, a graphologist, hypnotist, and gay rights activist. On Halloween 1970, he organized a "witch in" event in Central Park that the authorities tried to ban. He then started the Witches Liberation Movement and, later, the Witches Anti-Defamation League, demanding reparations from the Catholic Church for their role in the historical persecution of witches.

In 1974, Martello complained to a reporter, "Today, witches are treated like refugees from the psychiatric ward, but for the first time in history, modern witches are fighting for their constitutionally guaranteed civil rights."

That said, there was nothing actually illegal about practicing witchcraft as a religion - in most states - by 1974. The old state laws about obtaining money by fortune-telling, palmistry, and mediumship were still in place but were being updated and tinkered with here and there. But the laws were rarely enforced and didn't affect the new witch religion.

In addition to Martello's more radical movement, others did some real good. One women's rights group called itself WITCH -

the Women's International Conspiracy from Hell. They picketed the 1968 Miss America contest, and on Halloween one year, one part of the group dressed up as witches to picket and humorously hex Chase Manhattan Bank in an action called "Up Against Wall Street." The movement also funded self-defense classes for women and created a referral line for women's health services.

Women from WITCH protesting at Chase Manhattan Bank during the "Up Against Wall Street" movement.

(Below) Playboy Bunny Starr Maddox appeared in the magazine promoting her belief in Wicca in 1970.

Two clear indications that modern witchcraft had firmly become part of American culture was when it was featured in *Playboy* and recognized by the Internal Revenue Service.

In 1970, Playboy Bunny Starr Maddox, a member of a Wicca coven in Miami, was photographed in glamorous witch poses alongside one of her in her Bunny costume. Starr told journalists that Wicca bothered her parents more than her being a Bunny did. "They're strict fundamentalists, and they don't like witchcraft, she said. They once sent their minister to talk to her, but he came up with an excuse to leave when she asked him about religion. A couple of years later, Starr was in Chicago promoting a Playboy production of *Macbeth* - which really must have been something to see - and she confided that she had been burned at the stake for witchcraft in a previous life.

In 1972, the IRS certified that the Church and School of Wicca was a religious association and therefore was tax-exempt. Gavin and Yvonne Frost founded the church in Missouri in 1968. They created the first -- and longest-lasting -- correspondence course for witchcraft, which I'm sure many of us saw in the backs of magazines and even comic books while growing up.

Who were all these new modern witches? They were nearly all white, urban, middle-class, and female. Coven members were homemakers, lawyers, dentists, nurses, and professionals with graduate degrees and were mostly in their twenties and thirties.

The media coverage pioneered by Sybil Leek and carried on by others helped normalize interest in the movement, but outside large cities, those wanting to join a coven faced challenges for many years. Wanting to be a witch was not something you talked to your parents about over Sunday dinner or pinned up on the bulletin board at the local grocery store. Because of this, advertisements began appearing in regional papers' personal columns in the 1970s. Those interested in Wicca left telephone numbers and addresses where those who shared their interests could call or write.

Unfortunately, things got even more challenging in the late 1970s and into the 1980s and early '90s. Wicca was starting to find its place at the same time fears of satanic cults were fueled by the counterculture's darker side. Roman Polanski's atmospheric film *Rosemary's Baby* caused a sensation in 1968 with its creepy paranoia that a New York occult group was engineering the birth of a satanic messiah. Then, the following year, the Manson murders shocked America, further worrying the country about the emergence of satanic cults.

Scare stories multiplied soon after. "Hippie commune witchcraft blood rites told," screamed one headline from the *Los Angeles Herald-Examiner*. It reported that police in Santa Cruz were concerned about the growth of witchcraft cults that sacrificed animals and turned people into "Satan's Slaves." And the stories just kept spreading.

In 1972, Christian evangelist Mike Warnke published a best-selling book called *The Satan Seller*, in which he shocked and fascinated readers with his purported former life as the leader of a satanic cult in the late 1960s, practicing magic, invoking demons, taking drugs, indulging in wild orgies, and committing rape. The book was exposed as a pack of lies, but the damage had been done. Scores of other "I Was a Satanist" books followed over the next two decades.

Christian evangelist Mike Warnke wrote a book claiming to be a Satanist and witch in 1972. The book was nothing but lies but managed to scare a lot of people about witchcraft.

Followers of Wicca came forward to denounce such stories as having anything to do with witchcraft. "Too many people in the United States confuse it with Satanism, and how could it be?" one spokesperson told a journalist. "Witchcraft, real witchcraft, doesn't recognize the existence of Satan or the Devil. That's a Christian concept."

But such statements didn't matter. By then, an increasingly powerful evangelical mob had already started to stoke the fires of misinformation and suspicion.

And then came the 1980s, when things really spun out of control.

"SATANIC PANIC"

It was in the 1980s when all the trouble started.

Of course, it started long before that - as far back as Salem in 1692, when being accused of being a witch had fatal results. Most Americans believed that nothing like that could ever happen again. But it did. In fact, in the 1980s, witches and Satanists were everywhere. A hysteria - much like the one that gripped the people of Salem - seized the country. The hysteria was spread by fundamentalist Christians, radical religious groups, television talk show hosts, and many otherwise well-intentioned people and organizations who feared that a vast underground network of witches was infiltrating the country.

They claimed these groups were spreading their evil message through rock-n-roll music, were kidnapping and abusing children, and might even be responsible for murdering thousands of people who went missing every year. Those missing persons, they believed, had fallen victim to satanic cults who used them for blood sacrifices to the Devil. The evidence for such an underground was obvious, they claimed, and pointed to a handful of murders carried out by delinquents in black t-shirts, questionable child abuse cases, and "recovered memories" of what came to be known as Satanic Ritual Abuse.

The end result of the "witch hunts" of the 1980s and early 1990s were scores of people being accused of crimes they did not commit, the destruction of families caused by "repressed" memories of things that never happened, and a nationwide panic that witches were waiting on every corner to kidnap children.

It all sounds very familiar, doesn't it?

If there was a single thing that can truly be credited with starting what became known as "Satanic Panic" in the 1980s, it was the publication of a book called *Michelle Remembers,* co-written by a Canadian psychiatrist named Dr. Lawrence Pazder and his patient, Michelle Smith. I discovered this book when I was starting my first year of high school and confess to being terrified by the contents. Not only did I believe that what I was reading was possible, but I was also convinced that it had all taken place. Like so many others at the time, I was fooled by the startling, horrific contents of the book, but my gullibility would not last for long.

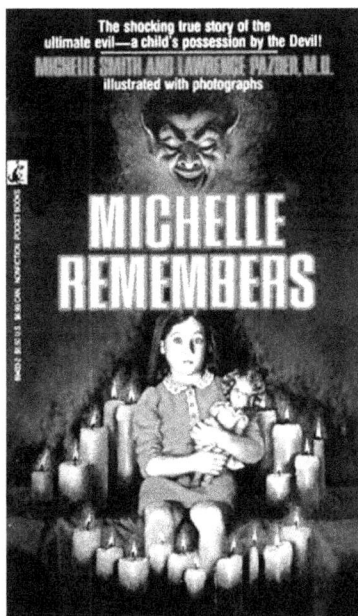

The book that helped to launch the "Satanic Panic" of the 1980s. This book also turned out to be nothing but nonsense, but it once again painted witchcraft in a bad light ~ even though witchcraft and Satanism have no connection with one another.

Within a few years, I began to realize, as many others also did, that the satanic hysteria of the 1980s had very little basis in truth. Unfortunately, though, the movement was only just beginning. It was just too colorful and too sensational for the talk show hosts and television evangelists to let go of, and they found that by ignoring the facts and spreading half-truths, they could keep their audiences glued to their seats - and utterly terrified that devil-worshipping boogiemen were around every corner waiting to get them.

In a nutshell, *Michelle Remembers* tells the story of a little girl whose mother turns her over to a witchcraft cult in Vancouver in the 1950s. The book is put together as a narrative, flashing back and forth between the past and present, and offers the version of events that Smith retrieves from her "recovered memories" during her therapy. It documents her mother's involvement with the cult, the many magic rituals that the young Michelle was forced to attend and participate in, and the many horrifying events that occurred during a time when she was literally held prisoner by the cult. During the rites, Smith was allegedly tortured, locked in cages, sexually assaulted, witnessed several murders, and was covered in the blood of slain infants and adults. She was eventually rescued thanks to the intervention of Jesus and the Virgin Mary. The archangel Michael then shows up and erases all her memories of the events "until the time is right."

I know what you're thinking - but I swear it seemed real to me when I was 13.

Anyway, when people started looking closer at the story, it began to fall apart. It took years, but eventually, the book was completely debunked. By then, though, the damage was done.

Michelle Remembers was the first book of its kind, but its success would inspire dozens of copy-cat titles, and it would become an important part of the controversies regarding Satanic Ritual Abuse and repressed memories. Satanic Ritual Abuse first made headlines after the book's publication and referred to physical and sexual abuse that reportedly occurred during occult or satanic ceremonies. The phenomenon began in the early 1980s, mainly in the United States, but spread to other parts of the world, impacting how the legal, therapeutic, and social work professions dealt with allegations of abuse.

Other books about repressed memories followed, and in the hysteria that accompanied their publication, no one thought to ask why earlier ritual abuse cases had not come to light. Too many people just accepted that the stories were true. They provided the model for all the allegations of ritual abuse that followed, like the 1983 McMartin Preschool case in California, a horrific incident in which preschool children were coached into lies about the owners of the school they attended. It turned into arrests, court cases, and ruined a lot of lives - much like the witchcraft trials of the seventeenth century.

Yes, history does sometimes repeat itself.

The trial went on for years, and eventually, everyone involved was acquitted on all accounts. One of the defendants spent five years in jail without ever being convicted of anything.

It was the media and social workers who helped fan the flames of the "witch hunt" in the McMartin case, and they continued to spread the word about so-called Satanic Ritual Abuse in the months and years to come. Psychologists began speaking at conferences about Satanic Ritual Abuse as a nationwide conspiracy.

In another scenario that's hauntingly familiar - if you denied the existence of an underground satanic movement were probably part of the conspiracy.

In 1986, a social worker named Carol Darling argued in a grand jury hearing that the conspiracy reached the government's highest levels. Her husband, Brad Darling, gave conferences about the satanic conspiracy, which he alleged dated back for centuries.

By the late 1980s, the recognition that mental health workers had given to Satanic Ritual Abuse led to the formation of Christian psychotherapy groups, exorcist organizations, multiple personality claims, and the development of groups for "survivors" of abuse. Thanks to all the attention, federal funding was provided for conferences supporting the idea of Satanic Ritual Abuse, offering an opportunity for prosecutors to exchange views on the best ways to secure convictions on cases that might be many years old. Many cases were prosecuted based on an adult's "recovered memories" of alleged childhood assaults.

Perhaps predictably, alleged incidents began to be reported all over the country, the majority of which came from memories allegedly "recovered" by a therapist who had studied the techniques used to retrieve the hidden memories their clients had buried.

Conservative religious groups targeted anything that might make people susceptible to "demonic influences" - like books, films, and, notably, rock music. The righteous folks launched an aggressive campaign against a score of iconic rock acts accusing them of deliberately planting subliminal satanic messages in their music. Of course, the messages were said to be audible only when the albums were played backward.

The media continued to add fuel to the fire. In 1987, Geraldo Rivera produced a national television special on satanic cults, claiming that "there are over one million Satanists ffiin the United Statesffl linked in a highly organized, secretive network." This show, along with others that began appearing at the time, were subsequently used by religious groups, psychotherapists, social workers, and law enforcement agencies to promote the idea that witches were engaged in a conspiracy to commit serious crimes across the country.

Perhaps the groups that benefited the most from the claims of satanic conspiracies were conservative Christian organizations, which were enthusiastic in promoting rumors of Satanic Ritual Abuse. Just as the Church had been quick to condemn the accused during the witchcraft scares hundreds of years before, religious fundamentalists in the late 1980s used "Satanic Panic" to frighten believers and bring new members into their churches. Christian psychotherapists began working with patients to "recover" lost and repressed memories, and soon after, lurid stories of black robes and murdered babies began to appear. Religious groups were instrumental in starting, spreading, and maintaining rumors about Satanic Ritual Abuse through sermons about its dangers, by way of lectures by purported experts, and by prayer sessions and special showings of programs like Geraldo Rivera's 1987 "exposé."

Eventually, though, even the sensationalistic media couldn't ignore the fact that there was little hard evidence that could confirm the thousands of alleged accounts of Satanic abuse or that a vast underground conspiracy existed that was covering everything up. Media coverage began to turn negative toward the end of the 1980s, and the Panic finally ended between 1992 and 1995. By the end of the 1990s, allegations of ritual abuse were finally being met with skepticism, and belief in Satanic Ritual Abuse finally stopped being given much credence in mainstream professional psychological circles.

But the damage was already done.

It took years for Wicca and witchcraft to recover, but they did. New covens formed, along with new traditions, and many were once again focused on aggressive feminist elements. Witches were encouraged to fight the patriarchy and regain power over their bodies and souls. This form of Wicca focused on the goddess of the hunt, Diana, and it was part of a major explosion of interest in witchcraft in the wake of the 1980s.

Since that time, Wicca has taken firm roots in American culture. It has become federally recognized as a religion, including in the military, and there are at least 5 million practitioners in the United States alone - although that number is definitely skewed since many witches prefer to work alone or in small covens.

Let's just say there are a lot of pagans, witches, Wiccans, conjurers, hex doctors, and cunning folk in America in these modern times.

10. ONE LAST NIGHT
IN SALEM

Guilt about what happened in Salem in 1692 was an itch that some could not resist scratching.

In 1946, Georgia industrialist H. Vance Greenslit petitioned the Massachusetts legislature to pardon one of his Salem descendants and six others who were executed for witchcraft. They refused and did so again in 1946 and 1953, although the petition was finally granted in 1957.

After Greenslit ended his pursuit of a pardon, a Salem resident named John Beresford Hatch began a one-made crusade to have the British parliament exonerate all those who were executed at Salem. He sent numerous letters to Buckingham Palace and the Prime Minister's office. In 1960, he petitioned Congress, the State Department, and the Massachusetts legislature to pressure the British government to respond. A letter to the British consul in Boston received a curt reply - Her Majesty's Government no longer had jurisdiction over witch trials. A letter sent to then Prime Minister Harold McMillan suggested that he and Hatch meet at Gallows Hill in Salem "to settle once and for all time" the exoneration of the accused. He never received a reply.

Then, in 1992, a new monument was installed in Salem to honor those who'd been executed there. It was unveiled by Arthur Miller - writer of *The Crucible* - and Holocaust survivor and human rights campaigner Elie Wiesel gave a speech. The event was a somber moment to remind the nation about the dangers of persecution and prejudice.

Meanwhile, the popular image of the witch was changing - and not just because of the rise of Wicca. There was an alternative to the satanic image that evangelists were peddling.

In November 1964, Joy Miller, an editor at the *Associated Press,* complained, "This may go down as the year of the kook, the year weirdo achieved status, the year Halloween lasted on the calendar." She was grumbling about the success of *The Addams Family* and *Bewitched*, which had both started airing on ABC that year. The old films about vampires, werewolves, and the living dead used to send shivers up the spine, but now television was normalizing such figures of supernatural fear, she wrote. "The ghoul next is pure Pollyanna, and the witch is a homebody who conjures up dinner by a twitch of her pretty nose."

By the 1960s, witches were sexy, overshadowing the old stereotypes represented in *The Wizard of Oz* and Disney's *Snow White*. Young, beautiful witches had been depicted in nineteenth-century literature, but the advertising industry, film, and television provided the makeover in popular culture.

In the romantic comedy, *I Married a Witch*, knock-out Veronica Lake plays Jennifer, a seventeenth-century Salem witch who was burned at the stake - perpetrating the mistaken belief that witches were burned at the stake in America. Her spirit remains in the tree where she was burned until one day in 1942

Veronica Lake in *I Married a Witch*

when it's hit by lightning, and she's set free to seek revenge on the descendant of her Puritan persecutor, played by Frederic

Kim Novak and Jimmy Stewart in *Bell, Book & Candle*

March. True love overcomes hate, though, and the film ends happily with the marriage between Lake and March.

Bell, Book, and Candle, in 1958, presented a modern-day witch played by Kim Novak. She lives in Greenwich Village with her cat familiar and finds herself attracted to her neighbor, played by Jimmy Stewart. The problem is that she will lose her powers if she falls in love.

The idea that a good witch could be both nubile and domesticated came across strongly in the most influential sexy witch of the era, Samantha Stephens, in *Bewitched*. ABC made 254 episodes between 1964 and 1972. Elizabeth Montgomery played Samantha, married to her mortal husband, Darren, played by Dick York for most of the series. He was the

Elizabeth Montgomery in *Bewitched*, a show that became essential to the changing view of witchcraft in America.

bane of existence to Samantha's mother, Endora, played by Agnes Moorehead. Samantha's cavalcade of crazy relatives dropped in for visits and were played by actors like Bernard Fox as Dr. Bombay, Alice Ghostley as Esmerelda, Paul Lynde as Uncle Arthur, and many more. Much of the comic relief came from the nosy next-door neighbor, Gladys Kravitz, who was sure that something strange was happening at the Stephens' house.

I'm not going to lie – I absolutely loved this show in re-runs as a kid and still love it now.

In June 1970, the cast of *Bewitched* made a rare venture out of the studio to film scenes in Salem for two Halloween-themed episodes. A statue of Samantha seated on a broom is one of the most photographed images in Salem today.

And it's no surprise. When the show came to town, one of the producers told the press, "The directional traffic signals which carry the face of an old hag on a broom will be changed to a prettier profile of Samantha."

Salem was just about to have a witchcraft renaissance.

The commercial exploitation of the 1692 witch trials started in the 1890s when a local jeweler began making and selling "Salem Witch Souvenir Spoons," depicting witches, nooses, cats, brooms, and the moon. A few years later, a number of businesses in town began using a brand - "made in Witch City." In 1940, the makers of a line of women's toiletries called "Early American Old Spice" launched a marketing campaign illustrated with a beautiful woman hanging from a gnarled old tree, a rose clasped in one hand, and a verse beneath her that read:

Hung! As a witch -
Much too much for the Puritans of Salem -
Her charming witchery quite overcame them.

Readers who saw this ad in one of their favorite magazines were excited at the prospect that they, too, could possess the "radiant charm that baffled our Founding Fathers."

I'll assume they didn't expect to be hanged for it.

In 1889, Parker Brothers produced a board game called "Ye Witchcraft Game," but people were upset enough that they decided to pull it from production a few years later. That wouldn't be a problem seven decades later, though. In 1970, a Salem company presented "Witch Pitch" at the American Toy Fair. Players tossed little discs into a revolving cupola on a stereotypical witch's house. The packaging announced it was "Made in Witch City, U.S.A."

Small-scale tourism in Salem had started around the turn of the last century, but there had long been a battle between those who wanted to promote the town's rich history without witches and those who wanted to further exploit the brand with huge potential. Those scales tipped wildly in the 1970s. The Halloween episodes of *Bewitched* were a tremendous influence. When the town's chamber of commerce finally fully embraced the "Witch City" brand, the Wiccans started arriving in droves.

Leading the way was a Californian named Laurie Cabot, who opened "A Witch Shop" in 1971 and started selling Wiccan paraphernalia and witch-related curios. Like Sybil Leek, she courted the media, wrote popular books, and even managed to brand herself successfully as the "Official Witch of Salem," a title she's managed to hang onto for decades, mostly thanks to national television and press exposure.

Laurie Cabot

In 1986, after the release of the film version of *The Witches of Eastwick*, John Updike's novel about suburban women delving into the occult, Laurie established the Witches' League for Public Awareness to counter negative images of her religion in popular

Salem, Massachusetts, today is known as the "Witch City" and the "Halloween Capital of the World," thanks to brilliant marketing by the business and tourism leaders of the town.

(Left) In honor of the way that Bewitched changed the view of Salem and witchcraft in general, a statue of Elizabeth Montgomery as Samantha was unveiled in 2005.

culture and the media. She said of the movie, "Here are three women who have nothing better to do, because they are so frustrated sexually, than to get involved with witchcraft. They are not witches. If they are anything, they are weekend Satanists. They don't do one witchy thing in the whole film."

Laurie Cabot no longer has a shop in Salem, but her presence is still felt, primarily due to all the other witch shops, tours, and businesses that followed in her wake.

As you might imagine, not everyone in Salem is thrilled with its image as "Witch City." As far back as 1977, some city council members protested the moniker but were overruled by those who realized that witchcraft was the town's proverbial bread and butter.

Salem caters to all aspects of dark tourism, including promotion of its historic cemeteries. Three of them are linked to the witch trials of 1692, including the Howard Street Cemetery, where Giles Corey was pressed to death by rocks.

The embrace of witchcraft during this time was partly due to the commercialization of Halloween. Halloween, introduced to America by the Irish, had once been a somewhat violent affair with drinking, fighting, and often dangerous pranks.

By the 1960s, though, the more innocent version of trick-or-treating had become popular and was ripe for commercialization. Soon, supermarkets, drug stores, and department stores began offering costumes, candy, and hundreds of special Halloween items for parties.

It took a while, but Salem finally saw this as an opportunity not to be missed. In 1982, a group of business people devised "Haunted Happenings" for the holiday, advertising the town as the "Halloween Capital of the World." The initiative grew until it began attracting the hundreds of thousands who flock there today.

Popular culture has continued to make witchcraft appealing, just as it did with Samantha in Bewitched. Over the years, we've had *Teen Witch, Sabrina, the Teenage Witch, Charmed, A Discovery of Witches, The Mayfair Witches, The Chilling Adventures of Sabrina, American Horror Story*, and even a historical series called *Salem*, which spent three seasons delving into the witch trials. You'll find them in theaters, too, *Hocus Pocus,*

Hellbender, Suspiria, Gretel and Hansel, The Craft, two of my favorites - *The Autopsy of Jane Doe* and Robert Egger's *The Witch* - and many more.

They have become such a part of our culture that we often forget to look back and see where it all came from and how it all started.

Today, witchcraft and folk magic are more popular than ever. In recent years, interest has soared regarding folk traditions, backwoods healing, and the old gods. Many look to the past for answers in a new and troubling world.

But it's in the past that we also find warnings of the intolerance of religious fanaticism. The days of witch trials and hangings may be over, but the demonizing of witchcraft still takes place every day by fundamentalists and conservative Christian groups.

Like the Catholic church and the Puritans did hundreds of years ago, they still attempt to link witchcraft to the Devil because - as I have already stated - the perception of witchcraft is always in the eye of the beholder.

To some Christians, witchcraft is always the work of the Devil. But it's a lot like what I say about Christianity -- one man's religion is another man's cult.

Since 1692, the narrative regarding witchcraft had been distorted by the constant manipulation of history and slanted by racial and religious prejudice. Much of the story of witchcraft in the growth of America has been conveniently forgotten or obscured by myth-making and hate.

The preoccupation that so many have with Salem often hides some uncomfortable truths about the people who built the United States - and the god they worshipped. Thousands of Americans, indigenous people, and immigrants from Europe and Africa were persecuted, abused, and murdered as witches, largely because their religion was different from those who persecuted them.

That same religious intolerance remains today as a reminder that even after several centuries, most of society still does not understand the core beliefs of witchcraft and folk magic.

It's pretty simple:

As long as it harms no one, do what you will.

After a long and bloody history, those who practice witchcraft just want to be afforded the same rights as everyone else - to practice their beliefs as they choose. It's a small but important need, but I'd say after all they have endured over the years, it's one they deserve.

TROY TAYLOR
WINTER-SPRING 2023

BIBLIOGRAPHY

Adler, Margaret - *Drawing Down the Moon: Witches, Druids, Goddess-Worshippers, and Other Pagans in America,* New York, NY, Penguin, 1997

Alvarado, Denise - *The Magic of Marie Laveau*, Newburyport, MA, Weiser Books, 2020
------------------------ - Witch Queens, *Voodoo Spirits, and Hoodoo Saints*, Newburyport, MA, Weiser Books, 2022

Anderson, Jeffrey E. - *Conjure in African American Society*, Baton Rouge, LA, 2005

Baker, Emerson W. - *The Devil of the Great Island: Witchcraft and Conflict in Early New England*, New York, NY, 2007

Ballard, H. Byron - *Root Branches and Spirits: The Folkways of Witchery of Appalachia*, Woodbury, MN, Llewellyn Books, 2021

Berger, Helen - *A Community of Witches: Contemporary Neo-Paganism and Witchcraft in the United States*, Columbia, 1998

Bird, Stephanie Rose - *Stick, Stones, Roots, and Bones: Hoodoo, Mojo, and Conjuring with Herbs*, Woodbury, MN, Llewellyn Books, 2019

Birnes, William J. and Joel Martin --- *The Haunting of America*, New York, NY, Forge Books, 2009

Boyer, Paul and Stephen Nissenbaum - *Salem-Village Witchcraft: A Documentary Record of Local Conflict in Colonial New England*, Belmont, CA, 1972
-- - *The Salem Witchcraft Papers*, New York, NY, 1977

Buckland, Raymond - *Buckland's Complete Book of Witchcraft*, Woodbury, MN, Llewellyn Books, 2002

Cavendish, Richard - *The Black Arts*, New York, NY, Capricorn Publishing, 1967

Cavendish, Richard (Editor) *Man, Myth and Magic Series: An Illustrated Encyclopedia of the Supernatural*, New York, NY, Marshall Cavendish Corporation, 1970

Chireau, Yvonne P. - *Black Magic: Religion and the African American Conjuring Tradition*, Berkely University Press, 2003

Clifton, Charles A. - *Her Hidden Children: The Rise of Wicca and Paganism in American*, Lanham, 2006

Davies, Owen - *America Bewitched*, London, UK, Oxford University Press, 2013
--------------------- - *Oxford Illustrated History of Witchcraft and Magic*, London, UK, Oxford University Press, 2027

Dell, Christopher - *The Occult, Witchcraft, and Magic*, New York, NY, Thames & Hudson, 2016

Demos, John - *Entertaining Satan: Witchcraft and Culture of Early New England*, London, UK, Oxford University Press, 1996

Foulds, Diane E. - *Death in Salem*, National Book Network, 2010

Frazer, James George - *The Golden Bough: A Study in Magic and Religion*, Oxford University Press Edition, 2009

Gaskill, Malcolm - *The Ruin of All Witches: Life and Death in the New World*, New York, NY, Alfred A. Knopf, 2021

Gettings, Fred - *Encyclopedia of the Occult*, London, UK, Rider and Co., 1986

Godbeer, Richard - *The Devil's Dominion: Magic and Religion in Early New England*, Cambridge MA, Yale University Press, 1992

Godsen, Chris - *Magic*, New York, NY, Farrar, Straus and Giroux, 2020

Goldhagen, Shari, Editor - *Witches: Then and Now*, Miami, FL, Centennial Books, 2021

Greenwood, Susan - *The Illustrated History of Witchcraft and Magic*, Wigston, UK, Anness Publishing, 2011

Guiley, Rosemary Ellen - *The Encyclopedia of Witches and Witchcraft*, New York, NY, Facts on File, 1999

Hall, David D. - *Worlds of Wonder, Days of Judgement: Popular Religious Beliefs in Early New England*, New York, NY, 1989

Hammond, Amberrose - *Mysterious Michigan*, Charleston, SC, History Press, 2022

Hawthorn, Ambrosia - *Spellbook for New Witches*, Emeryville, CA, Rockbridge Press, 2020

Hill, Douglas and Pat Williams - *The Supernatural,* London, UK, Aldus Books Limited, 1965

Hofer, Peter Charles - *The Devil's Disciples: Makers of the Salem Witcraft Trials,* Baltimore, MD, Johns Hopkins University Press, 1996

Horowitz, Mitch - *Occult America,* New York, NY, Bantam Books, 2009

Hutcheson, Cory Thomas - *New World Witchery,* Woodbury, MN, Llewellyn Books, 2021

Hutton, Ronald - *The Triumph of the Moon: A History of Modern Pagan Witchcraft,* Oxford University Press, 2001

Karlsen, Carol - *Devil in the Shape of a Woman: Sinners and Witches in Puritan New England,* Ithaca, NY, 1997

Kelden - *The Witches' Sabbath,* Woodbury, MN, Llewellyn Books, 2022

Kitteridge, George Lyman - *Witchcraft in Old and New England,* Cambridge, MA, New York, NY, Athenaeum, 1972

Kriebel, David - *Powwowing Among the Pennsylvania Dutch: A Traditional Medical Practice in the Modern World,* University Park, 2007

LaMonica, Lisa - *Witches and Warlocks of New York*, Essex, CT, Globe Pequot Press, 2022

Levin, David - *What Happened in Salem?*, New York, NY, Harcourt, Brace & World, 1960

Lewis, Arthur - *Hex*, New York, NY, Trident Press, 1969

McGinnis, J. Ross - *Trials of Hex*, Davis, CA, 2000

Mankey, Jason - *The Horned God of the Witches*, Woodbury, MN, Llewellyn Books, 2021

Mar, Alex - *Witches of America*, New York, NY, Farrar, Straus and Giroux, 2015

Milnes, Gerald C. - *Signs, Cures, and Witchery: German Appalachian Folklore*, Knoxville, TN, 2007

Murphy, Michael - *Fear Dat*, New York, NY, W.W. Norton and Co., 2015

Murray, Dr. Margaret Alice - *God of the Witches*, Reprint edition - Originally published in 1933
---------------------------------- - *The Witch-Cult in Western Europe*, Reprint edition - Originally published in 1921

Museum of Witchcraft and Magic - *Of Shadows*, London, UK, Strange Attractor Press, 2026

Norton, Mary Beth - *In the Devil's Snare: The Salem Witchcraft Crisis of 1692*, New York, NY, Alfred A. Knopf, 2002

Ocker, J.W. - *A Season With the Witch*, New York, NY, W.W. Norton, 2016

Richards, Jake - *Backwoods Witchcraft*, Newburyport, MA, Weiser Books, 2019

Roach, Marilynne K. - *Six Women of Salem*, Boston, Ma, Da Capo Press, 2013

Shone, Sherry - *Hoodoo For Everyone*, Berkely, CA, North Atlantic Books, 2022

Smith, Michelle and Lawrence Pazder - *Michelle Remembers,* New York, NY, St. Martin's Press, 1980

Stollznow, Karen - *God Bless America*, Durham, NC, Pitchstone Publishing, 2013

Streeter, Michael - *Witchcraft: A Secret History* - London, UK, White Lion Publishing, 2020

Timbers, Frances - *The History of Magic and Witchcraft in the West*, Havertown, PA, Pen and Sword Books, 2019

West, Michael William - *Sex Magicians*, Rochester, VT, Destiny Books, 2021

Weston, Brandon - Ozark Folk Magic, Woodbury, MN, Llewellyn Books, 2021

Wheatley, Dennis - *The Devil and All His Works*, New York, NY, American Heritage Press, 1971

Wilson, Colin - *The Occult: A History*, New York, NY, Random House, 1971

White, Thomas - *Witches of Pennsylvania*, Charleston, SC, History Press, 2013

SPECIAL THANKS TO:

April Slaughter: Cover Design and Artwork
Becky Ray: Editing and Proofreading
Samantha Smith
Athena & the "Aunts" ~ Sue, Carmen & Rocky
Brianna Snow
Orrin and Rachel Taylor
Rene Kruse
Rachael Horath
Bethany Horath
Elyse and Thomas Reihner
Lisa Taylor and Lux
John Winterbauer
Kaylan Schardan
Maggie and Packy Lundholm
Cody Beck
Tom and Michelle Bonadurer
Lydia Rhoades
Susan Kelly and Amy Bouyear
Cheryl Stamp and Sheryel Williams~Staab
Joelle Leitschuh and Tonya Leitschuh
Jami Kennedy
Scott and Hannah Robl
Jake and Emily Fink
Dave and Donna Nunnally
And the entire crew of American Hauntings

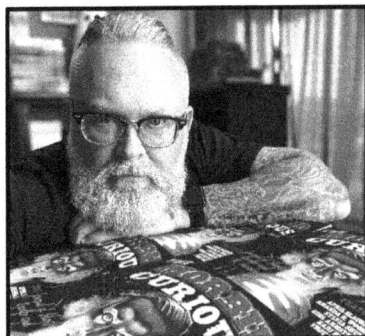

ABOUT THE AUTHOR

Troy Taylor is the author of books on ghosts, hauntings, true crime, the unexplained, and the supernatural in America. He is also the founder of American Hauntings Ink, which offers books, ghost tours, events, and weekend excursions. He was born and raised in the Midwest and divides his time between Illinois and wherever the wind decides to take him.

See Troy's other titles at:
www.americanhauntingsink.com

www.ingramcontent.com/pod-product-compliance
Lightning Source LLC
Chambersburg PA
CBHW062042080426
42734CB00012B/2531